PRESENTED TO:

_____

FROM:

_____

"As you therefore have received Christ Jesus the Lord, so walk in Him, rooted and built up in Him and established in the faith, as you have been taught, abounding in it with thanksgiving."

COLOSSIANS 2:6-7

INTRODUCTION

I'm tempted to open this little book by saying: "Welcome to another uncertain year!"

The last couple of years have been difficult, and the next twelve months are full of unpredictable events. Who knows what will next befall us? People everywhere are on edge.

But I don't feel uncertain or on edge, and neither should you. So instead, I'm going to say: "Welcome to a *certain* year!"

I'm certain Jesus is in charge. I'm certain His Word will sustain us, His Spirit will revive us, His angels will watch over us, and His plans will unfold as He has decreed them. The Lord's promises are as certain as His character, and His presence is as sure as sunshine. I'm persuaded nothing can separate us from the love of God found in Christ Jesus our Lord—not for a day, not for a moment. Surely goodness and mercy will follow us, not just every day, but every minute.

None of us are immune from stress and tension, but when we know how to walk with the Lord in the light of His Word, we're in the best possible place. The prophet Isaiah said, "The Lord…He awakens Me morning by morning. He awakens My ear to hear" (Isaiah 50:4). In this way we're "renewed day by day" (2 Corinthians 4:16).

Let's live every single day this year *with* Jesus, *for* Jesus, and *like* Jesus.

I'm not going to tell you how many days I've been on this earth—I had a significant birthday last year—but from a lifetime of experience, I can tell you the song I learned in childhood is true: *Every day with Jesus is better than the day before!*

And of that, I'm certain!

David Jeremiah

JANUARY

JANUARY 1
A Better Life

Blessed are the pure in heart, for they shall see God.
MATTHEW 5:8

C. S. Lewis said, "Integrity is doing the right thing, even when no one is watching." The truth of the matter is that Someone is always watching. God in heaven sees our thoughts, our actions, our mistakes, and our guilt when we fail. One of the great assurances found in Scripture is that in spite of our failures and sin, God loves us and encourages us to be better. How often have we heard a young child say, "Daddy, I want to be like you!" What a blessing for an earthly father to hear those words from his child. That is what God wants to hear from us—not that we are perfect—but that our desire and goal is to be like Him.

Do you have someone in your life who makes you want to be a better person in one or more ways? We should all be so blessed. People who knew Jesus felt that way about Him. The phrase, "Go and sin no more" (John 8:11) is emblematic of what happened to many people who encountered Jesus in their life. It was hard to be around the Son of God without being motivated to be better, especially to be a purer person.

If you are a Christian, Jesus is with you every moment through the Holy Spirit's presence in your life. Let His presence, and His Word, be the primary shaping influence in your life this year—you will have a better life as you spend every day with Jesus.

So it was that for a whole year they assembled with the church and taught a great many people. And the disciples were first called Christians in Antioch.

ACTS 11:26

In Acts 11, Barnabas was overseeing the work in the local church at Antioch, and he needed an assistant. He recruited Saul of Tarsus, who was coming to be known as Paul. They devoted an entire year to the project of growing the church and teaching the Word of God. The effort was so successful that people began calling these believers by the name of Christ Himself—Christ-ones, or Christians.

Imagine what would happen if you devoted a whole year to personal Bible study! It would produce a new you! Millions of people around the world take online courses in their homes. They build specific time into their daily schedules to work on their degrees. What if you said to yourself, "This year I'm going to become a student in the School of God's Word. I'm going to build time into my daily schedule to become proficient in Scripture."

There are all kinds of resources available to help you make that change, but it starts with two things: an open Bible and a pen. As you begin this new year, make it your goal to be a student of Scripture and let His Word dwell in you richly each day.

*You have delivered my soul from death,
my eyes from tears, and my feet from falling.*
PSALM 116:8

One troubled man finally said, "I'm tired of being sad."
Sometimes we have to make an emotional stand, buttressed by
prayer, and put the sadness behind us. Those who are in Christ
don't stay sad forever. In Psalm 116, the writer had been in deep
physical trouble. He had experienced so much pain he thought
he was dying (verse 3). His life had fallen into "trouble and
sorrow" (verse 3). But he had turned his problems into prayers
(verse 4), and God had helped him.

Everyone faces seasons of pain, trouble, or sorrow, and
sometimes we can't keep from crying. In fact, weeping is one
of the ways we express our feelings and process our emotions.
But you can trust in this promise: God is listening to the cry of
your heart and sees the tears falling from your eyes. He is your
helper and deliverer.

God hears and answers our prayers. He will deliver your
soul from death, your eyes from tears, and your feet from
falling. Beginning today, make the choice to no longer live in
sadness and allow the joy of the Lord to turn your mourning
into dancing (Psalm 30:11).

JANUARY 4
The Brevity of Life

But, beloved, do not forget this one thing,
that with the Lord one day is as a thousand years,
and a thousand years as one day.
2 PETER 3:8

The word *year* in the Bible typically describes a period of time which, for us, seems to pass quickly. We're often amazed at how fast our birthdays approach, and we shake our heads at how quickly our children grow up. The older we grow, the more we realize the brevity of life.

It's helpful to remember that our God does not experience time as we do. His eternal nature is never flustered by how slowly or how quickly time is passing. To Him, a day is like a thousand years and a thousand years as a day.

For us, as His children, it means the brevity of our earthly life is countered by the endless nature of our eternal life. If you're missing a loved one in heaven, don't brood over your memories of past happiness. Look forward to future fellowship! If you're feeling poorly, don't give up; look up. Focusing our attention on Almighty God and the eternal future He has planned for us makes the reality of the present fit into its proper perspective. We can then respond to His words in Revelation, "Surely I am coming quickly," with "Even so, come, Lord Jesus!" (22:20)

JANUARY 5
Time and Eternity

For a thousand years in Your sight are like yesterday when it is past,
and like a watch in the night.

PSALM 90:4

When it came to keeping time, the Romans divided the night into four "watches"—four periods of three hours from sunset to sunrise. This was in contrast to the Jewish standard of measuring the night by three watches of four hours each. But whether measuring by Jewish or Roman standards, a watch in the night was very short—a matter of a few hours.

In Psalm 90, Moses meditated on time and eternity—man's time compared to God's eternity—and said that in God's sight a thousand years is like yesterday, a brief "watch in the night." We think a thousand years is a terrifically long period of time, and to us, it is! But to God a thousand years is as brief as a few hours, a watch in the night. Why is that true? Because God is "the eternal God" (Deuteronomy 33:27). He is not measured by time as we are.

God sees all of time as one event. He knows your tomorrows as well as you know your life today and your yesterdays. Therefore, you can trust Him with whatever tomorrow brings—God holds your future in His loving hands.

JANUARY 6
Be Sure!

But these are written that you may believe that Jesus is the Christ, the Son of God, and that believing you may have life in His name.

JOHN 20:31

Most biblically-based preachers and teachers avail themselves of insights gained from the original languages of the Bible. But one preacher, known for his facility with Greek and Hebrew, told his congregation, "My greatest concern is not that you don't understand Greek or Hebrew, it's that you don't understand English!"

When the Bible says something over and over, in plain English, and is still not believed, there is a problem deeper than language. For instance, the Bible says in many verses and in many ways, that those who place their faith in Jesus Christ, the Son of God, can be assured of eternal life. The apostle John said explicitly that he wrote in order that his readers might know that they can have eternal life through faith in Christ (John 3:16; 20:31; 1 John 5:13). Apparently, some still doubted their salvation. Can a Christian be assured of his or her salvation? Yes!

If you have doubts about your salvation, continue to read and meditate on the verses in Scripture that were written to give you assurance of your faith. They were written so that you might know and be sure!

JANUARY 7
Ministers of Reconciliation

Therefore, having been justified by faith,
we have peace with God through our Lord Jesus Christ.
ROMANS 5:1

A couple of modern cultural maxims reflect an important biblical principle: "It takes one to know one" and "You can't give what you don't have." In other words, personal experience and possessions dictate what we can pass on to others. And that is especially true when it comes to having peace in our heart. Since having peace in this world depends first on having peace with God, that's where we must start.

The New Testament makes it clear that our own peace with God comes by being "justified by faith," which results in our reconciliation with God. Once we are reconciled to God, the peace we enjoy can be shared with others. In fact, another way to describe our role as peacemakers is as ministers of reconciliation—that is Paul's description of those who have been reconciled to Christ (2 Corinthians 5:18).

Do you have peace with God today? It comes through faith in Jesus Christ. Once you have been justified by faith and experience peace with God, you can become a peacemaker to the world by sharing what you have—a relationship with Jesus Christ.

JANUARY 8
Make Disciples!

Go therefore and make disciples of all the nations, baptizing them in the name of the Father and of the Son and of the Holy Spirit.
MATTHEW 28:19

When Jesus sent His disciples to minister, various words and phrases were used: teach, heal, cast out demons, baptize, preach, and more. But the most comprehensive of all the action words Jesus gave to His followers at different times is the one found in the Great Commission, given after His resurrection and before His ascension: "Make disciples."

"Make disciples" is the only imperative command in Matthew 28:19–20. Involved in that process are baptizing and teaching, corollary activities to making disciples. But all these activities assume obedience to "Go therefore." Having gone, followers of Jesus were to make disciples—additional followers and learners—in all the nations of the world. Making disciples is not the same as making converts. Converts come from *decisions*; disciples come from *dedication*. And it takes one to make one.

To obey Jesus' final commands, we must go and share the Gospel with others so they will also go and "make disciples of all the nations." We are not saved to sit and contemplate; we are saved to go and share.

JANUARY 9
Retreat

And when He had sent the multitudes away, He went up on the mountain by Himself to pray. Now when evening came, He was alone there.
MATTHEW 14:23

Our lives are filled with family, friends, work, appointments, ministry commitments, and more. Children have sports practices and music lessons weekly. Parents work forty hours a week and serve at church too. Many of us rush from commitment to commitment without taking time to rest.

Jesus understands the busyness of life. In Matthew 14 we read that Jesus escaped the crowd and went to a deserted place by Himself, only to have the crowd follow Him (verse 13). When Jesus saw the crowd, He was filled with compassion, healed the sick, and fed the people. After He cared for the crowd, Jesus sent the disciples and the multitude away. Then He once again went to spend time alone in prayer. Yet after a time of refreshment alone, He returned to His ministry, to the work He was on earth to do— "to serve, and to give His life a ransom for many" (Mark 10:45).

While many of our activities and commitments are necessary and good, we need time away in prayer just as Jesus did. Take the time today to find refreshment through Scripture and prayer, and if possible, schedule a time for a spiritual retreat to experience the renewal of both your body and spirit.

JANUARY 10
Word of Wisdom

All Scripture is given by inspiration of God, and is profitable for doctrine, for reproof, for correction, for instruction in righteousness.

2 TIMOTHY 3:16

Foxfire magazine began in 1967 as a quarterly publication by students in the mountains of north Georgia. The focus of the articles was on primitive Appalachian culture and lifestyles. As articles accumulated, they were gathered and published in *The Foxfire Book* in 1972. The book was so successful that a total of thirteen volumes have been published through 2021. The books represent "the bible" for how to live and prosper in a simple, back-to-the-land lifestyle.

God's Holy Word, the Bible, is like that for the Christian life. There is hardly a question in life that God's Word does not provide direction on what we should do or how we should live. Just as skill is needed to live a simple, mountain lifestyle, so skill is needed to live wisely in this world. In fact, the Old Testament word for *wisdom* is actually the Hebrew word for *skill*. God wants to give us skill to make wise and godly choices on our journey.

Do you have a question or need direction or wisdom for making a decision? Start with God's Word—it was given to make us wise (Psalm 111:10).

JANUARY 11
Good Gifts

If you then, being evil, know how to give good gifts to your children,
how much more will your Father who is in heaven
give good things to those who ask Him!
MATTHEW 7:11

In this sentence, Jesus acknowledged the inherent sinfulness of the human heart. He plainly called us "evil." He knew the truth of Jeremiah 17:9: "The heart is deceitful above all things, and desperately wicked; who can know it?" Yet Jesus also knew there is still common grace in the world. There is some goodness in most parents. It is natural to want to care for our children (and grandchildren) and meet their needs.

Our Lord's primary point is God's care for us. If we, fallen humanity, want to care for our children and give them good things, how much greater is God's desire to care for us? He is the perfect, sinless, eternal, infinite Father—our Abba Father.

But there is a secondary point as well. As followers of Christ, we should realize the urgency of meeting our children's needs and giving them what is best beyond material needs such as food and clothing. They are God's blessing to us, and we need to give them what is needed most—they need all the patience, prayers, and promises from God's Word that we can give them.

And Jesus said to them, "I am the bread of life. He who comes to Me shall never hunger, and he who believes in Me shall never thirst."

JOHN 6:35

Type "bread making" into Amazon, and thousands of book titles will pop up. You can learn how to make artisan bread, sourdough bread, no-knead bread, and more. The possibilities seem endless, yet there are only four main ingredients for baking bread—flour, water, yeast, and salt. Other ingredients, such as sugar, herbs, or cheese, may be added, depending on the recipe. But with only four simple ingredients, you can make a loaf of bread for your family.

Only one ingredient, however, is needed for salvation—the Gospel. Jesus said, "I am the living bread which came down from heaven. If anyone eats of this bread, he will live forever; and the bread that I shall give is My flesh, which I shall give for the life of the world" (John 6:51). When we take Jesus Christ spiritually and make Him a part of us, Jesus satisfies our hunger and gives us eternal life. The Bread of Life promises not only eternal life but a rich abundant life (John 10:10). And this Bread from heaven is far more satisfying than any bread fresh from the oven—with Christ we will never hunger again.

JANUARY 13
Walking the Talk at Home

And you, fathers, do not provoke your children to wrath,
but bring them up in the training and admonition of the Lord.
EPHESIANS 6:4

In one family, the dad spends all his time landscaping the yard. In another, the mom lives on the phone. In another, parents read Bible stories and pray with their children every night. And in yet another family, the parents talk about how much they love their church family and friends. It reminds us of the saying, "Be careful what you do, 'cause little eyes are watching you.'"

It's not hard to notice what a person's priorities are. It matters less what we say and more what we do. Saying is important at the right times, but we need to spend more time doing in the home than talking; our actions speak louder than our words. If someone interviewed our children and asked them, "What's the most important thing to your dad and mom?"—their answers might be revealing. When we manifest the fruit of the Spirit in our home (Galatians 5:22–23) on a consistent basis and lead our family in the things of the Lord…our children will notice.

As we imitate Christ and our children imitate us, they will reap the benefits of the fruit of the Spirit as they learn about God and His Son not only from what we say but from what we do.

JANUARY 14
A Nudge

And say to Archippus, "Take heed to the ministry
which you have received in the Lord, that you may fulfill it."
COLOSSIANS 4:17

Do you ever need a nudge to do something? Psychologists claim that twenty percent of us are habitual procrastinators, and the other eighty percent occasionally struggle with putting things off. Several books have been written to help people overcome procrastination, but those who need the books never get around to opening them! They need a nudge.

So did Archippus.

This man is mentioned twice in the Bible. He lived in the town of Colossae and attended the church that met in Philemon's home. Paul called him "our fellow soldier" (Philemon 1:2). But in writing to the Colossians, Paul cryptically devoted one verse to his fellow soldier: "Tell Archippus: 'See to it that you complete the ministry you have received in the Lord'" (Colossians 4:17, NIV).

Put your name there in place of Archippus. God has something great for you to do. Don't put it off. God is waiting to use you. View this verse as a nudge. Complete the work God has given you—and begin today!

JANUARY 15
A Generous Gift

By this we know love, because He laid down His life for us.
And we also ought to lay down our lives for the brethren.
But whoever has this world's goods, and sees his brother in need,
and shuts up his heart from him, how does the love of God abide in him?

1 JOHN 3:16–17

Last year a waitress in Massachusetts received a five-thousand-dollar tip from a customer. She initially thought a decimal point was missing, but when she looked at the bottom of the receipt, she realized the tip really was for five thousand dollars, not fifty dollars! Through social media, the waitress was able to thank her customer saying, "I already thoroughly enjoy my job, but you just made it that much better."[1]

An unexpected financial gift of five thousand dollars would make most of our weeks or months. But Christ gave us the greatest gift we could ever receive—the gift of His life. In the same way, He calls us to give generously to each other. The love of God is displayed when we give to others. You may not be able to leave a generous tip, but perhaps you can donate some food to a food bank or help a neighbor with their yard work. Jesus' generous gift of salvation compels us to love others by being His hands extended to meet the needs of others wherever and whenever we can.

[1] "Waitress Gets $5,000 Tip From Billionaire in Challenge Gone Viral," *KIRO 7 News*, February 3, 2020.

JANUARY 16
The Voice of the Spirit

But the Helper, the Holy Spirit,
whom the Father will send in My name,
He will teach you all things.
JOHN 14:26

In this day of smart phones and social media it has become increasingly difficult for us to discern our own thoughts and feelings. In order to keep up with life, it seems we must travel at the speed of society, never stopping to take a deep breath and listen to the Holy Spirit's leading. As frustrating as this may be, it is not a new challenge.

When Jesus walked the earth, He was constantly surrounded by a multitude of people; but He knew that the most important relationship He could invest in was with His Father, for it was His voice that would lead and guide Him. Therefore, He spent a large amount of time in prayer and conversation with God.

A lady was once asked how she knew the voice of the Spirit. She answered, "How do you know your husband's step and your child's cry from the step and cry of all others?" For her, the voice of the Spirit was as familiar as the unique sounds of her husband and child.

To become sensitive to the Spirit's leading, spend time getting to know His voice. The more intimately we know Him, the easier it will be to hear His voice above all others.

It Takes a Lifetime

But solid food belongs to those who are of full age...those who by reason of
use have their senses exercised to discern both good and evil.

HEBREWS 5:14

It has been said that the new birth takes but a moment;
spiritual maturity takes a lifetime.

Nowhere is this more clearly demonstrated than in the
Parable of the Sower where Jesus warns His disciples about the
many different ways in which God's Word would be received.
He said some would fall by the wayside, being snatched up
by the devil as soon as the Word entered their heart. Others
would receive the Word with joy but fall away during a time
of temptation. Still others would hear the Word, yet remain
entangled in the cares of the world, making it impossible for
them to bring any spiritual fruit to maturity. Finally, Jesus told
of the ones who, "having heard the word with a noble and good
heart, keep it and bear fruit with patience" (Luke 8:11–15).

Spiritual maturity is a continual process of growth that
takes time and patience. As you remain rooted in the Word and
nourished through prayer and fellowship with the Lord, you
will see your faith grow and mature as never before.

JANUARY 18
Living Water

Whoever drinks of this water will thirst again,
but whoever drinks of the water that I shall give him
will never thirst. But the water that I shall give him will
become in him a fountain of water springing up into everlasting life.

JOHN 4:13-14

Physical water has two properties—hydrogen and oxygen. They are both tasteless, unseen elements. But what happens when you put them together? They form the vast oceans that surround the largest mass of our great world. And without those two elements put together in what we call water, we can't live.

When Jesus met the Samaritan woman at the well in Sychar, He engaged her in a conversation about living water. However, the woman was focused on physical water. It took her some time to understand that living water is spiritual. When the woman asked Him a question about worship, Jesus said, "Those who worship [God] must worship in spirit and truth" (John 4:24). The spiritual, living water which Jesus was talking about and to which He pointed the Samaritan woman also has two properties—the spirit and the truth.

Living water never runs out, and it quenches our thirst completely. So if you're thirsty and seeking, your spiritual thirst won't be met with physical water. Instead, come to Jesus, receive Him, and discover the refreshment you seek.

JANUARY 19
Verses or Chapters?

Your Word I have hidden in my heart.
PSALM 119:11

Michael Billester visited eastern Poland during the late 1930s and gave a Bible to one of the villagers while there. The villager read it, was converted, and passed the book to two hundred others who were all saved because of it. When Billester returned in 1940, the group gathered for a worship service, and he suggested they all recite a few Bible verses they had memorized. A man stood up and said, "Perhaps we have misunderstood. Did you mean verses or chapters?" Billester was astonished to learn that they had memorized whole chapters of the Bible. In fact, together, the two hundred villagers knew almost the entire Bible by heart.

View memorizing Scripture as important as these Polish villagers did. Value its power and effectiveness in your life as much as Jesus did when He used it to defend Himself against Satan's temptations.

Remember the true purpose for memorizing Scripture—"that you may be able to stand against the wiles of the devil" (Ephesians 6:11). Make it a priority to spend some time imprinting the Word of God on your heart and mind.

Be strong and of good courage, do not fear nor be afraid of them;
for the Lord your God, He is the One who goes with you.
He will not leave you nor forsake you.
DEUTERONOMY 31:6

How many emotions are swirling around inside you? In the old days, we were taught human personalities were composed of six emotions that mixed together, like primary colors, to create a range of feelings. A study published in the *Proceedings of the National Academy of Sciences of the United States of America* suggests that there are 27 basic emotions. The list is too long to print here, but it includes: amusement, anxiety, awe, boredom, calmness, disgust, envy, excitement, fear, horror, sadness, and sympathy.

Our emotions can overwhelm us, but we shouldn't let them overwhelm the truth of God. When you experience fear, sadness, anxiety, or confusion, turn your attention to the Word of God. There are two chapters in the Bible, Deuteronomy 31 and Joshua 1, where the Lord tells us again and again that He will never leave us nor forsake us.

These are good chapters to read when your emotions are giving you trouble. Don't give in to your swirling emotions, place your trust in God's comforting presence to lead and guide you.

JANUARY 21
No Limit to Forgiveness

I acknowledged my sin to You, and my iniquity I have not hidden.
I said, "I will confess my transgressions to the Lord,"
and You forgave the iniquity of my sin.
PSALM 32:5

Most nations have *periods of prescription* in their legal systems—more commonly referred to as "statutes of limitations." Such statutes designate a specific period of time when charges must be brought against someone accused of committing a civil or criminal crime—the purpose being to ensure a speedy resolution of the charges for the sake of the accused.

Thankfully for us, there is no statute of limitation for when sin must be confessed in order to receive God's forgiveness. Let's say you sin and fail to confess it to God, then ten years later you come under conviction about that sin. Is it too late to confess it? Has God's grace period run out? Certainly not! No such limitation exists. King David waited almost a year before confessing his adultery and complicity in murder to God—and he only confessed then because he had been found out (2 Samuel 11–12). But God still forgave him.

Don't wait to confess your sins to God. When you wait to confess your sin, you carry the weight of your guilt and shame with you each day. Remember, He is ready and willing to forgive all who come to Him (1 John 1:9).

"The Kingdom of Heaven Is at Hand"

And as you go, preach, saying, "The kingdom of heaven is at hand."
MATTHEW 10:7

When John the Baptist began his ministry, he preached (Matthew 3:1). And when Jesus followed on John's heels, He did the same thing: He preached (Matthew 4:17). After Jesus ascended to heaven, His followers in Jerusalem did what they had been taught: They preached (Acts 4:2; 5:42). And after Stephen's martyrdom, when the Church was driven from Jerusalem, Acts 8 is evidence of their single-minded focus on preaching (verses 4–5, 12, 35, 40). Then Paul was converted and "immediately he preached the Christ in the synagogues, that He is the Son of God" (Acts 9:20).

Regardless of who, when, or where, the early followers of Jesus preached! In the early stages, John and Jesus "declared, announced" that the Kingdom of God was at hand. After the resurrection, preaching became more focused: proclaiming the good news/tidings of Christ's identity, death, burial, and resurrection for the sins of the world (1 Corinthians 15:1–4). Why did they focus on preaching? Paul answered that question with another question: "And how shall they hear [and call and believe] without a preacher?" (Romans 10:14–15).

Wherever you go today, "Preach the word! Be ready in season and out of season" (2 Timothy 4:2), for "The kingdom of heaven is at hand."

JANUARY 23
Tell God Everything

I cry out to the Lord with my voice;
with my voice to the Lord I make my supplication.
PSALM 142:1

When reading the New Testament, we sometimes wonder: "Was the apostle Paul thinking of such-and-such Old Testament event when he wrote those words?" That could be the case when we see an example (Old Testament) and exhortation (New Testament) to pour out our concerns to God.

When David was anointed king, King Saul tried to kill David to block his ascension to the throne. On one occasion, David hid in "the cave of Adullam" (1 Samuel 22:1) to escape the murderous Saul. In Psalm 142, we have a record of David's prayer to God while he was hiding from Saul. And what a prayer! Surely it is an example of what Paul wrote about in Philippians 4:6–7—don't be anxious, but through prayers and supplications let your concerns be made known to God. And just as David was guarded in a "stronghold" while he prayed (1 Samuel 22:4), so the believer is guarded by the peace of God as we commit our concerns to Him (Philippians 4:7).

Don't be afraid to tell God your deepest needs and concerns. By example and exhortation, the Bible instructs us to bring everything to God in prayer and supplication.

His Permanent Purpose

"No weapon formed against you shall prosper, and every tongue which rises against you in judgment you shall condemn. This is the heritage of the servants of the Lord, and their righteousness is from Me," says the Lord.

ISAIAH 54:17

Isaiah 53 is one of the most theologically important chapters in the Old Testament. It contains the portrait of the Servant of the Lord—the coming Messiah who would suffer on behalf of His people. The Servant—revealed eventually as Jesus Christ—saw that many would be opposed to Him (Isaiah 50:8–9). Yet He also saw that He would be vindicated by God: "Surely the Lord God will help Me" (verse 9).

Interestingly, after the Servant's presentation in Isaiah 53, He is never referred to again in the singular. Rather, it is His "seed" (Isaiah 53:10), His spiritual offspring, who take center stage. It is "the heritage of the servants of the Lord" that "no weapon formed against [them] shall prosper" (Isaiah 54:17). God's purposes for His people will never be canceled (Isaiah 55:10–11).

If God has called you for a purpose, and He has, you can be assured of this: Nothing will prosper against you and God's purpose for your life.

JANUARY 25
Known and Loved

Before I formed you in the womb I knew you;
before you were born I sanctified you; I ordained you.

JEREMIAH 1:5

It's mind-boggling to imagine what God was doing before the creation of the universe. Since He is from everlasting to everlasting (Psalm 90:2), He existed before "time" began. But only God Himself can understand that. Yet we do have a few hints about it from the Bible. We know the Father, Son, and Holy Spirit enjoyed rich fellowship, for Jesus prayed about the glory and love He shared with the Father before the world began (John 17:5, 24).

Ephesians 1:4 says that God chose us in Christ "before the foundation of the world." And Matthew 25:34 says that God has prepared a kingdom for us "from the foundation of the world."

God also knew you and planned your life in advance, so you could live with purpose and fulfillment. Before He formed you in the womb, He knew you and set you apart to serve Him. The apostle Paul said the same thing in Galatians 1:15.

Hallelujah! Jesus has a lifetime of purpose stored up for you. Don't waste a moment of it—seek His guidance and move forward into His perfect will for your life.

JANUARY 26
The Faithful Son

If we are faithless, He remains faithful; He cannot deny Himself.
2 TIMOTHY 2:13

What if the sun decided one day not to shine its warm, life-giving rays on your spot of earth? What if morning never came? What if you couldn't count on the sun rising?

Not once in thousands of years has the sun been unreliable. In times of war and peace, in times of love and hate, in times of revival or depravity, it still rises. Its dependability is unaffected by the fickle, undulating tides of human thought and behavior.

The Creator is far more faithful than the creation. God will keep His promises, honor His commitments, and care for His children, no matter what. Numbers 23:19 says: "God is not a man, that He should lie, nor a son of man, that He should repent. Has He said, and will He not do? Or has He spoken, and will He not make it good?"

God expects His children to be faithful, but His faithfulness to us isn't dependent on our faithfulness to Him. If you've failed God—if you've been faithless—confess it to Him and seek His forgiveness. But don't doubt His faithfulness. "The sun shall no longer be your light by day, nor for brightness shall the moon give light to you; but the Lord will be to you an everlasting light, and your God your glory" (Isaiah 60:19).

O Lord, Your Name is Faithful and True, and I am trusting You today.

JANUARY 27
Ravenous for Revelation

Your words were found, and I ate them,
and Your word was to me the joy and rejoicing of my heart.
JEREMIAH 15:16

Nutritionists warn that skipping too many meals can interfere
with our body's appetite and cause us to develop strong food
cravings, especially for sugar and carbohydrates. The same thing
can happen spiritually. If we begin skipping our regular time
of personal Bible study, we might lose our healthy appetite and
begin feeding our mind with mental junk food.

It's normal for a healthy soul to crave a few morsels from
the book of Proverbs, which are simple and easy to digest.
Other times we need a long, slow, hot meal from Ephesians
or Ezekiel. Are you ever hungry for the Sermon on the
Mount? Thirsty for the worship of the Psalms? Ravenous for
Revelation?

The entire Bible—Genesis to Revelation—is a pantry for
the soul. It's God's menu for our mind and heart, manna for
every morning and bread for every night. When we hunger
and thirst for Scripture, God feeds and sustains us with His
nourishing Word.

JANUARY 28
Soaring to Strength

But those who wait on the Lord shall renew their strength;
they shall mount up with wings like eagles,
they shall run and not be weary, they shall walk and not faint.

ISAIAH 40:31

The Andean condor is the world's largest soaring bird. With a wingspan of more than ten feet, condors can soar for up to five hours, covering one hundred miles, without flapping their wings once! In one study, a group of condors spent just one percent of their time aloft flapping their wings.[2]

The prophet Isaiah had never seen an Andean condor, but he had certainly seen eagles and other soaring birds in the Middle East. It is no wonder that he used the image of a soaring eagle to represent the one who waits on the Lord. Once aloft, it is the power of the wind that keeps the eagle soaring, not the power of the eagle itself. In the Christian life, it is the wind of the Spirit of God that gives us power to run and not be weary, to walk and not grow faint.

Renew your strength as you wait upon Him in prayer and Bible study each day.

[2] "Andean Condor Can Fly for 100 Miles Without Flapping Wings" *The Guardian*, July 13, 2020.

JANUARY 29
Set Apart for a Purpose

And when forty years had passed, an Angel of the Lord appeared to [Moses] in a flame of fire in a bush, in the wilderness of Mount Sinai.

ACTS 7:30

Readers of the four Gospels, the accounts of Jesus' life and ministry on earth, are familiar with the time He spent alone. It was apparently not unusual for Him to withdraw from the crowds, even from His own disciples, to spend time alone with the Father (Luke 5:16). The interesting thing is that this practice of isolation was not uncommon among those learning from and about God.

The apostle Paul is a good example. After his conversion to Christ, he immediately withdrew into the wilderness of Arabia before returning to Damascus (Galatians 1:17). In total, he ministered some fourteen years in relative obscurity before being embraced by the leaders of the Jerusalem church (Galatians 1:21–2 2:2). An even longer period of obscurity was endured by Moses—forty years as a shepherd in Midian before God called him to go back to Egypt to lead the Hebrews out of captivity.

Sometimes God sets us apart in order to prepare us for what is coming next. Nothing happens by chance—there is always a purpose in His plan for His children.

Common Blessings and Burdens

He makes His sun rise on the evil and on the good,
and sends rain on the just and on the unjust.
MATTHEW 5:45

In Matthew 5:45, Jesus spoke of God's fairness and graciousness. Every morning the sun gives another day's life to all humanity, whether evil or good. Refreshing showers fall on the lawns of committed Christians and of their pagan neighbors. While some blessings are reserved only for the children of God, others are common to the entire world.

In the same way, some burdens are borne by believers, such as persecution or sorrow over lost souls. But other burdens are shared by all humanity; being a Christian doesn't make us immune from trials. Even seasoned Christians need to remember this, or else we'll find ourselves thinking, "Why is this happening to me? If God loves me so, why am I in such painful straits? Why don't other people have these problems I'm facing?"

Sorrow is universal; but for the believer, it is redemptive because God turns it to good. Dr. F. B. Meyer wrote, "In suffering and sorrow God touches the minor chords, develops the passive virtues, and opens to view the treasures of darkness, the constellations of promise, the rainbow of hope, the silver light of the covenant."

Trust God's sovereign plan for your life today and rejoice in His loving care—He is with you—rain or shine.

These all died in faith, not having received the promises, but having seen them afar off were assured of them, embraced them and confessed that they were strangers and pilgrims on the earth.

HEBREWS 11:13

Is anything harder in life than keeping promises? Making promises is easy; keeping them is another matter. Sadly, everyone has broken a promise—or at least not kept a promise as well as they would have intended. And our experience of promise-breaking makes us wonder about God and His promises: If we don't always keep ours, does He?

The first twelve verses of Hebrews 11 list ordinary people who received promises from God but never experienced their fulfillment before they died: Abel, Enoch, Noah, Abraham, Isaac, Jacob, Sarah, and others. *But they didn't doubt God.* They were "assured" by the promises and "embraced" the promises and died believing the promises as "strangers and pilgrims on the earth." We are like them. We have been given "great and precious promises" (2 Peter 1:4), some of which may not be fulfilled in our lifetime. That is why we are called to "walk by faith, not by sight" (2 Corinthians 5:7).

Be assured by God's promises. Embrace God's promises. Live and, if need be, die, trusting God's promises. God is faithful and true, and so are His promises.

FEBRUARY

FEBRUARY 1
Joy in the Word

I rejoice at Your word as one who finds great treasure.
PSALM 119:162

El Dorado was the name given by Spaniards in the sixteenth century to describe a mythical king of native people in Colombia, South America. The myth grew from referring to a man, to a city, to a kingdom, and finally to an empire of gold. Treasure hunters from England and Spain searched all over Colombia, Venezuela, Guyana, and northern Brazil—and all came up sad and disappointed. There was no city or kingdom of golden treasures to be found.

But there is a treasure of joy waiting to be discovered between the pages of Scripture—the treasure of God's Word. Could anything be more valuable than a Book that answers mankind's most important questions: Where did I come from? What is my purpose? What is right and wrong? What is my destiny? These questions, and more, are the foundation of man's questioning about our purpose and place here on earth—and the answers are there for us in Scripture. In good times and bad, we can rejoice knowing the answers to all of life's biggest questions are there for the reading.

Solomon penned these words about the treasure of God's Word: "If you seek it like silver and search for it as for hidden treasures, then you will understand the fear of the Lord and find the knowledge of God" (Proverbs 2:4–5, ESV).

FEBRUARY 2
Don't Be Shaken

Then a voice came from the throne, saying, "Praise our God, all you His servants and those who fear Him, both small and great!"
REVELATION 19:5

Imagine a moment when terrible earthquakes rattle vast portions of the planet, causing entire cities to collapse. When evil reigns on earth and war engulfs the Middle East. What should we do when that time comes?

That's a great time to look up, for your redemption draws nigh.

Revelation 17 and 18 describe such a moment, when the empire of the Antichrist will crumble just as he's on the verge of destroying the nation of Israel. The world will literally be at the point of Armageddon. And at that terrible moment, a loud voice will call from the throne of heaven, saying: "Praise our God, all you His servants and those who fear Him, both small and great!" The choirs of heaven will burst into loud shouts of "Alleluia!" And Christ will return to resolve all the issues of earth, judge evil, and establish His kingdom.

Praising God brings perspective to our problems, restores hope for the hurting, and creates confidence during chaos. Whatever earthquake is rocking your life today, praise our awesome and unshakable God. He's on His way to help.

FEBRUARY 3
Be an Ambassador

[Jesus] sent them to preach the kingdom of God and to heal the sick.
LUKE 9:2

Most nations send ambassadors to live in the capital of other countries around the world. Ambassadors only have the authority granted to them by their country's government. But their status is official. When they speak, they speak for their nation. And when they act, they are expected to act as their own government would act.

The apostle Paul said that he, and his coworkers, were "ambassadors for Christ, as though God were [speaking] through us" (2 Corinthians 5:20). When Paul spoke, he spoke the Word of God. Christ had commissioned him to go and speak—to represent the Kingdom of God to the world (Acts 9:15; 23:11; 26:15–18). Paul wasn't the first kingdom ambassador to be sent by Jesus. He had sent the twelve disciples (Matthew 10; Mark 6; Luke 9), and then another group of seventy (Luke 10). He sent them to do the same thing He had been doing: Preach about the kingdom and heal the sick.

Like Paul, we are Christ's ambassadors sent to represent the King and His kingdom in the world. He is with us every moment helping us fulfill our mission, even until "the end of the age" (Matthew 28:20).

FEBRUARY 4
New Beginning

And Jesus went about all Galilee, teaching in their synagogues,
preaching the gospel of the kingdom, and healing all kinds of sickness
and all kinds of disease among the people.
MATTHEW 4:23

During His earthly ministry, Jesus not only instructed and inspired people by His powerful presence and wisdom, but he cast out demons and healed the sick and lame. After meeting Jesus, the blind could see; the deaf could hear; the lame could walk; the demon possessed were set free; and their sins were forgiven! Jesus gave them a new beginning! They were no longer the outcasts of society, forced to beg for their daily food; they were restored to a new life in their community, and freed from their sin.

For those who come to Christ today, a new life in Christ is ours as well. Second Corinthians 5:17 says, "Therefore, if anyone is in Christ, he is a new creation; old things have passed away; behold, all things have become new." Through Christ's sacrifice, we are set free from the weight of our sin and the burden of shame. No longer in darkness, we now walk in the light of God's love and the newness of life (Romans 6:4). It is a new beginning.

If we would judge ourselves, we would not be judged.
1 CORINTHIANS 11:31

Jonathan knew he shouldn't use the company computer to access questionable websites, but he did it anyway. As a result, his boss appeared in his office one day, asked for his keys and files, and summarily marched him outside the building, firing him. Jonathan was humiliated, but he had no one to blame but himself. If he had evaluated and corrected his behavior, others would not have done so. If he had judged himself, he would not have been judged.

To judge our sins means seeing them in their true light as God sees them. It means to hate those sins and to know that God wants to put them out of our life. It means to honestly acknowledge moral failures in our life and to deal with them through genuine, lasting confession and repentance.

King David did this in Psalm 32:3–5: "When I kept silent, my bones grew old through my groaning all the day long. For day and night Your hand was heavy upon me; my vitality was turned into the drought of summer. I acknowledged my sin to You, and my iniquity I have not hidden. I said, 'I will confess my transgressions to the Lord,' and You forgave the iniquity of my sin."

Does anything in your life need to be evaluated and corrected today? Repentance not only brings relief, it brings restoration to our relationship with Christ.

Powder Keg

Therefore submit to God. Resist the devil and he will flee from you.
JAMES 4:7

"Lord, deliver me from that evil man—myself." So prayed the great theologian, Augustine, in the fifth century. Most of us feel that way. Though eager to live a disciplined life, we struggle with the conniving, debasing tendencies of the "flesh." When the Bible talks about the "flesh," it isn't talking about our physical bodies, but about our sinful natures. When we become Christians, our "old selves" don't disappear. We inherit a new Christ-like nature, but the old nature still hangs on with pit-bull determination.

Dr. W. A. Criswell said: "We sit on a veritable magazine of powder, this old nature, this unregenerate self.... Our worst enemy is the old self." We can't gain mastery over sinful tendencies just by turning over a new leaf, making resolutions, or finding accountability partners—though those things are helpful. We must walk in the Spirit. That means daily submitting every aspect of our lives willingly to Christ, consciously living under His control.

Ask the Holy Spirit to guide and direct your path each day so that your life will reflect the Lord Jesus Christ. "Put on the Lord Jesus Christ, and make no provision for the flesh, to fulfill its lusts" (Romans 13:14).

Not I, but Christ!

Let integrity and uprightness preserve me, for I wait for You.
PSALM 25:21

The eighteenth-century English minister, Matthew Henry, wrote, "Cast not away your confidence because God defers His performances. That which does not come in your time, will be hastened in His time, which is always the more convenient season. He is not bound to keep our time, but He will perform His word, honour our faith, and reward them that diligently seek Him." [3]

Sometimes it can seem like God does not "show up" when we want Him to. But as Henry states, God simply defers His performances at times in order to teach us the concept of active waiting. God's desire is not for us to stop serving Him simply because we are waiting for His answer. He wants us to seek Him and be about His business while we wait, for it is in those precious times of waiting that we learn to be dependent upon God alone.

Keep doing what is right, living in a godly manner, knowing that the Lord will answer your questions in His time. Don't be anxious and move forward in haste, but wait patiently for God's guidance and direction. The answer will come in His time.

[3] http://dailychristianquote.com/dcqpatience-waiting.html.

But God demonstrates His own love toward us,
in that while we were still sinners, Christ died for us.

ROMANS 5:8

Thermopylae is the ancient Greek location of numerous battles of antiquity, most notably between the Greeks and the invading Persians in 480 B.C. A vastly outnumbered Greek army—including the 300 Spartans—were tasked with delaying the hundreds of thousands of invading Persian warriors. Knowing they were doomed to defeat, they went to Thermopylae to die. Such was the Spartan ethic: Life was consummated in a noble death.

Such was Jesus' ethic: He came into the world to die for sinners. (And not just to die, but to conquer death and live forever—1 Corinthians 15:54–55.) Such was His love for us that He "set [His] face like a flint" (Isaiah 50:7) and "steadfastly set His face to go to Jerusalem" (Luke 9:51) to die the death of a sinner. Why did He do this? Because "greater love has no one than this, than to lay down one's life for his friends" (John 15:13).

We may never be called to die physically for another person, but we are called to die to ourselves by putting others' needs ahead of our own. Such was His love for us!

FEBRUARY 9
Leap of Faith

The God of my strength, in whom I will trust;
My shield and the horn of my salvation,
My stronghold and my refuge.
2 SAMUEL 22:3

In 2021, an apartment building in France caught fire, trapping two brothers, aged three and ten, several floors above the ground. A crowd gathered, and the boys had to jump into the arms of those far below them. The older boy dropped his little brother into the crowd while thick, black smoke billowed from the apartment. Then the ten-year-old hesitated. The crowd yelled for him to jump, and, gathering all his courage, he leapt into the air. Both boys were caught, and neither was harmed.

We never know when or if we'll be called upon to exercise sudden courage. If we put ourselves in the ten-year-old's shoes, would we have the courage to leap off a burning ledge? Hopefully we would if situation called for it.

But God gives us spiritual boldness like He gives grace—just when it's needed. If you're facing something frightening, take comfort and "Be strong and of good courage" (Deuteronomy 31:6). Don't be afraid. The eternal God is your refuge and underneath are His everlasting arms. He is your strong refuge.

But Simon answered and said to [Jesus], "Master, we have toiled all night and caught nothing; nevertheless at Your word I will let down the net." And when they had done this, they caught a great number of fish.

LUKE 5:5–6

When a highly recruited basketball player arrives on a college campus to play for the first time, some of the fans may have heard of him, but they have probably never seen him play. During the season opener, if the new player plays well, he will no doubt demonstrate to the crowd why he was recruited by his performance on the court. By seeing his skills, the fans will realize this is no regular basketball player; he has the talent to help their team win.

When Jesus called Peter, James, and John as His disciples, they had been fishing all night but had been unable to catch any fish. Jesus told them to go "out into the deep and let down your nets for a catch" (Luke 5:4). The men reluctantly obeyed, and they caught "a great number of fish" (verse 6). It was a mighty moment in the lives of these men. They discovered that nothing was impossible for Jesus—even knowing where the fish were to be found—and they "forsook all and followed Him" (Luke 5:11).

Jesus' miracles during His earthly ministry demonstrated not only who He was, but the power that He had to forgive sin, to heal the sick, and in this case to allow some weary fishermen to bring in a mighty catch after spending hours toiling with no success. What a powerful Savior we serve!

FEBRUARY 11
All Have Come to Pass

For the Lord our God is He who brought us and our fathers
up out of the land of Egypt, from the house of bondage, who did those
great signs in our sight, and preserved us in all the way that we
went and among all the people through whom we passed.
JOSHUA 24:17

Every book of the Bible has a unique purpose. Many times you can find a key verse that drives this home. For example, the purpose of the book of Revelation is stated right at the beginning of the book: "to show His servants—things that must shortly take place" (Revelation 1:1). In the book of Joshua, the underlying purpose and theme is found in Joshua 23:14:

"And you know in all your hearts and in all your souls that not one thing has failed of all the good things which the Lord your God spoke concerning you. All have come to pass; not one word of them has failed."

"Not one word of them has failed." What a tremendous thought! God promised ancient Israel that they would have a homeland, that He would guide them by His presence, provide for their needs, and bring them to their new home. Not one promise failed.

God's faithfulness is as certain as the sun rising in the morning—He keeps His promises.

And He sat down, called the twelve, and said to them,
"If anyone desires to be first, he shall be last of all and servant of all."

MARK 9:35

In his short novel, *Journey to the East*, German author Hermann Hesse told the story of a group of men on a mythical journey. One of the main characters is Leo, a servant who handles all the group's menial tasks and needs—until he disappears. Without Leo the journey falls apart and is abandoned. Years later, one of the original journeymen discovers that Leo, the servant, was the head of the league that had sponsored the journey. He was a powerful and noble leader but had exercised his leadership by being a servant to others.

This fictional parable illustrates perfectly what Jesus taught His disciples about leading through service. When Jesus discovered the disciples arguing about which among them was the greatest, He set them straight: The greatest is the least; the last is the first; the leader is the servant. It's another of the paradoxes in the Kingdom of God—the opposite of how the world thinks. Instead of praying that God would allow you to lead others, pray for opportunities to serve others. Only through humble service are true leaders born.

[Nothing] shall be able to separate us from the love of God
which is in Christ Jesus our Lord.
ROMANS 8:39

Imprinting occurs when some birds or mammals are born and they bond with the first thing they see. Most notably, baby ducklings hatched from an incubator are known to imprint on the humans who raise them, making them inseparable.

Another kind of imprinting is described by Jesus in John 10:27–28: "My sheep hear My voice … and they follow Me…. And they shall never perish; neither shall anyone snatch them out of My hand." If we have been born again, we will follow Christ. And nothing shall ever separate us from the love of God which is in Christ. God is "stuck with us" for eternity! Paul details a long list of forces that might seek to break the bond between Him and us (Romans 8:35–39). And he concludes the list by saying that nothing can separate us from God's love. His love not only saves us but keeps us secure forever.

Give thanks that you are secure in God's love. Then, look for ways to help others discover the unconditional love of God—it is the greatest love story ever told.

FEBRUARY 14

True Love

For if when we were enemies we were reconciled to God through the death of
His Son, much more, having been reconciled, we shall be saved by His life.
ROMANS 5:10

The sixteenth-century English Bible translator, William Tyndale, was detained by royal authorities in Belgium and condemned to die. He was tied to a stake, strangled to death, and his body was burned. His last words were reported: "Lord! Open the king of England's eyes." Not a prayer of vengeance, judgment, anger, or regret—but a prayer of love, that the king of England's eyes would be open to spiritual truth. That is consistent with Paul's description of unconditional love in 1 Corinthians 13:7: Love "hopes all things, endures all things." And Jesus' words in John 15:13: True love will lay down its own life (self-interests, desires) for the life of another. Jesus Himself, while dying on a cross, asked God to forgive those who put Him there (Luke 23:34).

These are all examples of unconditional love—the kind of love God demonstrated when He sent His only Son to die on the cross for us (John 3:16; Romans 5:10). Love for one's enemies is unconditional love—it goes against our nature to love someone who doesn't love us in return—but it is how God loves. His love is unchangeable, constant, and unconditional. And we are called to love like He loves. We show God's love when we love "in spite of" what someone has said or done and we put others' needs ahead of our own. That is true love.

FEBRUARY 15
Aren't You Scared?

Where, O death, is your victory?
1 CORINTHIANS 15:55, NIV

A young boy was seen cutting across a cemetery lot just around dark and was later asked by an observer, "Aren't you scared?" "No," said the boy. "I only cut through here to get home."

The boy didn't see any reason to fear the cemetery; the only thing he focused on was how quickly he was going to get home.

In the same way, we have no reason to fear death; it is merely a shortcut to our heavenly home. The Bible tells us that the instant we are absent from this life and this body, we are present with the Lord (2 Corinthians 5:8). In other words, we are literally carried from this life to the next in the arms of the One who created us … we are never alone, even for a moment. What a comforting thought!

When we accept the Lord as our personal Savior, our eternal home in heaven is secured. Rejoice in that fact and keep your eyes firmly fixed on Christ, so that, like the little boy, you will have no reason to fear the shortcut home.

FEBRUARY 16
No One Like You!

Now you are the body of Christ, and members individually.
1 CORINTHIANS 12:27

For $75,000 you can buy Spot, the mass-produced robotic dog that can walk, climb stairs, and open doors. He doesn't need housetraining, feeding, or a daily walk. And he can be helpful in difficult situations. He has cameras in his eyes, is rust-proof, and can operate in terrible weather. He isn't safe for children, and he isn't unique. Every Spot is essentially like every other Spot—and he's not really alive.

God has created billions of beings who are alive. He put cameras in our eyes, a beating heart in our chests, and remarkable physical systems that defy the finest robotic innovators. And we don't rust.

Furthermore, we aren't mass produced. Each of us is uniquely created by God with our own personalities, gifts, talents, backgrounds, faces, fingerprints, and backgrounds. We all have one purpose—to glorify God and enjoy Him forever—but individual ministries. There is no one like you. There never has been, and there never will be. You are an important member of the Body of Christ—put your gifts and talents to use for the Kingdom today!

FEBRUARY 17
Go Into All the World!

And He said to them, "Go into all the world and
preach the gospel to every creature."
MARK 16:15

Our modern English words "ethnic" and "ethnicity" come from the Greek word *ethnos* which meant people groups. When Jesus told His disciples to go and make disciples of "all nations" (Matthew 28:19—*ethne*), He wasn't referring to political nations. He was referring to "all the world's peoples"—the Gentiles of the world. And in Mark's version of the Great Commission—"preach the gospel to every creature"—the same thing is meant: preach to all creation (Greek *ktisis*—creature or creation).

In other words, Jesus' Gospel was not just for Jews. Since the days of Isaiah the prophet, the Servant of the Lord was destined to come as a "light to the Gentiles" (Isaiah 42:6; 49:6; 60:3; Acts 13:47; 26:23). It has never been easier to take the Gospel to every person, every ethnicity, every creature, than it is today. In your neighborhood and workplace, you likely have people representing a diversity of ethnicities from around the world. Can you share the Gospel with them?

To be a missionary today, you only have to leave your front door. The world has come to us; introduce them to Jesus.

But none of these things move me; nor do I count my life dear to myself, so that I may finish my race with joy, and the ministry which I received from the Lord Jesus, to testify to the gospel of the grace of God.

ACTS 20:24

The great gift of humankind is the ability to be moved, to be inspired, by art, music, people, architecture, nature, poetry, acting, and more. But we are also inspired by fear. Godly motivations move us to dream big; unwise motivations inspire us to retreat.

The apostle Paul said something profound about inspiration: "But none of these things move me." He was talking about the fear of persecution from those who opposed his ministry in Jerusalem. But he wasn't "moved" by their threats—or, more generally, anything that might befall him in the future. Why? Because he didn't count his life dear to himself. That is, he viewed his life as belonging to God, not to himself (1 Corinthians 6:19–20). Paul was moved primarily by one thing: "the ministry which [he] received from the Lord Jesus, to testify to the gospel of the grace of God."

The greater our God-given dream—our vision, our ministry—the less we will be moved by the things of this world.

Intense Love

And this is love: that we walk in obedience to his commands.
2 JOHN 1:6, NIV

Bible teacher Donald Grey Barnhouse told the story of a young son of a missionary couple in Zaire who was playing in the yard when suddenly he heard his father's voice ring out, "Philip, obey me instantly! Drop to your stomach!" The boy did so immediately. "Now crawl to me as fast as you can!" The boy obeyed. "Now stand up and run to me!" Philip ran into his father's arms. When the young boy looked back at the tree he had been playing near, he saw a large deadly snake hanging from one of the branches. His instant obedience had saved his life!

You can almost feel the intensity of this father's love as he asks his son for complete trust and obedience in order to avoid impending danger. It is no different with God. He sees what we cannot; and when our life is headed for peril, He cries out to us with the intense love of a father trying to save his child's life.

So when you hear God's voice commanding you to obey, remember it is the loving, caring voice of your Heavenly Father who desires only the very best for you. Obedience is the key.

Son of My Right Hand

And so it was, as her soul was departing (for she died),
that she called his name Ben-Oni; but his father called him Benjamin.
GENESIS 35:18

Many children are being saddled with strange names nowadays, such as the boy whose sports-minded parents named him Espn. In colonial times, parents sometimes opened the Bible at random and selected the first word they saw, which led one child to be named Notwithstanding Griswold.

There were some strange names in the Old Testament, too. In Genesis 35, as Rachel struggled in childbirth, she named her son Ben-Oni, which means "Son of My Sorrow." Imagine having a name that would constantly remind you that your birth had caused your mother's death! Graciously, the boy's father, Jacob, discarded that name and called him Benjamin, which means "Son of My Right Hand"—a designation of honor in the home.

Often we suffer trials in life. Times of trouble can leave us bitter, causing us to contend with negative emotions. But those are the times when we need to trust the Lord to bring honor out of suffering and triumph out of tears. Allow the trouble to make you better, not bitter. Through faith we can view our experiences through God's perspective—it is an illuminating view.

Trusting in God's promises is a winning strategy. Remember: It was the tribe of Benjamin that not only produced Israel's first king but also the great apostle Paul.

FEBRUARY 21
Peter and John

For we cannot but speak the things which we have seen and heard.
ACTS 4:20

The Sanhedrin simply didn't know what to do with Peter, John, and the other disciples. These apostles, who had recently been cowardly and craven, were now as bold as lions. They were enflamed by the resurrection of Jesus and filled with the Holy Spirit. Fleeing was no longer an option. When the council commanded them to cease their teaching, Peter replied, "Whether it is right in the sight of God to listen to you more than to God, you judge. For we cannot but speak the things which we have seen and heard" (Acts 4:19–20).

Many forces are trying to silence Christians in the world today. Though two thousand years have passed, the age long opposition to the Gospel still exists. In some lands, it takes the form of overt persecution. In others, secular forces seek to intimidate believers into silence.

But the Word of God cannot be silenced. The followers of Christ will always find a way to proclaim the Good News. We do not retreat and flee, but stand firm as soldiers ready for battle. The Gospel is unstoppable in this world. "Watch, stand fast in the faith, be brave, be strong" (1 Corinthians 16:13).

FEBRUARY 22
Onward Christian Soldier

And whoever does not bear his cross
and come after Me cannot be My disciple.
LUKE 14:27

Entering boot camp for basic military training used to mean being stripped of all your identity. Everything was taken from you—including your hair—and you were given back only what you would need to be a good soldier. You were even told what to think: "When I want your opinion," the drill sergeant would bark, "I'll give it to you!"

Not to compare the Christian life with the military... but wait—even Paul drew that comparison (2 Timothy 2:3). There is discipline, training—and especially sacrifice—in both the military and the Christian life. When Jesus was recruiting and training His own kingdom soldiers, He told them they would only need one thing in order to follow Him: a cross. He didn't say to bring your checkbook, your 401(k) retirement portfolio, your dreams and aspirations, or your hobbies. He just said to take up your cross and follow Him. The point of that drastic charge was simple: Following Jesus means giving up what we will eventually lose to receive something imperishable and assured—eternity with Him.

The Christian soldier carries only one possession into battle: The cross of self-surrender to Jesus.

*But it is good for me to draw near to God; I have put my trust
in the Lord God, that I may declare all Your works.*

PSALM 73:28

We express gratitude when we find a service or repair person who instills confidence. It's not the fancy truck or high-tech gear that they have; it's that they are there to help us when we need them. They may not advertise on the radio or television, and they may not have a web page or social media presence, but they stay busy because one satisfied customer tells a friend, who tells a friend, and so on.

Similarly, the longer we walk with God, the more our confidence in Him grows. The attractions and distractions of this world lose their appeal as we turn to Him in quietness and strength. He is there when we need Him and He never fails to meet our needs. This reality began to dawn on the disciples when some of those following Him were offended by His teaching. He asked the disciples, "Do you also want to go away?" And Peter replied, "Lord, to whom shall we go? You have the words of eternal life" (John 6:66–68).

The more we embrace God's perspective and spend time with Him, the more our confidence in Him grows. *Jesus, Jesus, how I trust Him!*

Now God worked unusual miracles by the hands of Paul.
ACTS 19:11

After World War II, a group of German students volunteered to rebuild a severely damaged cathedral. It contained a large statue of Jesus, with outstretched arms and the words "Come unto Me" inscribed on it, but it was missing both hands. Since it proved impossible to reattach the hands, they decided to leave them off. And they changed the inscription to read, "Christ has no hands but ours."

The most well-known metaphor used by the apostle Paul for the followers of Jesus was the Body of Christ. First, though Jesus' literal body is absent from the earth, He is still ministering through the corporate body of His followers. Second, a body has many unique parts, which the New Testament writers compared to individual Christians. Some are ears, some are hands, some are feet—all working in harmony to do the work of Jesus in the world. If you are a follower of Jesus, you have been given grace (a spiritual gift), through the Holy Spirit, to do what Jesus would do if He were here today. Through you, the hands of Jesus minister to others and leave an imprint of His love—changing lives forever—through the power of the Holy Spirit. Be the hands of Jesus today.

FEBRUARY 25
The Light of the Word

Your word is a lamp to my feet and a light to my path.
PSALM 119:105

Many young people today can't imagine trying to find their way without the assistance of GPS in their cars and on their phones. Gone are the days of unfolding printed maps as we drive or making unexpected stops at gas stations to ask for directions.

Those of us who are Christians are like modern users of GPS; we can't remember a day without the guidance of the Bible in our lives. Attempting to navigate through life with no direction, no markers, no signs, no moral or spiritual boundaries to ensure we stay on the right path—it seems impossible for those of us who depend on God's Word. The psalmist put it best, calling God's Word a "lamp" and a "light" for our path. In the psalmist's day, a small oil lamp only illuminated a few feet of the path at night. And it can be that way with Scripture. We know which steps to take today by trusting that our steps will become clearer as we walk by faith.

Make God's Word your trusted source for guidance and direction by studying it daily and obeying it continually.

When Disasters Come

*Against its will, all creation was subjected to God's curse. But with eager
hope, the creation looks forward to the day when it will join
God's children in glorious freedom from death and decay.*

ROMANS 8:20–21, NLT

Nowhere on earth is truly safe. One couple moved from
California to Missouri to avoid earthquakes only to be killed in
a tornado. Natural disasters occur every single day—wildfires,
earthquakes, floods, landsides, tornados, hurricanes, blizzards,
and all the rest. On average, natural disasters kill sixty thousand
people globally each year. The Bible teaches that when Adam
and Eve sinned, a curse fell over the earth (Genesis 3:17). Since
then, all of creation has groaned and labored as with birth
pangs (Romans 8:22).

That's why Jesus came, suffering in our place at Calvary, and
then rising from the dead—providing a way of redemption for
our sin. His sacrifice frees us from the curse of sin and offers
eternal protection from the disasters of life. One day He will
create the new heavens and a new earth, free from natural
disasters, death, disease, drought, and sin.

God rules over every area of life, including natural
disasters. We can fully trust in the One who died for us and will
one day establish the new heavens and new earth—our home
for all eternity.

*Put on the whole armor of God, that you may be able to
stand against the wiles of the devil.*
EPHESIANS 6:11

Though we are not promised salvation for imitating Jesus, once we come to know Him and we grow in our relationship with Him, we discover the power of His life as a model for ours. His love, faithfulness, generosity, and sacrifice are benchmarks for our lives, His followers.

And we discover His power in another area as well: defending ourselves from the attacks and deceptions of Satan. The apostle Paul exhorted the Ephesians to put on the "whole armor of God" in order to stand against the devil. And part of that armor is the sword of the Spirit, the Word of God (Ephesians 6:17). Using the Word, the "sword of the Spirit," is how Jesus defeated Satan's temptations in the wilderness (Matthew 4:1–11). Three times Satan tempted Jesus and each time Jesus responded with a principle of Scripture from Deuteronomy. When Satan spoke a lie, Jesus responded with the truth. That was all it took to defeat the devil, and "he departed from [Jesus] until an opportune time" (Luke 4:13).

Don't fear the devil. Instead, fear (respect and revere) God and His Word, against which nothing can stand.

FEBRUARY 28
Rewards

And whatever you do, do it heartily, as to the Lord and not to men, knowing that from the Lord you will receive the reward of the inheritance.
COLOSSIANS 3:23–24

The dictionary offers two definitions for the word *reward*. The first is a sum of money given for the detection of a criminal. The other is an award given in return for faithful service. The second definition describes the biblical concept of our heavenly rewards. In a way we don't fully understand, God will reward His faithful servants for their earthly lives and labor. Some of these rewards are described as crowns. The Bible talks about the Victor's Crown (1 Corinthians 9:24–27); the Crown of Rejoicing (1 Thessalonians 2:19); the Crown of Righteousness (2 Timothy 4:8); the Crown of Life (James 1:12); and the Crown of Glory (1 Peter 5:4).

Perhaps the greatest possible reward in heaven will simply be the words from Jesus: "Well done, good and faithful servant" (Matthew 25:21).

Let's labor for His Name's sake without becoming weary (Revelation 2:3), and trust God to richly welcome us into heaven when our earthly work is done.

MARCH

MARCH 1
Remember His Works

For You, Lord, have made me glad through Your work;
I will triumph in the works of Your hands.
O Lord, how great are Your works! Your thoughts are very deep.
PSALM 92:4–5

Journals and diaries have been kept for centuries. Well-known historical figures like England's Samuel Pepys and the Dutch-German Jewess Anne Frank kept personal records that have been published and read by millions throughout the years.

The Psalms of Scripture, in a way, are like David's (and others') journals in which they recorded their thoughts, prayers, and praises to God. For example, Psalm 143 records David's reflections at a time of trouble in his life. In the midst of explaining his needs to God, he says this: "I remember the days of old; I meditate on all Your works; I muse on the work of Your hands" (verse 5). He is strengthened in his current trial by *remembering what God had done for him in the past.* And thus the power of a written record of God's works is demonstrated—it gives a reason to praise Him for the past and trust Him for the future.

When you are calling out to God, let His past give you hope for the future—remember His great works.

For in the time of trouble He shall hide me in His pavilion; in the secret place of His tabernacle He shall hide me; He shall set me high upon a rock.

PSALM 27:5

You wouldn't think a song about trouble would become a Broadway musical classic. But "Ya Got Trouble," from the 1957 Broadway musical *The Music Man*, did just that. It's a rousing number in which a slippery salesman tries to convince the town to ward off the dangers to young people about temptations like pool halls: "Trouble starts with a capital *t*, and that rhymes with *p*, and that stands for pool!"

Instead of singing and dancing when trouble appears, most people adopt a more fearful perspective: What's going to happen? Will I make it through? Ironically, the psalmist David poured out his troubles to God in song, though of a more serious type. And rather than retreat in fear, David advanced into songs of faith. In situations where he was least likely to worship God—when hurting or in trouble—David demonstrated an amazing ability to worship Him all the more.

If you are facing a trial today, read Psalm 27 and let David's words of praise fill your heart with confidence and hope.

MARCH 3
Green Pastures

He makes me to lie down in green pastures;
He leads me beside the still waters.
PSALM 23:2

God chose to clad the earth in green. Genesis 1:30 talks about the "green herb[s]" and Deuteronomy 12:2 speaks of the "green tree[s]." Psalm 23:2 says, "He makes me to lie down in green pastures." The writer of Psalm 52 said, "But I am like a green olive tree in the house of God; I trust in the mercy of God forever" (verse 8). Jesus taught the multitudes as they sat "down in groups on the green grass" (Mark 6:39).

Green reminds us of growth, and we grow the fastest when we sit down on the green grass, as it were, and listen to Jesus. What a beautiful pastoral scene to contemplate. Imagine sitting at the feet of Jesus as He teaches, giving wonderful, life-changing lessons as we listen to Him and soak in every word He speaks.

You can do that every day as you open your Bible and read of the love Jesus has for you! Step into green pastures as you sit at the feet of Jesus each day!

Let not your heart be troubled; you believe in God, believe also in Me.
JOHN 14:1

In today's world, it is easy to be troubled. There is unrest in many nations. There are viruses and other diseases exploding around the world. Just when we think the world's militaries are at rest, new tensions develop on neighboring borders. Living in a fallen world will always present reasons to be troubled.

When the patriarch Job had his troubles, one of his friends "comforted" him by reminding him that "man is born to trouble, as the sparks fly upward" (Job 5:7). That is realistic, but of small comfort. Jesus had more of a remedy. When He was preparing to leave earth to return to heaven, His disciples were understandably troubled. They had pinned their hopes on Jesus being their divine deliverer. So He told them, "Let not your heart be troubled; you believe in God, believe also in Me." In other words, make your belief count; let your confidence in God, and in Me, settle your hearts. The apostle Paul repeated the same advice in Philippians 4:6–7: "Be anxious for nothing." Commit your anxieties to God and let His peace guard your heart and mind.

What is your remedy for a troubled heart? Take God's prescription for trouble by trusting in Him—He is your remedy for trouble.

MARCH 5
The Praise of Men

For they loved the praise of men more than the praise of God.
JOHN 12:43

When King Belshazzar hosted a drunken feast for a thousand of his nobles and officials, using the sacred vessels from the temple in Jerusalem, he was no doubt praised and lauded by those seeking to curry his favor. But the praise of men can be a dangerous thing—especially when it is preferred over praise from God. For when tragedy or judgment strikes, the praise of men cannot save or bestow mercy.

The same thing happened in Jesus' day. The apostle John records that among the religious rulers in Jerusalem "many believed in Him." But they would not confess their faith openly because of the Pharisees, "lest they should be put out of the synagogue." In other words, "they loved the praise of men than the praise of God" (John 12:42-43). They considered it best to be secret believers—maintaining their status among the non-believers while secretly professing to believe in Jesus. Perhaps they had missed what Jesus said as recorded in Matthew 10:32—He will confess before the Father those who confess Him before men.

Don't be afraid to live for Christ; don't prefer the praise of men over the praise of God.

MARCH 6
Living in the Light

God is light and in Him is no darkness at all.
1 JOHN 1:5

When eleven workers in China were rescued from a gold mine in 2021 after an explosion trapped them in darkness for two weeks, they had to have their eyes covered with a cloth as they were gradually exposed to the sunlight. It was determined that a sudden exposure to light too quickly would overwhelm their vision. In the same way, when we are shrouded by the darkness in our world today, we may be blind to the great blessings God has in store for us.

Living without Christ is like living in darkness. Unbelievers are unaware of what it is to truly live—with true joy, grace, and purpose. Like the miners, they are used to the darkness and have to cover their eyes to stay comfortable in the light of God's glory. But eventually, the miners were able to remove the cloth from their eyes so they could see the world around them once again—going from darkness to light. Imagine their emotions when they saw the brightness of the sun once again. Yet many in our world today still live in spiritual darkness. It is a reminder to shine God's light to others, so they may also find the light of His glory and begin living in the Light.

MARCH 7
One in Christ

There is neither Jew nor Greek, there is neither slave nor free, there is neither male nor female; for you are all one in Christ Jesus.
GALATIANS 3:28

W. C. Fields once quipped, "I'm free of all prejudices. I hate everyone equally." Well, in every heart there lurks a splinter of prejudice, causing us to view with discomfort or disdain someone different in some way from us. Jesus, being sinless, didn't fall into that trap. When He met the Samaritan woman by Jacob's well in Sychar, He effortlessly crossed every barrier that might have separated them.

He crossed the racial barrier, for the Jew of that day despised the Samaritans. He crossed the cultural barrier, for men of that era didn't initiate dialogue with unknown women. He passed the social divide because the two of them were from different lifestyles. He was a man; she was a woman. He was a rabbi; she was uneducated. He was a Jew; she was a Samaritan; He was moral; she was immoral. But Jesus loves everyone and takes no notice of race, language, gender, or social status. He died for all.

Being like Christ means that we prayerfully purge every trace of bias, partiality, preconceived opinions, or prejudice from our heart. Sadly, at times, there is some of that in every heart—but none in Christ's! Let His heart set the tone for our own—we "are all one in Christ Jesus."

MARCH 8
Knowing Our Place

That none of you may be puffed up on behalf of one against the other.
1 CORINTHIANS 4:6

The late NBC news commentator Tim Russert once described a meeting he had with Pope John Paul II. The Pope put his arm around Russert and said, "You are from NBC. They tell me you're a very important man." Taken aback, Russert said, "Your Holiness, there are only two of us in this room, and I am certainly a distant second." The Pope looked at him and said, "Right."

A degree of humility can keep us from stumbling in social settings. Humility is not only key in social settings but in spiritual service as well. As the writer of Proverbs said, "Pride goes before destruction" (Proverbs 16:18). Christians have been given the inestimable privilege of receiving gifts of grace from God—spiritual gifts which make it possible for us to serve Him in carrying out the ministry of Jesus. And if that isn't enough, someday we'll be given rewards in heaven for using those gifts faithfully! God provides the gifts, the power to use them, and the rewards. Where is the room for pride in such a plan? Our place is to humbly receive and employ what God has graciously given.

When we get ourselves out of the way, God can make our place in His plan known.

MARCH 9
The Greatest Architect

For he [Abraham] was looking forward to the city with foundations,
whose architect and builder is God.

HEBREWS 11:10, NIV

Who is the greatest architect of all time? Many experts would point to Antoni Gaudi of Spain, who designed the breathtaking church of the Sagrada Familia and other classic buildings and monuments in Barcelona. Gaudi had a deep reverence for God's creation, and he carefully studied the beauty and forms he saw in nature and sought to replicate them in his work. He would have said the greatest architect of all time is the Almighty Creator of heaven and earth.

According to Hebrews 11:10, our Almighty God not only created the universe, He is the architect and builder of the eternal city of New Jerusalem—our heavenly home.

It only stands to reason, then, that He can wisely plan our days. God has a blueprint for our lives, and when we humbly ask Him for help, He lovingly guides us. Through Jesus Christ, we have a preplanned, well-ordered life, full of purpose for each new day. As you place your trust in God and acknowledge Him in all your ways, He will direct your path (Proverbs 3:5–6).

An Act of Kindness

Greet Priscilla and Aquila, my fellow workers in Christ Jesus,
who risked their own necks for my life,
to whom not only I give thanks, but also all the churches.
ROMANS 16:3–4

Lily Ebert was a teenager in Auschwitz. She had nothing, not even a piece of paper. But one of the liberating American soldiers gave her a special gift. It was a German banknote on which he had scribbled the words, "As a start to a new life. Good luck and happiness." It was the first act of kindness Lily could remember, and she remembered it for years. At age ninety, she rediscovered the note while going through some papers with her great grandson. They quickly tracked down the identity of the soldier—Pvt. Hyman Schulman, a Jewish-American soldier who served as a chaplain's aide. Though Schulman passed away in 2013, Ebert is now in touch with his children.

Everyone needs a word of encouragement, an act of kindness, and the gift of friendship. Though we may not always be together, our bonds of fellowship are enduring. And our relationships are strengthened as we serve each other.

An act of kindness today may reverberate through an entire generation. Why not write a note or say a kind word to a someone today?

> *"Zacchaeus, make haste and come down, for today I must stay at your house."... But when they saw it, they all complained, saying, "He has gone to be a guest with a man who is a sinner."*
>
> LUKE 19:5, 7

Zacchaeus collected taxes for the Roman government, and a little extra for himself, making him an unloved person by the community. However, he wanted to see Jesus, and not only did He see Jesus, Jesus saw him. Jesus called him by name and went to his house. Unlike some people, Jesus wasn't afraid of what people would think if they saw Him with someone disliked by society. Jesus came "to seek and to save that which was lost" (Luke 19:10), and that meant that he was a friend of sinners.

Zacchaeus' encounter with Jesus changed his life! Zacchaeus demonstrated this change by giving half of his goods to the poor and repaying fourfold to those he had wronged. When we share the Gospel with those whom society dislikes, their lives can be changed, too. Too often, however, we stay inside our comfort zone of the familiar, instead of offering friendship to someone who is lost. But Jesus is a change-maker and it begins with being a friend of sinners! Just as Zacchaeus' life changed when he met Jesus, the lives of those around us will radically change when we introduce them to the ultimate change-maker—Jesus Christ!

The Angel of the Lord

And the Angel of the Lord appeared to the woman and said to her,
"Indeed now, you are barren and have borne no children,
but you shall conceive and bear a son."

JUDGES 13:3

Multiple times in the Old Testament Jesus appears as the Angel of the Lord to communicate a message to someone. In Genesis, He speaks to Abraham and tells him not to sacrifice Isaac on the altar he had built (22:12). In Judges, the Angel of the Lord appears to Gideon and tells him that he will save the Israelites from the Midianites (6:14). And later in Judges, He appears to Samson's parents to tell them they will have a son, who will deliver Israel from the Philistines (13:1-23).

Jesus does not appear to us today as the Angel of the Lord. Today Jesus speaks to us through Scripture. As we study His life in the Gospels, we learn to show compassion to those around us, to be salt and light in this world, and to love our enemies. And He also gave us the greatest commandment—to love God with all our heart, soul, mind, and strength—and to love our neighbors as our ourselves. His words to us in Scripture teach us how to live for Him as we patiently wait for His return.

When Jesus saw their faith, He said to the paralytic,
"Son, your sins are forgiven."
MARK 2:5

Recently a man went to the dentist suffering from a bad toothache. The dentist, in his examination, recognized the problem was more serious than a toothache and sent the man to a cardiologist where he was treated for heart disease.

Similarly, in the story in Mark 2, four friends carried a paralytic on a stretcher to Jesus. Unable to get through the crowds, these men lowered their friend through the roof; and the man descended right in front of Jesus. Looking at this man, the Lord detected a heart problem. This man needed forgiveness. Perhaps he had caused an accident that had hurt others and left himself paralyzed. Whatever had caused his physical condition, he had a serious heart condition—sin— that needed to be addressed first.

Jesus banished his sins forever, then proceeded to heal him completely.

Our problems and needs run deeper than we sometimes know; but when we walk with the Great Physician, He accurately diagnoses our needs and heals us completely.

MARCH 14
His Word, Our Hope

My soul faints for Your salvation, but I hope in Your word.

PSALM 119:81

"Can I get that in writing?" When you are shopping for a car, comparing prices between dealerships, you want a dealer's "best offer" to be put in writing—including how long the price is good for. As is often said in all manner of life situations, "If it's not in writing, it doesn't exist." But when it is in writing—the Declaration of Independence, a sales contract, a legal marriage certificate—the document provides a record of the past, assurance in the present, and hope for the future.

Some of those elements of human need—records, assurance, hope—must be part of the reason God committed His promises to writing. The result? Our Bible, the book containing the story of God's revelation and redemption of mankind. While some human documents can be violated or nullified, God's documents are infallible. Like God Himself, His Word is eternal and unchanging (Isaiah 40:8). While our soul may "faint" (grow weary with longing) for God's deliverance during this life, His Word guarantees His love and our salvation.

To have hope in His Word, we must know what His Word says. As our knowledge grows, the greater our hope and certainty will be for the future.

MARCH 15
Forced Perspective

The Lord is good, a stronghold in the day of trouble;
and He knows those who trust in Him.
NAHUM 1:7

Have you ever seen photographs that use the concept of forced perspective? It's a technique that employs optical illusions to make objects appear closer or farther away than they are—or to make them appear smaller or larger than they are in reality. Filmmakers used this in earlier days. For example, they would place a miniature model of a dinosaur close to the camera, and it would look gigantic to the moviegoers. Many tourists at the Leaning Tower of Pisa try this with their smartphones as well. They pose as if trying to hold up the leaning building.

The devil tries to use forced perspective on us too. He wants us to believe our troubles are much bigger than they are. If we look at our difficulties through the wrong lens, we'll magnify our burdens until they appear ready to topple onto us and crush us to death.

But the right concept of God shatters the devil's illusion. Our troubles shrink in the light of God's greatness. We are wise when we keep our focus on Jesus and find the correct perspective of Him.

The Law of the Lord is perfect, restoring the soul.
PSALM 19:7, NASB

After an extended workout at the gym, or a long bike ride on a scorching day, a refreshing sports drink can restore the body's electrolytes. After a grueling week to hit a project deadline at work, a long weekend can restore one's strength. And after a prolonged time of trouble, the Word of God can restore the soul.

Or so says the psalmist David, who, given his life's up-and-down path, should know. But restoring the soul is not all the Word of God can do. It can make the simple wise, it can bring joy to the heart, and it can enlighten the eyes (Psalm 19:7–8). And who wouldn't want more of those benefits? It is more valuable than gold and sweeter than honey (verse 10). Who would turn that down? But to get all those benefits, we must study to know more of the truths found in God's Word.

If those benefits appeal to you, don't miss a day reading and studying God's Word. The more you learn, the more you will be blessed!

MARCH 17
Patient and Prayerful

Your eyes saw my substance, being yet unformed.
And in Your book they all were written,
the days fashioned for me, when as yet there were none of them.

PSALM 139:16

The number one desire of Christians is to live according to God's will. And the number one question is, "How do I know His will?" The answer is two-fold. First, God's general will for all Christians is revealed in the pages of Scripture— instructions in righteous living for God's glory. But then there is the specific will of God for one's life.

Psalm 139:16 suggests that God has a plan for everyone's life, and the Bible is filled with examples. Jeremiah was told that God set him aside as a prophet. David was told he was to be Israel's king. Paul was commissioned as an apostle to the Gentiles. Moses was appointed to deliver the Hebrews from slavery to nationhood. Samuel was called as a child to be a prophet. Barnabas was confirmed by the Church to be a servant-leader, an encourager, to others. Solomon was commissioned to build the temple and rule over Israel. All these callings share one thing: *They came into their specific calling according to God's timing.*

Don't doubt that God has a specific purpose for your life. Just be patient and prayerful as you see it unfold.

MARCH 18
Courage in Three Dimensions

And from there, when the brethren heard about us,
they came to meet us as far as the Appii Forum and Three Inns.
When Paul saw them, he thanked God and took courage.

ACTS 28:15

Writer Kerry S. Walters suggests that *courage* is the quality that the Puritan writer, John Bunyan, called *valor*. This quality comes in three dimensions, and our Lord modeled all three. Walters wrote: "Jesus, who always and everywhere is the model for Christian comportment, Himself exemplified...three kinds of valor: physical courage in enduring bodily torture and cruel death following His arrest by Jewish authorities; moral courage when He defied Temple culture by chasing away the money lenders, and spiritual courage when, despite the shockwave of despair that overwhelmed Him on the Cross, He nonetheless persevered to the end."

The world around us can be intimidating, but the followers of Christ are not easily silenced. With grace and compassion, we are to speak and live as servants of Christ in a hostile world.

As we seek His will for our future, God will also give us the courage to accomplish His plan. Do what the apostle Paul did as he approached Rome: Go forward, thank God, and take courage.

She said to Him, "Yes, Lord, I believe that You are the Christ, the Son of God, who is come into the world."

JOHN 11:27

"Trading My Sorrows" was a popular praise song a few years ago, and it had a rather simple chorus: "Yes Lord, yes Lord, yes yes Lord."

That's a wonderfully biblical phrase. In Matthew 9:28, when the blind men came to Jesus requesting healing, He asked them, "Do you believe that I am able to do this?" They said, "Yes, Lord." When Jesus asked His disciples if they understood His parables, they said, "Yes, Lord" (Matthew 13:51). When Jesus spoke to the woman of Canaan who begged Him to help her daughter, she said, "Yes, Lord" (Matthew 15:27). When Jesus told Martha that He was the resurrection and the life, she said, "Yes, Lord" (John 11:27). And when Jesus said to Peter, "Do you love Me more than these?" Peter replied, "Yes, Lord; You know that I love You" (John 21:15).

In every way and at every moment, is that your heart's response? When you say, "Yes" to God, He will work in amazing ways in your life.

May your desire and prayer today be, "Yes Lord, yes Lord, yes yes Lord"!

Your Labor Is Not in Vain

Therefore, my beloved brethren, be steadfast, immovable, always abounding in the work of the Lord, knowing that your labor is not in vain in the Lord.
1 CORINTHIANS 15:58

John Calvin left a mark on the world that endures century after century, yet during his lifetime he often battled discouragement. He once said, "I am entangled in so many troublesome affairs that I am almost beside myself." On another occasion, he said, "Today hardly one in a hundred considers how difficult and arduous it is to faithfully discharge the office of pastor." And again he said, "In addition to the immense troubles by which I am so sorely consumed, there is almost no day on which some new pain or anxiety does not come."

John Stott called discouragement the "occupational hazard of Christian ministry."

Yet the Bible repeatedly tells us to eschew discouragement, to treat it like a sin, to resist and refuse it. "Do not fear or be discouraged," says Deuteronomy 1:21. The Lord is never discouraged—and we should follow His leading. Our life, love, and labor in the Lord is never in vain. Take God's promise in 1 Corinthians 15:58 and use it like a broom to sweep discouragement out of your heart.

MARCH 21
Storms of Obedience

Strengthening the souls of the disciples, exhorting them to continue
in the faith, and saying, "We must through many tribulations
enter the kingdom of God."

ACTS 14:22

One of the unexplained events in the book of Acts is why young John Mark deserted Paul and Barnabas on their first missionary journey (Acts 13:13). Could it have been because of their trials on the island of Cypress? A sorcerer named Elymas tried to prevent Paul and Barnabas from preaching to the Roman official. Maybe John Mark wondered if their mission was truly in the will of God.

It's natural to think that obedience leads to tranquility. But just the opposite is often true: Obedience to God can result in trials. Storms can come because we have been obedient, not necessarily because we are disobedient. That was certainly true of those in the New Testament. The four Gospels and Acts recount one attack and obstacle after another upon those who were wholly committed to fulfilling God's calling. Every follower of Jesus should get this matter settled in their heart: The deeper we go into the Kingdom of God, the more likely we are to be resisted.

If you are obeying God and experiencing a storm at the same time, you are following in the footsteps of the heroes of the faith. God will bring you through this storm of obedience.

MARCH 22
The Little Children

Let the little children come to Me, and do not forbid them;
for of such is the kingdom of heaven.
MATTHEW 19:14

The Gospels only give us representative moments in our Lord's ministry. John tells us that if everything Jesus did had been written down, there wouldn't be enough books in the world to contain the record of it. But even the Gospels in their brevity record *nine separate occasions* when Jesus ministered especially to children. The words "child" and "children" occur nearly one hundred times in the Gospels. Jesus loved children: He loved working with children, and He rebuked the disciples for preventing children from approaching Him. It's easy to picture our Lord with children running around His feet, sitting on His lap, and even in His arms and on His shoulders.

If you're working with children in your home or church, it is a blessed calling from God. None are so high in the Lord's work as those who stoop down to the level of children and minister to our Lord's little friends.

But immediately [Jesus] talked with them and said to them,
"Be of good cheer! It is I; do not be afraid."
MARK 6:50

Two artists were asked to create original paintings that represented their idea of peace. One artist painted a beautiful mountain scene: gorgeous colors, deer in the meadow, a bubbling stream—the absence of conflict. The other artist painted a dark picture of a violent storm that was crashing the ocean waves against the face of a cliff. But there, tucked into a nook in the cliff, was a bird resting quietly, its face buried beneath its wing, totally at rest in the midst of the storm.

There are two ways God can answer our prayers when we seek peace. He can remove the storms, as in the first painting, or He can give us peace in the midst of the storms, as in the second. Twice in His relationship with His disciples, Jesus gave them peace during storms. Once He calmed the storm (Mark 4:35–41), and once He came to them in the midst of the waves (Mark 6:45–52). We can ask Him to remove the storms of life, but we grow closer to Him when He walks with us through the storm and we discover His presence and peace that carries us through.

If you are seeking peace, you can have it. But let God decide how and when to give it to you.

MARCH 24
Food That Satisfies

And Jesus said to them, "I am the bread of life. He who comes to Me shall never hunger, and he who believes in Me shall never thirst.

JOHN 6:35

All of us get hungry, but not all of us know why. Most often, our body says, "I need food" when glycogen (carbohydrate) levels in the liver and muscles decrease and energy stores are depleted. That's "actual" hunger. "Perceived" hunger is when digestion empties the stomach of its last filling and mild cramps (hunger pangs) ensue as the stomach shrinks.

Everyone knows what it's like to be spiritually and emotionally hungry as well. We may be hungry for comfort or thirsty for love, hungry for forgiveness or thirsty for knowledge and truth. It takes a certain level of spiritual and emotional nutrition for us to meet those hunger and thirst needs that are common to the human experience. Having those needs met outside of God's provision is like eating a doughnut for breakfast: a quick fix that will shortly disappoint. God's provision for every spiritual need in the human race is Jesus Christ and His indwelling Spirit. He invites us to come to Him so we will never hunger or thirst again.

If you've been skipping spiritual meals lately, you may feel hungry—or famished. Don't settle for anything less than the Bread of Life.

Miracle of Multiplication

And He took the seven loaves and the fish and gave thanks, broke them and gave them to His disciples; and the disciples gave to the multitude.

MATTHEW 15:36

Everyone is familiar with the Seven Wonders of the Ancient World (the Great Pyramid of Giza, Babylon's hanging gardens, and others). Did you know that many refer to compounding interest as the eighth wonder of the world? Compounding is the seeming miracle that occurs when the interest on our savings also begins to earn interest and money multiplies seemingly miraculously.

Well, money doesn't multiply miraculously, but some things do. For instance, when Jesus took a few loaves of bread and fish from a young boy and fed thousands of people, that was miraculous multiplication. And when He takes our small, but faithful, contribution to His kingdom and causes much fruit to be borne, that's miraculous multiplication as well. We never know when the smallest action on our part will bring about a significant result. A word of witness or an act of generosity for the cause of Christ might change a life—or, in time, the world.

MARCH 26
The Son of God

The scribes and Pharisees watched Him closely, whether He would heal on the Sabbath, that they might find an accusation against Him. But He knew their thoughts, and said to the man who had the withered hand, " Arise and stand here." And he arose and stood.

LUKE 6:7–8

Members of the same family often look alike, sound alike, and act alike. Everything from hair color to facial expressions and speech patterns may be recognizable in family members. There have even been instances when siblings who were separated as babies meet each other as adults and are surprised to find out how much they resemble each other.

But Jesus isn't just similar to God. He is God. He says, "I and My Father are one" (John 10:30). Jesus not only stated His deity, but He also exhibited attributes of God while He was here on earth. He demonstrated His omniscience when He taught His disciples about His coming suffering, death, and resurrection (Matthew 16:21) and when He knew the thoughts of the religious leaders (Luke 6:7–8). His omnipotence is displayed when He cast the demons out of the man and into the herd of swine, and when He brought Lazarus back to life (Mark 5:1–17; John 11:38–44).

As fully God, Jesus knows all about us—He knows each fear, sorrow, and joy we experience. What comfort there is in knowing that as the Son of God, Jesus is ready to help and support us through life. And we are part of His family!

Love Your Enemy

"If your enemy is hungry, feed him; if he is thirsty, give him a drink;
for in so doing you will heap coals of fire on his head."
Do not be overcome by evil, but overcome evil with good.

ROMANS 12:20–21

Before telling us how to treat our enemies, Paul tells us that vengeance is the Lord's (Romans 12:19). It's not enough for us to step out of the way and let God's wrath come on our enemies. If we see our enemy, we have to take positive action toward him even though he's taking negative action toward us. We have to activate the principle of replacement. When someone does evil to us, we are to do good to them.

Jesus said the same in Matthew 5:44, "Love your enemies, bless those who curse you, do good to those who hate you, and pray for those who spitefully use you and persecute you." Not only did Jesus command us to love our enemies, He loved His enemies. His death and resurrection took the punishment for the sin of the world—past, present and future—including those who had Him crucified. When we know God and are filled with the Holy Spirit, we, too, can love our enemies. We can do good to them, in spite of the evil done to us, and demonstrate God's love to them.

MARCH 28
A Heavenly View

For our citizenship is in heaven, from which we also
eagerly wait for the Savior, the Lord Jesus Christ.
PHILIPPIANS 3:20

The brilliant scientist Sir Isaac Newton said that he could take his telescope and look millions and millions of miles into space. Then he added, "But when I lay it aside, go into my room, shut the door, and get down on my knees in earnest prayer, I see more of heaven and feel closer to the Lord than if I were assisted by all the telescopes on earth."[4]

Trying to live life in our own strength makes no more sense than trying to see God through a telescope. Still, there are times when we struggle unnecessarily through life, forgetful of the power that lies in communicating with the Creator.

In John 15:5, the Lord tells us, "I am the vine, you are the branches. He who abides in Me, and I in him, bears much fruit; for without Me you can do nothing." It is a fact: We cannot live this Christian life in our own strength. That fact does not stop us from trying, to be sure. It is an ongoing battle to die to self; but we must relinquish control and depend solely upon Christ, for it is only through Him that all things are possible.

[4] http://elbourne.org/sermons/index.mv?illustration+4434.

*[You] have put on the new man who is renewed in knowledge
according to the image of Him who created him.*
COLOSSIANS 3:10

Babylon's King Nebuchadnezzar ordered a giant statue of
gold to be built: ninety feet tall, nine feet wide. It might have
represented the king himself or it might have represented
Nebuchadnezzar's patron god, Nabu. Since kings of the day
ascribed divine status to themselves, the image—whether of a
king or the king's god—represented the divine on earth (Daniel
3:1–8).

We find a similar scenario in the Genesis creation story: God
created man in His own image (Genesis 1:26–27). The same word
for image—*tzelem*—is used both for God's image (a spiritual
image) and the image in Babylon (a physical image). What was
the purpose of God creating mankind in His image? Mankind
was to represent God throughout God's kingdom, or creation. As
Paul writes in Ephesians 4:24, Christians are a new creation "to
be like God—truly righteous and holy" (NLT).

Though originally marred by sin, we have been re-created
(born again) to reflect God's righteousness and holiness. When
others see us, they are to see the character of our God.

MARCH 30
Reach the Heart

Honor your father and mother . . .
that it may be well with you and you may live long on the earth.
EPHESIANS 6:2–3

Why is it so important for children to honor and obey their parents? It's not because we need well-behaved children, nor is it simply because we are adults and they are minors. God commands children to obey their mother and father because it is training for the respect and obedience needed for a healthy relationship with the Lord. And when a child understands that in being obedient to his parents, he is obeying Christ, then the heart of that child is impacted forever. Becoming acquainted with submission to loving authority and obedience to a caring parent makes it easier for a child to have a genuine desire to love, serve, and obey God.

Every word of the Bible was written for a specific purpose, and the command to "Honor your father and mother" is no exception. Jesus set the standard for obedience when He walked the earth. Not only did He put himself under the authority and leadership of His earthly mother and father, but He also obeyed His Heavenly Father even unto death to pay the price for our sins. Let's follow His example by honoring our parents and teaching our children to do the same.

MARCH 31
Life Begets Life

Even when we were dead in trespasses, [God] made us alive
together with Christ (by grace you have been saved).
EPHESIANS 2:5

Try this experiment to see the difference in life and death. Take three raw carrots and cut the tops off each, one inch from the end. Boil one of the tops for five minutes, bake another at 325 degrees Fahrenheit for five minutes, and leave the third carrot top raw. Then put all three tops in a dish containing a half-inch of water, keeping the water replenished as needed. After a few days, one of the carrot tops will begin to sprout. Guess which one?

Enzymes are the life force in raw food, and they are destroyed at temperatures exceeding 115 degrees Fahrenheit. When the enzymes are destroyed, food is no longer alive. Just so, human beings have a life force: the spirit, or the breath of life (Genesis 2:7). Man's spirit—his ability to connect to the life of God through God's Spirit—is dead because of sin. But when the Spirit of God enters into man at the moment of salvation, life is restored. Though man is "dead in trespasses," the Spirit of God makes us "alive together with Christ."

To live now and forever, eternally with God, be made alive by the Spirit of God through faith in Christ. Only life can beget life.

APRIL

APRIL 1

A Man of Sorrows

Jesus wept.
JOHN 11:35

Someone once said, "You may soon forget those with whom you have laughed, but you will never forget those with whom you have wept."

When we are experiencing sorrow, one of the greatest comforts is knowing that someone else has gone through a similar trial and has literally felt the sadness we feel. In such dark times of life, we tend to cling to those friends who have been where we are. Jesus is one such friend. He experienced the death of a very close friend, watched as some of His disciples openly betrayed Him, and kept silent as He was unjustly beaten and hung on a cross. He was "a Man of sorrows and acquainted with grief," and because of His humanity, He can relate to us on a very personal level when we are dealing with pain and grief (Isaiah 53:3).

If you are in a time of sadness and sorrow and feel that no one understands you, there is One who does—Jesus. He experienced the pain of rejection, loss, and more. You can trust that He will walk with you through your darkest hour.

APRIL 2
Reason Together

"Come now, and let us reason together," says the Lord,
"though your sins are like scarlet, they shall be as white as snow;
though they are red like crimson, they shall be as wool."
ISAIAH 1:18

This is a very colorful verse. It mentions scarlet, red, crimson, and white. For the sake of time, let's just focus on scarlet. For centuries, scarlet has been a color that signifies wealth and power.

How ironic that the color really came from a bug!

The finest scarlets in antiquity came from a tiny scale insect called Kermes, which was a type of parasite among the oak trees throughout the Mediterranean world. The male insects were very small and could fly away, but the females had no wings. When collected, they were found to contain thousands of eggs, and their offspring were brilliant red. The insects were captured, dried, and ground into powder, which was used to form the scarlet dye.

In a remarkably similar way, sin is a parasite to the human soul, and it dyes us—and it causes us to die. The devil wants to stain us through and through.

Only the scarlet blood of Christ can counteract the stain of sin and make us white as snow.

*For You formed my inward parts; You covered me in my mother's womb.
I will praise You, for I am fearfully and wonderfully made; marvelous are
Your works, and that my soul knows very well.*

PSALM 139:13–14

The Intelligent Design movement suggests that the existence of an orderly, purposeful creation implies the necessity of an organized, purposeful design, and therefore a Designer.

If we apply that idea to human beings, who innately display the ability and desire for meaning in their lives, it suggests a Creator who created them for that purpose. There are certainly plenty of biblical examples: Abraham was called to create a chosen people; Moses was called to shape that people into a nation; Jeremiah was called to be a prophet to the nation; David was called to be their king; Jesus was called to redeem Jews and Gentiles alike from sin; Paul was called to deliver Jesus' Good News to Gentiles and their kings…to cite a few examples. Psalm 139:13–16 pictures God creating humans and ordaining the days of their lives—He is our Divine Designer.

If you are seeking God's specific purpose for your life, ask Him to show it to you. Ask in faith as a son asking his Father for his daily provision for food, and it will be supplied to you (Luke 11:9–11).

APRIL 4
Even a Little Is Enough

He replied, "If you have faith as small as a mustard seed,
you can say to this mulberry tree, 'Be uprooted
and planted in the sea,' and it will obey you."
LUKE 17:6, NIV

Many Christians know that George Müller cared for more than ten thousand orphans in his lifetime in England and was a man of astounding faith. But not all know that he was not always such a faithful man. His early life in Prussia was marked by lying, gambling, drinking, and imprisonment for fraud. At age fifteen, he gave his attention to cards and drinking with friends while his mother lay dying.

This is also the same George Müller who, later in life, would sit his orphans down at a table with empty bowls and thank God for the food He would provide. And God always did. George Müller's life demonstrates that faith is a learned discipline. Faith does not come naturally but supernaturally. The natural man believes when he sees, but the supernatural man sees when he believes. And Jesus taught that it does not take as much faith to see as we might think—faith as small as a tiny seed can see mountains move.

If you are lacking great faith today, exercise the faith you have and then ask God for more. More faith, more fruit—believing God is a self-perpetuating experience.

APRIL 5
Strength by Faith

For when we were still without strength,
in due time Christ died for the ungodly.
ROMANS 5:6

Imagine the foolishness of a politician or social reformer going to a cemetery to preach his message: "Be better, be just, be tolerant, be committed, be stronger," he would call out. His response would be the same as when the living are exhorted to live strong lives without the empowerment of God. Physically dead people have no strength by which to act, nor do those without the Holy Spirit.

When Peter and John went to the temple in Jerusalem one afternoon, they encountered a man crippled from birth begging for money outside the temple gate. He was totally without strength in his legs—he was carried there by his friends each day. Peter and John had no money to give him, so they gave him what he needed more: strength and an opportunity to praise God. The man's healing, and his exuberant praise, is a beautiful picture of what Christ has done for us. When we lacked spiritual strength due to sin, Jesus died for us, removing the sin and giving us new strength in the Spirit. All we need to do is believe in Him.

Your strength is not needed to receive God's strength. Just as the crippled man learned: His strength is sufficient for your needs.

APRIL 6
Hunger Pains

Now the next day, when they had come out from Bethany,
[Jesus] was hungry. And seeing from afar a fig tree having leaves,
He went to see if perhaps He would find something on it.
MARK 11:12–13

This verse reminds us that Jesus in His humanity became hungry. The Gospels don't tell us that His stomach growled or His head hurt or any other signs that He was hungry, but we can assume His body responded the same way ours does when we are in need of nourishment.

When our body tells us we are hungry, many of us head to the kitchen to prepare a snack or a meal. Our focus is on satisfying our physical hunger as quickly as we can. Satisfying our immediate physical needs can serve as a reminder of our spiritual sustenance that comes from God. Those who partake of the Bread of Life and the Living Water will never hunger or thirst again—Jesus provides all we need—both for living today and for eternity.

At mealtimes, as you thank God for the daily provision of food and pray for loved ones near and far, thank Him for the gift of Jesus, who satisfies every longing of the soul, and for the hope of eternity with Him. If you are suffering hunger pains, the question is, what are you hungry for?

APRIL 7
Jesus' Biography

For by Him [Jesus] all things were created that are in heaven and that are on earth, visible and invisible, whether thrones or dominions or principalities or powers. All things were created through Him and for Him.
COLOSSIANS 1:16

Biographies often begin with when and where the subject of the book was born. On occasion the author will jump to later in the person's life and then fill in the details of their early years as the story progresses. When someone asks us what books of the Bible they should read to learn more about Jesus, we often point them to the Gospels—Matthew, Mark, Luke, and John—where we read about Jesus' life here on earth. The Gospels provide a good biography, if you will, of Jesus' life on earth. However, we find Jesus throughout the entire Bible, including at Creation in Genesis 1.

His "biography" is the entire Bible, not just the Gospels. The apostle Paul tells us, "All things were created through Him" (Colossians 1:16), and the apostle John says, "All things were made through Him, and without Him nothing was made that was made" (John 1:3). How amazing to think that the Creator of the universe willingly gave up His home in heaven to become a man, to suffer and die on the cross, conquering sin and death to redeem you and me from the penalty of our sin. What a biography!

APRIL 8
The Loyal Disciple

Now there was leaning on Jesus' bosom
one of His disciples, whom Jesus loved.
JOHN 13:23

The Greek word *agape* is one of the most important words in the New Testament. It means "unconditional love"—the no-strings-attached love with which God loves us. *Agape's* Hebrew parallel in the Old Testament, *hesed*, is less familiar but no less important. It means "loyal love" and describes God's everlasting love for His people Israel (and Israel's spiritual descendants, the Church).

Loyalty is almost a lost value in today's world. Everything seems to be for sale including friendship, affection, and devotion—the things which make up loyalty. Even Jesus' disciples found themselves lacking in loyalty on the day Jesus was crucified—all the disciples except one, that is. The disciple named John seems to have had a devotion to Jesus which the others lacked prior to His resurrection. John was the only one of the original band of disciples who stood at the foot of the cross in Jesus' final hours. John was loyal to the very end. Every Christian should ask himself, "Would I have been there with John? Will I be loyal to Jesus regardless of the price?"

The deeper our understanding of God's *agape*, the deeper the manifestation of our *hesed*.

APRIL 9
Precious Moments

Trust in the Lord with all your heart.
PROVERBS 3:5

Only God can make us more than we are, and He often uses critical "faith moments" in our life to accomplish the job. Looking back, can you name one special moment that has defined your life? Perhaps it was the day you gave your life to Jesus. Perhaps it was when you trusted God at a crucial time.

Moses experienced his defining moment at the burning bush. David experienced his defining moment when Samuel anointed him king of Israel. Esther's defining moment came when she risked her life to save the Jewish people. Peter's defining moment came when Jesus called him to become a fisher of men, and Paul always referred to the Damascus Road experience of Acts 9 as his defining moment.

Perhaps you're facing a defining moment in your life right now. You are either in a crisis or a crossroad. You can either trust God and press on by faith, or you can lean on your own understanding and go your own way. God's Word gives this trusted counsel: "Put your trust in the Lord your God and you will endure" (2 Chronicles 20:20, NASB). Take the road less traveled: "Trust in the Lord with all your heart."

APRIL 10
What If?

But now Christ is risen from the dead,
and has become the firstfruits of those who have fallen asleep.
1 CORINTHIANS 15:20

What if . . .?

What if the body of Jesus were still moldering somewhere in a Middle Eastern grave? The apostle Paul envisions that scenario and shows us the dire consequences: "If Christ is not risen," he wrote in 1 Corinthians 15, "your faith is futile; you are still in your sins! Then also those who have fallen asleep in Christ have perished" (verses 17–18). All is lost, he said, and all hope is gone. "If in this life only we have hope in Christ," we are pitiable indeed (verse 19).

"But," Paul quickly added in verse 20, "now Christ is risen from the dead!"

Without the Resurrection, we're like the Swiss philosopher Henri-Frederic Amiel who wrote, "Melancholy is at the bottom of everything, just as at the end of all rivers is the sea. Can it be otherwise in a world where nothing lasts, where all that we have loved or shall love must die?"

With the Resurrection, we can say with full hearts, "He is risen, He is risen indeed!"

No longer do I call you servants, for a servant does not know
what his master is doing; but I have called you friends,
for all things that I heard from My Father I have made known to you.
JOHN 15:15

Research says, on average, we have 12 social interactions per day. Another source estimates that a city dweller will interact with around 80,000 people throughout the course of their life. Additional inquiry found that we make 29 true friends throughout our lifetime yet only 6 of them actually last.[5] One study suggests that most people can have up to 5 intimate bonds, 15 close friends, and 150 casual friends at a time. All those numbers tell us one thing—we are constantly connecting and disconnecting from one another in our society.

There are continually people coming in and out of our life. Some are constant, and some are temporary. We never know who will stick by our side through life's twists and turns. But we do know one thing—Christ is our constant Friend. He has promised to never leave us nor forsake us (Hebrews 13:5). If we are ever feeling alone, we can rejoice in the fact that the Creator of the universe, Yahweh, the Almighty God calls us His friend.

[5] https://www.her.ie/life/prepare-to-lose-some-friends-new-study-shows-only-six-will-last-the-distance-177276.

Then [Jesus] went out from there and came to His own country.... And many hearing Him were astonished, saying.... "Is this not the carpenter, the Son of Mary, and brother of James, Joses, Judas, and Simon?"

MARK 6:1–3

After seeing how many homeless men struggle to find jobs, David Palmer founded Purposeful Design in Indiana, which creates custom furniture. Purposeful Design's mission is "to help rebuild lives of individuals broken by addiction or homelessness, equip them with valuable work skills, and provide the gift of work." Palmer says, "We're not here just to teach woodworking or offer a paycheck but to get under the skin. That begins with heart change. Otherwise...we feel like we're putting a Band-Aid on a terrible wound."[6] Purposeful Design is creating more than custom furniture for clients; they are teaching their employees about Jesus, the Carpenter.

For thirty years the Lord was not ashamed to be a carpenter. He worked with His hands doing the tasks that were given to Him. But Jesus did more than work with His hands. He allowed His hands to be nailed to the cross to take the punishment for our sin. Jesus' life brought hope to a hurting world and the hope of heaven one day, changing our lives today and for all of eternity. He was so much more than a Carpenter!

[6] "Our Story," *Purposeful Design*, https://pdindy.com/our-story/.

So it was that the beggar [Lazarus] died, and was carried by the angels to Abraham's bosom. The rich man also died and was buried.

LUKE 16:22

Prince Philip, Duke of Edinburgh, husband of Britain's Queen Elizabeth II, died in April 2021, at the age of 99. The family said how grateful they were that his passing was peaceful—Prince Philip died in his sleep. Speaking to the press, his daughter-in-law, Sophie, Countess of Wessex, said, "It was like someone took him by the hand and off he went."[7]

Could that "someone" have been one of God's angels? According to a story told by Jesus, it is not beyond our consideration. First, Scripture is clear that God's angels are sent as ministering spirits to serve those who will inherit salvation (Hebrews 1:14). Second, in Jesus' story, angels came to carry a poor beggar from his deathbed to "Abraham's bosom." Question: Was this story of Jesus a fictional parable or a true account? Jesus didn't say. Even if it was fictional, Jesus' parables always related factual perspectives on life. One of the ways angels minister to believers is to escort them home to heaven when they die.

How do you feel about the end of life on earth? An angelic escort to heaven is yet another reason for the believer not to fear death!

[7] "Philip's Death 'Like Someone Took Him by the Hand and Off He Went,'" *Daily Mail*, April 11, 2021.

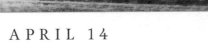

APRIL 14
Joseph of Arimathea

And Joseph took the body and wrapped it in a clean linen cloth,
and laid it in his own new tomb, which he had cut out in the rock.
MATTHEW 27:59-60, NASB

Christian novelist Bodie Thoene once worked for Hollywood film star John Wayne as a script writer. Wayne read an article she had written and liked it; a relationship developed, and she began writing for Wayne's production company. Later, when Thoene asked the famous actor why he had been so generous toward her, he answered, "Because somebody did it for me."

Receiving seems to stimulate giving. That was true for a man in the four Gospels, Joseph of Arimathea. He was a prominent member of the Jewish council in Jerusalem, meaning he was wealthy and well-respected. But like another member of the council, Nicodemus, Joseph had become a disciple of Jesus, albeit a secret one for fear of retaliation from the Jews. But when Joseph watched Jesus suffer and die for him, he could remain a secret follower no longer. He went to Pilate and got permission to bury the body of Jesus in his own, new tomb. Joseph was transformed by Jesus' generosity toward him. That ought to be true of everyone who claims to be His follower.

Don't be a silent follower of Jesus, step forward and show His love to others as He has shown His great love to you.

*So will the Son of Man be three days
and three nights in the heart of the earth.*
MATTHEW 12:40

A little boy walked up to a lady sitting under an umbrella on the beach: "Are you a Christian?" "Yes, I am," she replied. "Do you read your Bible every day?" "Yes, I do." "Do you pray often?" Yes, again. "Well," the lad concluded, "will you hold my quarter while I go swimming?"

Trustworthiness is developed by telling the truth and, more importantly, never failing to do what has been promised. It only takes one unkept promise or one lie to destroy credibility and become an untrustworthy person. Take the resurrection of Jesus, for instance. Many times during His three-year ministry on earth He foretold that He would be killed but would rise from the dead after three days. And that's exactly what happened! That may be the most astounding self-fulfilling prediction ever made. The fact that Jesus was raised from the dead exactly as He foretold gives us confidence in everything else He said. If there is anything Jesus said that you are tempted to question, remember the Resurrection. He proved His word is good.

A. M Hunter said it this way: "Christ either deceived mankind by conscious fraud, or He was himself deluded, or He was divine. There is no getting away from this trilemma."

APRIL 16
Becoming Like Jesus

*Beloved, now we are children of God; and it has not yet
been revealed what we shall be, but we know that when He is revealed,
we shall be like Him, for we shall see Him as He is.*

1 JOHN 3:2

The German Formula One racecar driver Michael Schumacher
won seven World Drivers' Championship titles before retiring
in 2012. A post-career skiing accident left him with a severe
brain injury from which he continues to fight back to health.
His son, Mick Schumacher, has followed in his father's
footsteps as an up-and-coming Formula One driver. Early in his
career, Mick Schumacher was quoted as saying, "My dad's my
hero, that's for sure."

It's not unusual for children to want to be like a parent.
And it raises the question for every Christian, "Whom do you
want to be like?" In a way, God has answered that question for
every believer since He is conforming us to be like His Son,
Jesus Christ (Romans 8:29). Romans 8:28 says God uses "all
things" to accomplish His purpose in us—that purpose being
to become like Jesus. When will that process be complete?
When He comes to gather us to Himself: "When He is revealed,
we shall be like Him" (1 John 3:2).

Whatever happens in your life today, watch for moments
where you can become more like Jesus. Take every opportunity
to walk in His steps.

Therefore they sought to take Him;
but no one laid a hand on Him,
because His hour had not yet come.
JOHN 7:30

Jesus Christ entered into time so that we might enter into eternity. As God, Jesus is infinite, timeless, eternal, and from everlasting to everlasting. But when He descended into our world through the virgin birth, He subjected Himself to the limitations of time. He often spoke in John's Gospel of "His hour." He passed most of His years in the small town of Nazareth, then devoted about three years to ministry. The six hours He spent on the cross is a period of torturous death we can't even imagine, despite all the pictures we have seen and sermons we have heard. Then He spent three days in the grave, followed by forty days on earth following His resurrection.

These years, days, and hours provided our gateway into eternal life. He prayed in John 12:27: "Now My soul is troubled, and what shall I say? 'Father, save Me from this hour'? But for this purpose I came to this hour." And in John 17:1 as He was about to be arrested, Jesus prayed, "Father, the hour has come."

Because Christ came to earth for a specific time, we can be with Him in heaven for time and eternity. What an incredible thought! Treasure every moment today as you prepare for your eternal home with Him one day.

APRIL 18
Willing Obedience

And being found in appearance as a man, He humbled Himself
and became obedient to the point of death, even the death of the cross.
PHILIPPIANS 2:8

The head of a mission agency once met with a mother whose son served in Sudan. During their conversation, he was touched by her description of her son's heart for the people he served. The man visited the woman's home several months later; this time to tell her that her son had been killed in Sudan. The mother's response to this tragic news was, "I would rather have my son die in the middle of Sudan, alone, than to have him living here with me, disobeying God's will."[8] This mother valued her son's obedience to his Heavenly Father more than her own personal preference.

When Jesus came to earth, He willingly obeyed the Father. He said "I do not seek My own will but the will of the Father who sent Me" (John 5:30). Jesus was obedient His entire life here on earth. As He prayed to the Father in the Garden of Gethsemane, Jesus said, "Not as I will, but as You will" (Matthew 26:39). He did the will of the Father, even when it meant dying on the cross. Jesus' example of obedience challenges and motivates us to obey our Heavenly Father, even when obedience is difficult and results in suffering.

[8] "She Gave Her Children," *Ministry 127*, https://ministry127.com/resources/illustration/she-gave-her-children.

APRIL 19
The Benchmark of Our Faith

*And if Christ is not risen, then our preaching
is empty and your faith is also empty.*
1 CORINTHIANS 15:14

The Christian apologist and author C.S. Lewis made an interesting observation about Jesus' practice of saying to people, "I forgive you." It is natural for us to forgive people for things they have done to us. But what do we say if someone cheats you out of ten dollars and I say, "That's all right; I forgive him."

When a person goes around forgiving people who haven't done anything to harm that person, something seems amiss. The Pharisees caught the problem immediately when they said to Jesus, "Why does this man speak blasphemies like this? Who can forgive sins but God alone?" (Mark 2:7) Exactly. So Jesus was saying He was God. Now anyone could make that claim, and many have. What's needed is something to back up those claims. Jesus did many such things, all of which led up to the greatest proof of all: His resurrection from the dead. There are some things only God can do—like forgiving sin and conquering death. And Jesus did them all. The Resurrection is the ultimate, historical benchmark for your faith. Jesus is God—the Resurrection proves it.

Your faith can remain full because Jesus' grave remains empty—that is the best news imaginable.

APRIL 20
When God Was Determined

Him, being delivered by the determined purpose
and foreknowledge of God, you have taken by lawless hands,
have crucified, and put to death; whom God raised up.
ACTS 2:23-24

There's no word higher, greater, or possessing more authority than that of *sovereign*. Notice the last five letters: REIGN. The prefix, *sov*, means "super" or "above all." In his Pentecostal sermon in Acts 2, Peter stressed the sovereignty of God in matters related to the crucifixion of Christ. The Jewish leaders weren't in control of the events. Pontius Pilate wasn't the determining power. The Roman soldiers weren't in charge. None of the civil or religious powers wrecked the plan of Almighty God. Jesus was delivered to death "by the determined purpose and foreknowledge of God."

Notice the power of the word *determined*. The death of Christ was a determination made in heaven in order to provide the world with forgiveness of sin and eternal life. From eternity past, our Heavenly Father determined to love you, to save you, and to give you an eternal inheritance at the cost of the blood of His Son, whom He then raised from the dead.

Nothing is outside of God's determined sovereign rule, and that knowledge should make us feel safe and secure no matter what we encounter in our lives here on earth!

APRIL 21
It Is Finished!

So when Jesus had received the sour wine, He said,
"It is finished!" And bowing His head, He gave up His spirit.
JOHN 19:30

Imagine all the different "finish" points in sending men to the moon and back in the late 1960s. The design was finished; the training was finished; the launch was finished; the moonwalk was finished; the return was finished—it took many "finishes" for the whole project to be "finished."

And so it was with the work of Christ when He came to secure mankind's redemption. Let's look at three: the Cross, the Resurrection, and the Ascension. On the cross, Jesus said, "It is finished," referring to His death for our sins. He had said earlier that His mission was "to finish [the Father's] work" (John 4:34). But His death would have been incomplete without the Resurrection (1 Corinthians 15:14, 17). And the final "finish" in Christ's work came when He ascended to heaven forty days after the Resurrection (Acts 1:9–11). He came to earth, completed the Father's work, and returned to the Father in heaven.

Nothing remains to be done to secure our redemption for eternity. "It is finished." We just need to believe and embrace this gift.

For Christ has not entered the holy places made with hands,
which are copies of the true, but into heaven itself,
now to appear in the presence of God for us.
HEBREWS 9:24

Preaching through the Bible sometimes results in important events getting little attention. An example is the ascension of Christ into heaven forty days after His resurrection—one of the most important events in all of Christian theology. But going verse-by-verse through the New Testament means you only encounter three references to this important event: Mark 16:19; Luke 24:50–53; Acts 1:9–11. But an entire chapter of the book of Hebrews discusses the implications of the Ascension: Christ entering the heavenly sanctuary as our High Priest and Intercessor before the throne of God (Hebrews 9).

We should take great joy from the Ascension of Jesus and contemplate what it means for us. As our High Priest, Christ presented Himself to the Father and secured the eternal redemption of His Church by His own blood. As our Intercessor, Christ stands between us and God the Father, defending us against Satan's accusations (Romans 8:33–34).

Praise God today for what the Ascension of Christ means in your life: You are saved, sealed, sanctified, and secure forever.

[John the Baptist] said: "I am the voice of one crying in the wilderness: 'Make straight the way of the Lord,' as the prophet Isaiah said."

JOHN 1:23

God said, "I AM WHO I AM." Abraham said, "I am old." Jacob said, "I am Esau your firstborn." Moses said, "I am not eloquent." Gideon said, "I am the least in my father's house." Ruth said, "I am a foreigner." Nehemiah said, "I am doing a great work." Job said, "I am a brother of jackals." Jesus said, "I am the door, the light, the bread, the Good Shepherd." Paul said, "I am the chief of sinners."

How would you answer the question, "Who are you?" When John the Baptist was asked that question, he spoke without hesitation: "I am the voice." John was not confused, and he did not stutter. He knew exactly who he was and what he was called to do. He was "the voice." His calling was to speak—to announce the coming of the Kingdom of God and of the Messiah of Israel. It didn't bother John that he wasn't the Messiah—His only purpose was to prepare the way for Him. John was a satisfied man, confident and content in his knowledge of himself.

Can you say the same about yourself? If you're not sure about who you are and your calling in life, ask God for His insight. He has a purpose and plan uniquely designed just for you.

For if you forgive men their trespasses,
your heavenly Father will also forgive you.
MATTHEW 6:14

It was John Calvin who said, "A happy life depends on a good conscience." And another unknown sage once declared that a good conscience is like a "soft pillow"—the key to a peaceful night's sleep. It is no wonder that a good conscience is so highly valued; "good conscience" appears six times in the New Testament as something to be maintained.

One of the ways we maintain a good conscience is by settling things quickly between ourselves and others. As long as matters are unsettled—as long as we withhold mercy and forgiveness toward others—things cannot be settled between us and God. Regardless of who is at fault, whether ourselves or another, "If it is possible, as much as depends on you, live peaceably with all men" (Romans 12:18). Whether someone has something against us or we have something against another, we should settle the matter quickly (Matthew 5:23–26; 18:15). When we extend mercy to others, God continues to extend mercy to us.

Are there ongoing concerns that need to be settled between you and another? Take steps to make things right today. Then look forward to a "soft pillow" tonight.

APRIL 25
Trust in Him

*Fear not, for I am with you; be not dismayed, for I am
your God. I will strengthen you, yes, I will help you, I will
uphold you with My righteous right hand.*
ISAIAH 41:10

British missionary J. Hudson Taylor once wrote, "When I cannot read, when I cannot think, when I cannot even pray, I can trust." Our world is filled with unexpected turns. Life will continuously throw hurdles our way. In the midst of hardship, we must always remember we can trust in our Heavenly Father to carry us through the most difficult parts of the journey.

Many biblical characters reached the point of hopelessness. David cried out to God in the midst of crisis in Psalm 143. When Jesus was in emotional agony in the Garden of Gethsemane, He cried out to His Father (Mark 14:36). Elijah was discouraged and felt defeated and alone and cried out to the Lord in 1 Kings 19:4. In Jeremiah 20:18, Jeremiah wished he had never been born. When we are at our wits' end, when we have no strength left—when we cannot read, think, or even pray—we can trust in the One who has promised to deliver us.

Glorifying God

By this My Father is glorified,
that you bear much fruit;
so you will be My disciples.
JOHN 15:8

In a modern vineyard, there are three elements: the grapes, the vines, and the vintner—the winemaker. When a wine wins an award, it is not the grape that is honored, nor is the vine dug up and rewarded. Rather, it is the vintner, the winemaker, who is praised for the quality of the wine.

Jesus drew a similar parallel in John 15 in His teaching on bearing fruit. He said His followers are branches that bear the fruit; He is the vine and the Father is the vinedresser or vintner (verse 1). His point is that when we as believers stay connected to the true Vine, Jesus, we will bear much fruit. We stay connected by abiding in Jesus and allowing His words to abide in us (verse 7). The result is that the Father will be glorified when we abide in Jesus and bear much fruit. The glory is not ours; the glory is the Father's (verse 8).

God's will is for us to bear much fruit in His Name—that is how we glorify the Father.

APRIL 27
Marvelous Light

But you are a chosen generation, a royal priesthood, a holy nation,
His own special people, that you may proclaim the praises of Him
who called you out of darkness into His marvelous light.

1 PETER 2:9

Ken Block, a professional rally driver, fitted his off-road truck with 300,000 lumens of blinding light to make sure he can see everything on the darkest night and in the darkest places. How much is 300,000 lumens of light? The average car headlight pumps out 700 lumens on low, and 1,200 with the high beams turned on. A light in a football stadium uses 70,000 or more lumens. So if Ken Block heads down your street, you might want to don your sunglasses or pull your curtains.

Nothing, however, compares to the light Jesus sheds on our pathway as we proceed through life. The Lord Jesus radiates light, as we see on the Mount of Transfiguration in the Gospels and in the descriptions of Him in the book of Revelation. Our eyes aren't yet fitted for that brightness, but it filters onto our paths to brighten and illumine each step we take.

Walk in the radiance of His presence today.

APRIL 28
Be a Builder

Therefore let us pursue the things which make for peace
and the things by which one may edify another.
ROMANS 14:19

Say you're at a neighborhood gathering and you meet a new neighbor. When you ask about his line of work, he says, "I am the president of AAA Edification Company." If you are familiar with New Testament language, you might think he was in a ministry of some sort. But when you inquire, he clarifies: "We're in the building business—houses, apartments, office spaces, and the like."

That would be a reasonable, if not unlikely, name for such a company since edification means "to build up." The New Testament words edify and edification are based on a compound biblical word: house and build. More than a dozen times, the apostle Paul applied this "building" idea to Christians and the Church. On the large scale, he compared the Church to a building—a "holy temple in the Lord" (Ephesians 2:21). At the personal level, he exhorted all Christians to "build each other up"—to build up the Church by building up (edifying) the individual members (1 Thessalonians 5:11, NIV).

Look for ways today to build up—strengthen, encourage, love—other members of the Body of Christ. In doing so, you build up the whole Church.

APRIL 29
Abundant Life

The Spirit of God has made me,
and the breath of the Almighty gives me life.
JOB 33:4

Minnesota elementary school teacher Erin Durga found out that one of the school custodians, Patrick, had kidney failure and was looking for an organ donation. As soon as she heard about it, she decided she wanted to help—and soon after, she donated her kidney to him. Later Patrick said, "When I first woke up out of surgery, it was nothing I've ever felt before. It was a new life."[9]

When we receive the gift of salvation from our Heavenly Father, we receive a new life—it is unlike any emotion we have ever felt before! He made a donation—a sacrifice—to give us a second chance at life, so that we may have life more abundantly (John 10:10). He is the Source of our physical life, our spiritual life, and our heavenly destination for all of eternity. With the realization that this abundant life is available to all who will hear and accept His offer of salvation, it is our joy to take that knowledge to our friends, family, and former enemies. It is the Good News of the Gospel!

[9] Kyle Melnick, "A Third-Grade Teacher in Minnesota Donated a Kidney to Her School's Custodian," *The Washington Post*, December 2, 2020.

APRIL 30
The Attitude of the Spirit

Be made new in the attitude of your minds.
EPHESIANS 4:23, NIV

How would you define the word *attitude*? Wikipedia calls it "a psychological construct, a mental and emotional entity that ... characterizes a person... It is an individual's predisposed state of mind."[10]

The real question isn't how we define attitude, but how our attitudes are defining us. The Bible tells us that Christ wants us to be defined by His attitudes. Philippians 2:5 says, "You must have the same attitude that Christ Jesus had" (NLT).

Let's take that a step further. Isn't that the true implication of the fruit of the Spirit in Galatians 5:22–23? Maybe we could paraphrase it like this: "As you grow in Christ, the Holy Spirit will produce in you the very attitudes—the predisposed state of mind—of Jesus Himself, which is more love, more joy, more peace, more patience, more kindness, more goodness, more faithfulness, more gentleness, and more self-control."

Our attitude is important when it comes to our heart of obedience to the Father. If you have some unhealthy attitudes today, ask God to replace them with those of Jesus.

[10] "Attitude," https://en.wikipedia.org/wiki/Attitude_(psychology).

MAY

MAY 1
Peter's Mother-in-Law

When Jesus had come into Peter's house, He saw his wife's
mother lying sick with a fever. So He touched her hand,
and the fever left her. And she arose and served them.
MATTHEW 8:14-15

He touched her.... She arose and served them.

Those three verbs encompass the whole of the Christian life. When we ask Jesus to become our Savior, He touches us as surely as He touched the hand of Peter's mother-in-law in Capernaum. It brings to mind the Bill Gaither song "He Touched Me" that reminds us that we were shackled by a heavy burden beneath a load of guilt and shame, until the hand of Jesus touched us, and now we are no longer the same. We rise with new spiritual life. "And you He made alive," says Ephesians 2:1.

And we rise to serve.

Notice this woman's service began at home. She instantly began serving Jesus and Peter and her household. How our marriages would be transformed if we adopted an attitude of servanthood at home! Does the floor need sweeping? Do the dishes need washing? Does your spouse need a hug? Do your children need time and attention?

When He touches us, we become His servants who also bless others.

MAY 2

What I Wouldn't Give

For a day in Your courts is better than a thousand. I would rather be a doorkeeper in the house of my God than dwell in the tents of wickedness.

PSALM 84:10

You know it when it happens. It might be someone you feel could mentor you in your vocation. Or it might be a new friend with whom you establish an immediate connection. Or it might be the love of your life. Regardless of when and how, there are times when you think, "I'd give up next week for the chance to spend one more day with this person!"

The author of Psalm 84 felt that way, only he was ready to give up more than a week: He was ready to give up a thousand days for one day in God's presence. And a young Jewish man named Andrew, and his friend, followed Jesus as soon as they met Him and spent the rest of the day with Him (John 1:39). That's how most people today feel when they meet Jesus—they just can't get enough of Him. A lot of people who are not Christians would probably become Christians if they could just make contact with His irresistible presence. Many have given up a lot to spend as much time with Him as they can.

It's also easy to take His presence for granted, to forget what a pure pleasure Jesus can be, one-on-one. If it's been a while since you gave up something to be with Him, try doing it soon.

Now when Jesus looked at [Peter], He said, "You are Simon the son of Jonah. You shall be called Cephas" (which is translated, A Stone).
JOHN 1:42

Jerry Kramer played pro football for the Green Bay Packers under legendary coach Vince Lombardi. One day at practice during Kramer's first year, Lombardi ragged the rookie unmercifully, criticizing every move he made. By the end of practice Kramer was ready to quit. Afterward, Coach Lombardi approached Kramer, mussed up his hair, and said, "Son, one of these days you're gonna be the greatest guard in the league." Kramer said he suddenly felt ten feet tall!

When Jesus of Nazareth first met Simon of Bethsaida, the first thing He said to the young fisherman was, "You are going to become a rock!"—the literal translation of "You shall be called Cephas." Through all of Peter's missteps and failures as a disciple, perhaps it was that seed-thought that kept him going until he became the first to make known the Gospel to both the Jews and Gentiles (Acts 2:14–36; 10:1–48). How wonderful that God sees each of us in light of what we will become! He has promised to conform us to the image of His own Son (Romans 8:29).

The next time you look in a mirror, look beyond what you see and try to picture what God sees: The person He saved you to become.

MAY 4
God Is Working

It is my pleasure to tell you about the miraculous signs and wonders that the Most High God has performed for me.
DANIEL 4:2, NIV

It happened in the blink of an eye. The young pastor was pinned beneath eighteen hundred pounds of boxes and equipment, unable to move, believing that these could be his last few breaths. X-rays later revealed he had broken his neck in such a way that should have paralyzed him, and doctors gave him a 2 percent chance of ever walking again. But his young family and church congregation prayed as they had never prayed before, pleading with God and asking for a miraculous healing and full restoration. Forty days later, the young pastor walked out of the hospital and returned to preaching just two short months from the date of the accident.

When Jesus walked the earth, there was no doubt that miracles were very real; the physical evidence could even be seen by His strongest opponents. Today, however, people question whether or not God still uses miracles. Stories, like the one above, should dispel any doubt that they are indeed actively being used to change people's lives.

God is not through using miracles of all kinds. If you have a need that seems impossible, take it to the Lord and believe that He still works miracles today—God is still working.

"For I know the plans I have for you," declares the Lord, "plans to prosper you and not to harm you, plans to give you hope and a future."
JEREMIAH 29:11, NIV

There is a story told of a shipwreck survivor who washed up on a deserted island. After he had been there a few days, he built himself a hut and prayed to God for rescue. Each day he anxiously looked out over the horizon as he waited for God's deliverance in the form of a passing ship. One day, after returning from a hunt for food, he discovered that his hut was consumed in flames. He was devastated and believed it to be the worst thing that could have happened to him on the island; everything he had was gone. The next day however, a ship arrived and the captain said, "We saw your smoke signal."

Sometimes, when it seems our whole world is crumbling, it is difficult to believe that God is at work on our behalf. But just when we think all is lost, God unfolds His plan and teaches us that He had it under control the whole time.

Remember, God's ways are not our ways; His thoughts are unlike our thoughts; His plans are so much bigger than we could ever imagine or dream. Watch Him work out His unique plan for your life as it is revealed in His time. His plan is best!

MAY 6
Be Prepared

Therefore purge out the old leaven, that you may be a new lump, since you truly are unleavened. For indeed Christ, our Passover, was sacrificed for us.
1 CORINTHIANS 5:7

Men are good at preparing. They'll stay up late Friday night getting ready for Saturday's fishing trip. They'll spend hours organizing a basement workshop before beginning a project. They'll devote a week preparing for Saturday's tailgate party at the football stadium. And they'll religiously study the brackets for the college NCAA basketball tournament—March Madness—in preparation for watching this annual tournament.

The men of the Old Testament were charged by God with certain preparations as well: preparations for worship. At the first Passover, men were to select a perfect lamb, slaughter it, put its blood on the doorpost, roast the meat, and make sure the house was cleansed of leaven. Do men—or women—spend as much time preparing for worship today? What kinds of preparation should be made? Prayer, meditation on Scripture, repairing relationships, helping children get ready to appreciate the Sunday worship experience, preparation for the Lord's Supper—there are lots of ways to make worship more meaningful.

And He said to those who sold doves, "Take these things away!
Do not make My Father's house a house of merchandise!"
JOHN 2:16

"Cheap grace is the mortal enemy of our church." Those are the opening words of *The Cost of Discipleship*, written by the German pastor-theologian Dietrich Bonhoeffer. Many know him as the author of this and other books, but not all know that he was executed by hanging in 1945 for the part he played in resisting Adolf Hitler's Nazi government in Germany. As a Christian, he spoke out for what he knew to be true, though it cost him his life.

We could call Dietrich Bonhoeffer a modern Christian activist—and we could call Jesus of Nazareth the first one in history. When Jesus saw that the temple in Jerusalem had been turned into a marketplace where unscrupulous vendors were profiting from the guilty consciences of worshipers, His righteous anger took over. Driving them out, He cleansed His Father's house and incurred the wrath of those who valued their interests above God's.

The day may come when you are faced with something you know is not right. The temptation will be to pass by, to look the other way. But if you don't speak up for God, who will? By your actions and love stand up and show the lost the road to Christ.

When Jesus therefore saw His mother…
He said to His mother, "Woman, behold your son!"
JOHN 19:26

She was the twenty-fifth child in the English family of a religious dissenter; she had little education and lived in a male-dominated age; she married an older man and bore him nineteen children, nine of whom died. Her house burned down, her barn fell down, her health failed, and her pastor husband was either poor, jailed, or sick much of the time. But Susanna Wesley raised two sons named John and Charles who changed the world. She was a follower of Christ who raised her children to love and honor God.

A young Jewish woman named Mary didn't consider anything more meaningful than being the mother of the Son of God. From the beginning, she knew she was irreplaceable in the life of her child, and her sacrificial love remained strong to the end as she watched Him die for her and the world's sins. Jesus' efforts to care for Mary indicate just how much she meant to Him (John 19:27). It is the heart of mothers to sacrifice, and the need of mothers to be remembered. Surprise your mother this week with an unexpected token of love.

Motherhood is best defined by children who treasure their mother's love.

Blessed be the Lord, who daily loads us
with benefits, the God of our salvation!
PSALM 68:19

You'll need a special driver's license to get behind the wheel of the Belaz 75710. It's the largest dump truck ever manufactured. Even with nothing in its cavernous bed, it weighs an incredible 360 tons. Its tires are massive, and you have to climb a ladder to get to the driver's seat. But the Belaz 75710 isn't large enough to contain all the blessings God unloads into our life every day. He daily loads us with benefits, with blessings.

Our strongest emotions are often triggered by the things that most frustrate us. When something happens we don't like, feelings of anger or discouragement or anxiety surge through us. But it helps to remember Psalm 68:19. It helps even more to make a list of some of those blessings. Some are universal: the sunshine, the fresh air, the falling rain, the majestic thunder, the changing seasons, the starry sky. Others are very personal: a grandchild's hug, a positive comment on a term paper, a cup of hot tea, a kind note in the mail.

Today, count your many blessings—take the time to mention them by name—you will be blessed as you remember your daily benefits.

MAY 10
He Knows Your Name

I have redeemed you; I have called you by your name; you are Mine.
ISAIAH 43:1

We all remember the story of Zacchaeus who climbed into a tree so that he could observe Jesus as He passed by. When Jesus saw him, he specifically called Zacchaeus by name—no doubt shocking him to his core.

Worship leader and songwriter Tommy Walker wrote the memorable song, "He Knows My Name." The words of that song remind us that He, God, not only knows our name, He knows our every thought, sees each tear that falls, and hears when we call. What a blessed thought that is, that the God of heaven knows us so intimately.

Many of us are bad at remembering names, yet one of the greatest things we can say to someone is his or her name. Whether famous or obscure, it builds ties with people when we remember and use their names.

How wonderful that God knows our names. Have you ever noticed how often Jesus called people by their names in the Gospels: *Martha, Martha…. Go and tell John…. Blessed are you, Simon Bar-Jonah…. Lazarus, come forth!*

He knows your name; it's written on His heart, and He loves you today.

MAY 11
Day of Prayer

And when He had sent the multitudes away, He went up on the mountain
by Himself to pray. Now when evening came, He was alone there.
MATTHEW 14:23

Think of life's challenges in two categories: specific and general.
Specifically, we might be faced with a decision, a problem,
a need, or a burden. Generally, we are often faced with the
challenge of keeping life's priorities in order amidst the
busyness of life. Either case is a good reason to plan a spiritual
getaway to pray.

Jesus made time to pray for both reasons. In Luke 6:12, we
read that Jesus spent an entire night in prayer. We aren't told
why, but the next morning He chose His twelve disciples (verse
13). Did He set aside time to pray specifically about whom to
choose? Generally, we read of another prayer getaway—again,
no reason given (Matthew 14:23). But His night in prayer
followed the day of "feeding the five thousand"—an exhaustive
day of teaching and ministry. Perhaps that night in prayer was
simply to rest and refresh, alone in fellowship with God.

When was the last time you planned a spiritual getaway to
pray? Whether for an hour, a night, or a day—it will be time
well invested.

Whatever your hand finds to do, do it with your might.
ECCLESIASTES 9:10

A humorous sermon illustration gives an example of the wrong attitude toward work:

Manager: "I'm sorry I can't hire you, there isn't enough work to keep you busy."

Applicant: "You'd be surprised how little it takes."[11]

This is clearly an exaggeration in order to make a point, but some people truly have this mentality toward work; they don't take pride in the performance of their responsibilities, rather they take pride in their profession. According to the Bible, however, this is backward thinking; and even servants should do their best, not caring about their lowly position, but working with integrity unto their real Master, who is God (Colossians 3:23).

It is difficult not to get caught up in the pursuit for power and position. After all, in the eyes of the world, these are highly prized and sought-after treasures. But when we lock eyes with Jesus and turn a deaf ear to the praises of men, the only thing that truly matters is doing our work with an attitude that is pleasing and honoring to Him. The gift of work comes from God, so it is to Him that our efforts should be aimed.

[11] *Pulpit Helps*, Sept. 1990 (Chattanooga: Pulpit Helps).

MAY 13
David's Mother

Show your strength in behalf of your servant; save me,
because I serve you just as my mother did.
PSALM 86:16, NIV

We know David's father was Jesse, but we have little information about his mother. She is not mentioned by name in the Bible. On one occasion when David was running from the armies of Saul, he sought a place of refuge for his father and mother (1 Samuel 22:1–4), so she certainly knew of his triumph over Goliath and of Samuel's anointing him king of Judah. But we don't know if she lived long enough to see him reigning on the throne.

She certainly lived long enough to cast a powerful influence over his life. In Psalm 86, he indicates that he learned to serve the Lord by watching his mother. "I serve you," he said, "just as my mother did" (verse 16, NIV).

Our children are always watching us; from the first moment they open their eyes at birth to the last day we close our eyes in death. It's never too late to pray, to influence, and to set an example. Let's start today, serving Him in full view of all those we're allowed to influence.

MAY 14
Women Who Followed Christ

The twelve were with Him, and certain women who had been healed of evil spirits and infirmities . . . who provided for Him from their substance.
LUKE 8:1-3

Have you ever wondered how Jesus financed His ministry? When He left the carpenter's trade, He gave up His regular income, yet He still needed daily meals, an occasional change of clothes, money for taxes (which He once paid with a coin from a fish's mouth), and provisions for the twelve who left their livelihoods to follow Him.

It was a group of women who helped underwrite His earthly work. Having been touched and transformed by His power, they did what they could, giving from their means; and they provided the money He needed for His three-year mission.

If we'd been alive in those days, would we have given anything to Christ for His work? There's an easy way to answer that, of course. He is still alive and doing His work on earth. We can discern what we would have done then by seeing what we are doing now. If you aren't doing it now, begin today by giving to Christ's ministry here on earth—it has eternal benefits.

MAY 15
The Good Part

And [Martha] had a sister called Mary,
who also sat at Jesus' feet and heard His word.
LUKE 10:39

The great A. W. Tozer, author of many classics on the spiritual life, once wrote, "In an effort to get the work of the Lord done, we often lose contact with the Lord of the work." As we will see, being busy in God's work, to our own spiritual detriment, is not a modern mistake. Indeed, human beings are guilty of "not being able to see the forest for the trees"—losing sight of the big picture while focusing on details—in many areas of life.

In the first century, two sisters demonstrated the right and wrong way to prioritize what is most important. Mary and Martha opened their home in Bethany to Jesus and His disciples, presumably for a meal. Martha was scurrying about making preparations while Mary "sat at Jesus' feet and heard His word." Martha complained to Jesus that Mary wasn't helping enough, but Jesus gently rebuffed her complaint. He said that Mary had chosen the "good part," meaning focusing on Jesus and His teaching rather than housekeeping tasks.

Yes, the details of housekeeping and "the Lord's work" are important, but not at the expense of growing in intimacy with the Lord Himself. Let your pursuit of the work of the Lord begin with pursuing the Lord.

MAY 16
Failed, but Not Finished

And the Lord turned and looked at Peter. Then Peter remembered the word of the Lord, how He had said to him, "Before the rooster crows, you will deny Me three times." So Peter went out and wept bitterly.
LUKE 22:61–62

It doesn't happen often, thankfully, but it does happen: An employee makes a serious mistake that costs the company a large amount of money—and the employee is let go from his job. Whatever the reason for the mistake—negligence, poor judgment, or an honest error—the employer can't risk it happening again.

Aren't you thankful God has a different perspective on our failures? Granted, most of our failures may be small. But the principle of holiness is that to fail in one thing is like to fail in everything (James 2:10). If God judged us on our works, none of us could be saved. Before he came to understand grace, the apostle Peter probably thought he was finished when he denied knowing Christ three times. Yet Jesus, after the Resurrection, reached out to Peter and embraced him, recommissioning Peter in His service (John 21).

Never forget: We are saved by grace through faith, not by works. Our salvation, and our ministry, is the gift of God (Ephesians 2:8–10).

MAY 17
Advancing the Cause

To me, who am less than the least of all the saints, this grace was given,
that I should preach among the Gentiles the unsearchable riches of Christ.
EPHESIANS 3:8

The 34-year-old general was striking and handsome with blue eyes and reddish hair. Major General George McClellan gave the impression of strength and vigor, and, as one historian said, "Dashing about on a magnificent horse, he seemed omnipresent" on the battlefield. He had a brilliant mind; and when Abraham Lincoln told him that the supreme command of the Army was on his shoulders, he responded, "I can do it all." But he did very little; and for all his organization and personal charisma, he seemed unable to attack or advance his forces. Finally Lincoln gave up on him, saying, "If General McClellan does not want to use the army, I would like to borrow it for a while."

Many Christians are well-equipped, well-trained, and well-financed. No generation of believers has ever had more tools, more plans, more programs, or been more affluent. But are we really attacking the enemy and advancing the cause? Are we winning our friends to Christ? Are we witnessing for Him?

God has placed us where we are for a purpose—use the tools and gifts God has given you to advance His cause.

MAY 18
Walk Versus Talk

For a good tree does not bear bad fruit, nor does a bad tree bear good fruit.
LUKE 6:43

There is a long list of modern metaphors and sayings that have their origin in the Bible. One of the most widely known is the picture of a wolf disguising itself as a sheep: a wolf in sheep's clothing. That image comes from Jesus (not from the fables of the Greek Aesop), meaning you can't judge people by how they appear but rather by the evidence of their life.

In the same sermon, Jesus paralleled that image with another—the kind of fruit a tree bears: "You will know them by their fruits" (Matthew 7:16). He went on to expound that grapes don't come from thorn bushes or figs from thistles. Only "good" trees bear "good" fruit, and "bad" trees bear "bad" fruit. These weren't lessons on raising sheep or harvesting fruit, they were lessons about people. The works or fruit or actions of a person ultimately will reveal who he or she truly is. As Paul would later put it, these are the works of the flesh or the fruit of the Spirit (Galatians 5:16–26).

These ancient metaphors are directly relevant for us. If our walk does not match our talk, we will eventually be found out by the type of fruit we produce for the Lord.

MAY 19
Be Passionate, Not Passive

He who says he abides in Him ought himself also to walk just as He walked.
1 JOHN 2:6

Years ago when Brad Hathaway of Mattapoisett, Massachusetts, was in his mid-fifties, his doctor suggested he start walking as a way to deal with his diabetes and heart problems. Hathaway took the advice seriously and determined to walk around the circumference of the earth—not literally, but in equivalent distance. Day after day and year after year, Hathaway walked through rain and shine, anywhere from three to ten miles every day. Last fall, he finished mile number 24,901. To great local fanfare, he had walked the exact distance of the equator's band around the earth. His current age is 88.

"As time went on, walking got a little harder," he said. "I had a walking stick for a few years and now I have this walker to help me walk."[12]

It's impossible to make progress in our Christian walk if we don't make the effort to live with discipline, obedience, holiness, love, the input of truth, and the empowerment of the Holy Spirit. We have to work on our Christian walk. We're God's channels on earth, but we're not simply passive pipelines. We are onward-bound servants.

[12] Sam Read, "Massachusetts Man, 88 Will Have Walked About the Circumference of the World," *News Channel 19 ABC*, September 11, 2020.

MAY 20
A Higher Purpose

The Lord has made everything for its purpose.
PROVERBS 16:4, ESV

After competing in the 1924 Olympics, Eric Liddell knew that his calling didn't lie in world-class athletic competitions. The world told him he was built for running—at the highest level. But he knew, "God made me for China." Eric followed God's call to the mission field in China and used his skills to minister to the Chinese. Sadly, he died in a Japanese internment camp during World War II. His final words were, "It's complete surrender."

Feats that the world may see as great are unimportant when we have eternal vision. We don't know what plans the Lord has in store for us—but whatever they are, they will be far greater than anything the world wants us to do. His calling is more magnificent than anything we can imagine! We may be "built" for something in the world's eyes—but God made us for His specific purposes. As we wait on Him to reveal His plan to us, we need to wait patiently as we surrender to not only His timing but His will.

MAY 21
Overcoming Our Obstacles

Who is he who overcomes the world,
but he who believes that Jesus is the Son of God?
1 JOHN 5:5

The Bible is filled with overcomers. Abraham and Sarah overcame barrenness and had a child in their old age. Esther overcame her fear and saved her nation. Joseph overcame betrayal, slavery, and prison and went on to save nations from a seven-year famine. Daniel overcame captivity and a night with hungry lions and became the Lord's voice to the kings of Babylon. David overcame multiple attempts on his life, the loss of two sons, and a battle with a giant and became one of Israel's greatest rulers.

With God's help we can overcome obstacles that seem impossible. By man's standards, there is much we cannot accomplish—but with God, anything is possible! He will strengthen us through whatever we are going through. The Bible tells us we are able to defeat any trials we may face with the help of our Savior (Philippians 4:13). When you are dealing with hardship, turn to the One who is sufficient for any trial. God will help you overcome whatever difficulty you are facing, and you will become stronger and more effective for Him because of it!

MAY 22
"Greetings From Thailand!"

God is a just judge, and God is angry with the wicked every day.
PSALM 7:11

A convicted criminal named Oualid Sekkaki escaped from Belgium's Turnhout Prison in December 2019, and the authorities had no idea where he was until he sent them a letter. It contained his prison badge and a postcard that said, "Greetings from Thailand!" But officials kept looking for him, and he was arrested in Belgium in September 2020.

Wrongdoers can run from the law, and sometimes it's impossible to impose the kind of justice every case requires. Perhaps someone has wronged or abused you, and maybe they've never had to face the music for what they've done. But our omniscient and omnipresent God is angry with the wicked every day. That doesn't mean He's fuming with emotional frustration the way we become when we're angry. The wrath of God is His judicial response to evil. He will achieve justice for His children, so we can leave our cases with Him.

Romans 12:19 says, "Do not take revenge, my dear friends, but leave room for God's wrath" (NIV). Turn your case over to Him, let go of bitterness, and trust God to make things right.

MAY 23
This Is a Test

The testing of your faith produces patience.
JAMES 1:3

About a hundred years ago, a Bible college in Lestershire, New York, asked Walter Martin to help them compile a hymnal for school use. He moved there with his family and took up the assignment. One Sunday he left the house for a preaching appointment, but his wife Civilla felt ill and stayed home. That evening as Civilla thought about the struggles of life, she wrote the words to the poem, "God Will Take Care of You." Returning home, Walter read the poem and composed the music; and a great hymn was born.

The last stanza of this hymn says, "No matter what may be the test, God will take care of you." Our trials and troubles are often tests. Genesis 22:1 says that God tested Abraham. David said, "I know also, my God, that You test the heart" (1 Chronicles 29:17). Psalm 11:5 says, "The Lord tests the righteous."

If you're facing trials and troubles now, think of it as a test. God is testing the quality of your faith to see if you'll trust Him; and He's testing the extent of your dependability to see if you'll obey Him.

As we trust and obey Him, He will take care of us.

*Go home to your friends, and tell them what great things
the Lord has done for you, and how He has had compassion on you.*
MARK 5:19

In Mark 5, Jesus encountered the demoniac of the Gadarenes
who was naked, self-destructive, wild, and riotous—the very
things that characterize our society today. Jesus cast out the
demons, and people were amazed to see this man sitting
clothed in his right mind at the Lord's feet.

In his newfound devotion to Christ, he begged to follow
Jesus as a disciple. But Jesus told him to go home to his friends
and tell them what great things God had done for him.

Our loved ones are a difficult mission field; but Jesus has
done so very much for us, how can we remain silent? Of course,
our attitudes must radiate joy, and we must remember the
difference between sharing and nagging. Peter warned us to
be gracious and tactful, witnessing with a humble spirit rather
than constant sermons (1 Peter 3:1). Ask God for a burden for
friends and family, and then look for opportunities to tell them
of the great things the Lord has done for you.

MAY 25
"Whatever You Do"

Therefore...whatever you do, do all to the glory of God.
1 CORINTHIANS 10:31

The great composer, Franz Joseph Haydn, though weakened by age and confined to a wheelchair, was present one evening at the Vienna Music Hall where his piece, "The Creation," was being performed. As the piece progressed, the audience became so overwhelmed with emotion that when the passage "And there was light!" was reached, they arose and burst into applause. Struggling to stand, Haydn motioned for silence, pointed toward heaven and said, "No, no, not from me, but from thence comes all!"

We were created to praise God. It should be our aim to glorify Him through our thoughts, actions, and words, amounting to a life that is ultimately not about us but all about Christ. Haydn understood this well and carried it out wonderfully during his lifetime. He knew that the reason he was able to create such masterpieces was that God had blessed him with a gift. He spent his life using that gift to bring glory to the Lord.

Scripture tells us we are to "Give unto the Lord the glory due to His name" (Psalm 29:2). Whatever we do, let's do it to honor and glorify Christ Jesus the Lord.

MAY 26
No Matter the Illness

The Lord will strengthen him on his bed of illness;
You will sustain him on his sickbed.
PSALM 41:3

After Billy Graham's death at age 99, his last will and testament was made public. He said, "I ask my children and grandchildren to maintain and defend at all hazards and at any cost of personal sacrifice the blessed doctrine of complete atonement for sin through the blood of the Lord Jesus Christ once offered, and through that alone. I urge all of you to walk with the Lord in a life of separation from the world and to keep eternal values in view."

Then he wrote, "When you read this I will be safely with Jesus in Paradise. I will be awaiting the reunion of our family in Heaven."[13]

No matter what sickness we may face on earth, we can leave behind a testimony and joyfully look forward to a glorious Paradise. What a reunion, when we meet on the golden streets of the Celestial City! The Lord is preparing a place for us. His Holy Spirit will strengthen and sustain us in illness, and His blessed Word will prepare us for our eternal habitation.

[13] Jay Allmond, "Billy Graham's Last Will and Testament Revealed," *Baptist Press*, May 25, 2018.

MAY 27
His Ways, Our Ways

"For My thoughts are not your thoughts,
nor are your ways My ways," says the Lord.
ISAIAH 55:8

The preeminent lesson to be learned in the Christian life is to walk by faith. For years, we navigate this world on the basis of our five senses. Then we are called to subordinate our "sight" (our senses) to faith and trust: "For we walk by faith, not by sight" (2 Corinthians 5:7). Instead of believing what we see, we are called to trust what we can't see or sense. We are called to trust God's ways more than our own ways.

This trust challenge is seen throughout Scripture. When Israel was called from exile in Persia to return to Jerusalem, God told them they would one day summon nations to Him (Isaiah 55:5). How could a poor, captive nation summon other nations to God? Because God's ways are higher than our ways. Paul discovered this when his evangelistic mission was blocked by God, only to have a new door open instead—because God's ways were higher than his (Acts 16:6–10).

Walking by faith means trusting that God's ways are always at work, even when we can't see him working. The walk of faith is based not on our perceptions and ideas, but on God's character and promises.

MAY 28
Keep Going

I have glorified You on the earth. I have finished the work which You have given Me to do.
JOHN 17:4

An employer takes a trip out of town and leaves her assistant with a list of tasks to accomplish in her absence. If the employer returns and finds the tasks only partially complete, or completed in an unacceptable way, what does that mean? It means the assistant had little respect (fear, honor, awe) for the employer. The employer was not glorified by the assistant's performance. But what if the tasks are completed above and beyond the employer's expectations? The employer is glorified (honored) by the way the assistant valued the employer's assignment. The assistant may not have agreed with or enjoyed the tasks, but in order to honor the employer, the tasks were completed.

Jesus acted like the faithful assistant. When He was on earth, He accomplished the work that the Father had given Him to do. He "set [His] face like a flint" (Isaiah 50:7), letting nothing keep Him from glorifying the Father. He "steadfastly set His face to go to Jerusalem" (Luke 9:51) and died for the sins of the world.

Do the work God has called you to and keep going!

*Likewise, I say to you, there is joy in the presence
of the angels of God over one sinner who repents.*
LUKE 15:10

In 2021, the giant *Ever Given* container ship was stuck in
the Suez Canal for nearly a week, blocking an essential
international trade route for hundreds of ships and causing
economic turmoil. The entire world looked on, wondering what
could be done to oust the ship. Numerous diggers, tugboats,
dredging equipment, cranes, and more worked tirelessly to set
the ship free. Boats honked their horns in celebration after the
Ever Given was finally dislodged.

Just as it took multiple agencies and equipment to free
the container ship from the Suez Canal, it often takes work
from fellow Christians to play a part in the salvation journey
of someone who is lost. It could start with a simple "God
bless you" that sparks someone's interest in learning about
God. Perhaps someone sees a spirit of grace and forgiveness
in you that is not frequently seen in the world today. As the
Spirit prompts us, we are emissaries of God's love on their
path to receiving the gift of salvation. And when a lost sinner
yields to the Holy Spirit and is saved, there is celebration and
rejoicing—in heaven and on earth!

Create in me a clean heart, O God, and renew a steadfast spirit within me.
PSALM 51:10

In September of 2020, Nepalese climbers from an environmental organization spent 47 days collecting 2.2 tons of trash from Mount Everest. Tourism had dropped significantly because of the COVID-19 pandemic, so a group of people cleaned up garbage from the world's tallest mountain, along with cleaning up waste from the surrounding mountains as well.

Sometimes we have mountains of "trash" in our heart—and it takes time to identify and remove it from our life. It takes effort to eliminate selfish habits, sinful thoughts, and toxic traits. But thankfully, we don't have to do it alone. God wants to help us. When was the last time you examined your heart and brought everything to Christ in surrender? Choose today to ask God to wash away the trash and turmoil in your heart, and to renew a steadfast spirit in you!

MAY 31
Loving Like God Loves

A new commandment I give to you, that you love one another;
as I have loved you, that you also love one another.
JOHN 13:34

Every organization has a way of marketing or identifying itself. Political parties, sports teams, fraternal organizations, religious groups, corporations—all develop ways to define who they are. And members or adherents adopt those ideas or ideals and make them universally known.

Jesus gave His disciples just such a "brand," or identifying mark: love. In John 13:35, we have His words: "By this [sign] all will know that you are My disciples, if you have love for one another." But can't love be found as a trait in many different groups in society? Yes, but perhaps not the kind of love Jesus' disciples are to be marked by. In verse 34, Jesus made the love of which He spoke specific: "As I have loved you, that you also love one another." In other words, it's not just generic love—it's a God kind of love: sacrificial, enduring, generous, and unconditional. When we love those around us as Christ instructed, we manifest God's love in the world. As God has loved us, we are to love one another (John 15:12).

Being a witness for Christ ultimately involves a retelling of the Gospel. But before that opportunity arises, demonstrating God's love to others can be a first step.

JUNE

JUNE 1
Crystal-Clear Goals

Teach me to do Your will, for You are my God;
Your Spirit is good. Lead me in the land of uprightness.
PSALM 143:10

Many nations are battling infrastructure problems, and this extends to reservoirs. In America, for example, many of the nation's reservoirs are filling up with sediment. In the past, sand, silt, rocks, and debris floated down rivers and into the sea, but now they are being trapped behind dams, threatening our water supply. The point being...

If we're going to have the crystal-clear goals and plans of God flowing through our lives, we need pure sources. Our best ideas flow from the reservoir of prayer. Our most creative moments come from our time with the Creator. When we invest time with Him in prayer and Bible study, we gain clearer focus on our personal dreams.

In Psalm 143, David felt overwhelmed (verse 4), but he spread out his hands to God (verse 6). He said, "Cause me to know the way in which I should walk" (verse 8), and He asked for God to teach him and to lead him (verse 10).

God will lead you, teach you, and use you, even when you feel overwhelmed, as you spread out your hands to Him in prayer.

JUNE 2
20/20

I will guide you with My eye.
PSALM 32:8

In 2020, Ashley Winter, 37, of Hereford, England, set a new Guinness World Record after running a mile in 10 minutes 11 seconds while blindfolded. Perhaps you're wondering why anyone would run blindfolded. It was for a good cause. Winter suffers from keratoconus, a vision-impairing eye disease, and he was raising money for a foundation that supports medical breakthroughs in ophthalmology.

Pity those who run the race of life blindfolded! What if there was no divine plan for our life? What if every step was a gamble and every mile a riddle? What if we had to take our life journey without God's guidance?

Thankfully, there is a divine plan for us. God knows and orders the arrangement for every day. He knows tomorrow as well as He knows yesterday. And He invites us to ask Him for guidance at every point. He guides us with His eye, so that our own eyes can see the way.

If you're at a juncture now or facing some hard decisions, claim the promise of Psalm 32:8—He will guide you with His eye.

JUNE 3
Step Off, Step On

Do not set foot on the path of the wicked or walk in the way of evildoers.
Avoid it, do not travel on it; turn from it and go on your way.
PROVERBS 4:14–15, NIV

An ancient Chinese proverb says, "A journey of a thousand miles begins with a single step." Even long and difficult undertakings have a starting point; you can't begin a long journey at the halfway point. You must begin at the beginning.

The Bible speaks of journeys and paths, referring to the journey of life. It also speaks of first steps: "Do not set foot on the path of the wicked" (Proverbs 4:14, NIV). The point here is that the path of wickedness will not mysteriously turn into the path of righteousness. We must avoid the path of wickedness. Or if we are already on that path, we need to depart from it. Stepping off that path is what the Bible calls repentance and faith. The journey of life with God begins by stepping off one path and stepping onto another.

Repentance means to change one's mind, to turn and go in another direction. Such a choice is a step of faith—the first step on a lifelong journey with God.

For God so loved the world that He gave His only begotten Son,
that whoever believes in Him should not perish but have everlasting life.
JOHN 3:16

A nearsighted person can see things clearly that are close to them but not things that are far away. The opposite is someone who is farsighted, or in this case foresighted: having the ability to focus on things that are far away, or in the future. As Christians, we are called to focus on both—the present (near) and the future (far away). But sometimes we lose sight of the blessings yet to come.

Saints in the Old Testament were intentionally foresighted—they had a clearer vision of eternity than they had of the present. Hebrews 11:1–21 tells us of people like Abel, Enoch, Noah, Abraham, Sarah, Isaac, and Jacob. Their earthly lives ended without realizing the complete fulfillment of the promises of God in Christ, but they didn't mind. They knew they were aliens and strangers on earth, citizens of a better country—a heavenly one. And we should have the same kind of sight, focusing on the future as well as the present.

What are you focused on? Don't let your present circumstances, whether joys or sorrows, obscure your vision from the eternal blessings to come.

But the path of the just is like the shining sun,
that shines ever brighter unto the perfect day.
PROVERBS 4:18

For most of the day, there seems to be little change in the amount of light. But the magic hour of dawn is when we see a distinct change take place: Darkness is slowly invaded by light. It is slow, but it is also consistent. Once the light begins to appear, the darkness never overtakes it until the sun sets again at dusk.

Solomon used the dawn to illustrate the increasing light in which the righteous walk throughout their life. The "path of the just" becomes clearer and clearer as the light dawns, and for all of one's life the light "shines ever brighter unto the perfect day" in which darkness is done away with forever in eternity. When we first become a Christian, the light of the knowledge of God is just beginning to break in our heart. Things may not seem as clear as we want; we still stumble over obstacles in our path. But the longer we walk, the brighter the light shines.

Wherever you are on your path with God, as you walk faithfully with Him, He will shine more light on your path "unto the perfect day."

Serve Like Jesus

[Jesus], being in the form of God, did not consider it robbery to be equal with God, but made Himself of no reputation, taking the form of a bondservant, and coming in the likeness of men.

PHILIPPIANS 2:6–7

A British television franchise begun in 2009 has now been exported to nearly twenty nations around the world. The premise of *Undercover Boss* is that a high-ranking executive, sometimes the company CEO, goes to work undercover in one of the company's locations to get an inside look at internal workings. After a week or two, the undercover boss is revealed to the shock of employees—they never imagined a company president working alongside them in a menial task. Sometimes hardworking employees are rewarded with gifts or promotions for their service as witnessed by the boss.

In a very loose sense, Jesus was an "undercover boss" who left the glory of heaven to walk among humanity on earth (Philippians 2:6–8). To use His words, He came to serve, not to be served. His leadership style is one He recommended to His followers: The greatest among you must first become the least. The CEO of heaven and earth became like one of us—and even promises to reward us for our faithfulness (1 Corinthians 3:10–15)!

Wherever you go today, let your purpose be the same as Jesus' purpose: to serve rather than to be served. His servant's heart is a model for our own.

[We] shall see His face.
REVELATION 22:4

In 1951, a red-headed toddler named Ken Beeton fell into the Manning River in Australia. He was eighteen months old. A nine-year-old boy named Ken Gibson was walking along, saw the drowning child, and heroically managed to pull him to safety.

Seventy years passed, and Beeton, now 71, decided to find out what happened to his rescuer. He tracked down Gibson, now 78, and the two met face to face for an emotional reunion. "I might not have been here without him, so I'm saying thank you," an emotional Beeton said, to which Gibson smiled and replied, "You're welcome."

We've been rescued by the Stranger of Galilee who walked past just when we were drowning in our sins. One day we'll see Him face to face in New Jerusalem and say, "I wouldn't be here without You, so I'm saying thank You."

The Bible says we will see Him face to face (1 Corinthians 13:12). Let's anticipate the day when we will physically see the face of Christ. What a glorious thought!

JUNE 8
The Equation of Love

Love the Lord your God with all your heart, and with all your soul,
and with all your mind.... Love your neighbor as yourself.
MATTHEW 22:37, 39

Infinity. Ten. Two. One.

That's the biblical equation for love. It begins with
the limitless, boundless, bottomless, depthless love of an
eternal God (1 John 4:8). He loves with infinite love. Then in
seeking to show us how we should love, He gave us ten great
commandments. The first four show us how to love Him, and
the last six show us how to love each other (Exodus 20:1–17).

Jesus boiled it down to two great commands—to love the
Lord our God with all our heart, mind, soul, and strength—and
to love our neighbors as ourselves (Matthew 22:37–37).

And when we combine the two, we come up with one
word—love.

But it's not just any kind of love. Not the love of the pop
songs or the romance novels. Not the love of the world. God's
love is agape—self-sacrificing, self-giving, others-centered, and
God-honoring. When we discover this, we learn something.
The overwhelming priority of our life is love.

Is there someone who needs the encouragement of your
love today? Take a moment to make a phone call or write an
email—love makes a difference!

JUNE 9
No Limit on Limitations

For the one whom God has sent speaks the words of God,
for God gives the Spirit without limit.
JOHN 3:34, NIV

There appears to be no end to the number of limitations that can disrupt our lives. Our dreams, desires, and usefulness can be frustrated by physical frailties or unexpected disabilities; by unending financial problems; by geographical barriers; by legal restrictions; by family considerations; and more.

But you can do whatever God calls you to do despite your limitations, for He gave His Spirit to Jesus without limitations, and we are the extension of Jesus in this world.

In practical terms, that means we should stop worrying about what we can't do and start doing what we can do. We should do our tasks with enthusiasm, as working for the Lord and not for men (Colossians 3:23). We should wave off discouragement, and trust God to finish what He has begun in us.

Don't focus on your limitations. Acknowledge them, but focus on the unlimited grace, power, mercy, and plan of your Savior.

JUNE 10
Sharpening the Focus

Immediately there fell from [Saul's] eyes something like scales, and he received his sight at once; and he arose and was baptized.
ACTS 9:18

A funnel has a wide end and a narrow end. Those two ends can represent how differing people find their life's purpose. Some enter early in life at the narrow end, knowing exactly what they want to be or do. Others enter at the wide end and narrow their focus and activity over time. With our unique gifts and talents, we each follow our own path through life.

The apostle Paul took a mixed path. He was a tentmaker by trade (Acts 18:3), but that trade was only to support his true passion: understanding and teaching the laws of God. He was on a literal road—the road from Jerusalem to Damascus—in pursuit of that passion when God changed his focus, and thus his life. Instead of living as a teacher of law, he became a preacher of grace. He went from an accuser of the brethren (Acts 9:1), to an apostle of Jesus Christ. It was a miraculous transition.

Don't despair about your life's focus or purpose. Walk in the light God gives you today, trusting that further light will be revealed as needed.

But command Joshua, and encourage him and strengthen him;
for he shall go over before this people, and he shall cause them to
inherit the land which you will see.
DEUTERONOMY 3:28

A seventh grader named Journey Bowman in North Carolina wanted to make a difference in her school, so she started the POP, or Power of Positivity, program. She began putting positive and creative notes in the lockers of other students. "I wanted to write positive notes to make a difference in somebody's day," she said. "In turn, they might also choose to make a difference in someone else's day."

And that's what happened. One young man "who was not always very optimistic" wrote as many notes as he could, while another student, who was very shy, was able to express herself in writing. All the notes were anonymous, but the project changed the atmosphere of the school.

Moses wasn't able to cross the Jordan and lead Israel to conquer the Promised Land, but he had a vital assignment. His job was to encourage and strengthen Joshua, his successor.

The support and encouragement of others makes a difference in our lives and helps us cultivate our dreams. Why don't you POP into someone's life today with a word or note of encouragement!

JUNE 12
Sustainable Energy

To this end I strenuously contend with all the
energy Christ so powerfully works in me.
COLOSSIANS 1:29, NIV

It takes a lot of energy to keep our world powered up, lit up, and filled up. Scientists tell us that humans daily consume about 63,300,000 megawatt-hours of electricity. Approximately half our energy comes from oil and natural gas, and another quarter comes from coal and nuclear reactors. The remaining 25 percent comes from renewable energy sources.

Put all that together and multiply it by a billion, and it still wouldn't equal a split-second of the energy God makes available to His children for living the Christ-life in this world. Think of the phrase Paul used—all the energy Christ so powerfully works in me.

Is that true for you?

Jesus sends strength into our souls by the Holy Spirit, and that's why we're constantly told to be filled with the Spirit (Ephesians 5:18), to walk in the Spirit (Galatians 5:16), to pray in the Spirit (Ephesians 6:18), to love in the Spirit (Colossians 1:8), and to be in the Spirit on the Lord's day (Revelation 1:10).

The Spirit of God keeps moving us forward into His will for our lives.

Be Bold

Preach the word! Be ready in season and out of season.
Convince, rebuke, exhort, with all longsuffering and teaching.
2 TIMOTHY 4:2

An ancient Greek herald was an important, official member of the civic court. They had strong, authoritative voices, allowing them to be heard by crowds as they made official proclamations. They also had a peacekeeping role, settling civic disputes. As government representatives, the herald also had a religious role since gods and governors were so intertwined.

The verb form of Greek herald made its way into the New Testament as "proclaim" or "preach." But the connotation of "preach the word" was different from "announce the Gospel." When Paul told Timothy to "preach the word" in his role as pastor in Ephesus, he had the authority of the Word of God in mind. There were some in the church who were teaching incorrectly and causing trouble (1 Timothy 1:3–7), and Timothy needed to "convince, rebuke, exhort, with all longsuffering and teaching." Just as a Greek herald spoke with civic authority, so the herald of God's Word must speak with divine authority.

Like the apostle Paul, we should make known that we are not ashamed of the Gospel of Christ—it is the power of God unto salvation and the life transforming hope for the world (Romans 1:16).

JUNE 14
A Tall Yarn

He saved others.
MATTHEW 27:42

Would you believe giant balls of twine are scattered here and there around the world? The largest is said to be in Kansas, where a man named Frank Stoeber spent his life winding 1.6 million feet of twine into a massive ball, which is now a tourist attraction. Another man, Francis A. Johnson, spent years working on his ball of twine in Darwin, Minnesota. We could give other examples, but the lesson is as sharp as a needle. Many people spend their lives spinning their possessions into larger and larger bundles, which they'll only leave behind.

How much better to live as Jesus did—for others. Even His enemies said, "He saved others." Jesus lived for us, and He wants us to live for Him and to live for one another.

Look around you today. Perhaps you'll see a child needing a smile, a disabled person needing a boost, a weary worker needing a kind word, or a lonely person needing a call or note. Think of a way to encourage your pastor. Caring for others is the tie that binds. So look to Jesus and follow His pattern.

JUNE 15
Daily Faith, Daily Bread

Give us this day our daily bread.
MATTHEW 6:11

It is hard to imagine a shorter verse of Scripture that contains a larger history and summary of the dependence of God's people upon Him: "Give us this day our daily bread." Those are the words of instruction Jesus taught His disciples to pray in the Lord's Prayer. The attentive disciple, upon hearing those words, would have immediately remembered the account of God's provision in the wilderness for the redeemed Hebrew slaves.

For almost forty years, God provided manna for the Israelites to eat—a seed or grain-like substance on which they subsisted (Exodus 16). But that provision was a test of their faith in God's promise to provide (verse 4). They were to gather daily what they needed for only that day. In the same way, Jesus taught His disciples not to worry about tomorrow, but to trust God every day for our daily bread (Matthew 6:25–34). He reminded them that worrying brings nothing; but faith in God brings provision.

If you have a need, don't allow anxiety to replace your faith. Let your requests be made known to God and He will guard your heart and mind in Christ Jesus (Philippians 4:6–7).

JUNE 16
The Joy of Salvation

Restore to me the joy of Your salvation,
and uphold me by Your generous Spirit.
PSALM 51:12

We all know this well-known proverb: "You never miss
the water until the well runs dry"—and some of us have
experienced it. We never realized what a great friend a person
was until they moved away. We never realized the blessings of
our church home until a relocation took us to a new city. And,
it's possible, we never realized the joy of our salvation until we
found ourselves without that joy.

That's what happened to David, the king of Israel. We know
of his sins: adultery with Bathsheba and complicity in the
murder of her husband, Uriah (2 Samuel 11–12). It was not until
Bathsheba bore David a son that he repented of his sins. For
almost a year, he lived without the joy of his salvation—possibly
described in Psalm 32. In Psalm 51, we have David's heartfelt
prayer of confession to God. And in verse 12 we have his request
for what he had lost: "Restore to me the joy of Your salvation."

It's easy to take salvation for granted. But when sins,
attitudes, and behaviors lead us into darkness, we realize what
we have lost: joy. Thankfully, joy is only a prayer away.

JUNE 17
Greater Is He

You are of God, little children, and have overcome them,
because He who is in you is greater than he who is in the world.
1 JOHN 4:4

Perhaps Satan's greatest trick concerns his own identity. He has enabled the world to think of him as an impish demon, dressed in red, with a pitchfork and a pointy tail. He is pictured as sitting on one's shoulder, whispering suggestions into the ear—a cartoon character worthy of a laugh. But nothing could be more wrong.

Instead of a red-dressed imp, Satan is a powerful being, portrayed in Scripture like a "roaring lion, seeking whom he may devour" (1 Peter 5:8). He can destroy, divide, and discourage using that which reveals his character: lies, counterfeits, and deception. He was given the name "devil" (diabolos—accuser, slanderer) in Scripture because of his tactic of slandering us before God and slandering God before us. But for all his schemes and power, we do not need to fear him. For the God who is in us is greater than the devil who is in the world.

Be ready for spiritual battle by submitting to God and resisting the devil—and he will flee from you (James 4:7).

*For whoever desires to save his life will lose it,
but whoever loses his life for My sake and the gospel's will save it.*
MARK 8:35

The phrase, "No pain, no gain" has come to mean that success requires a willingness to reach for a goal. We can either desire safety—live a no-risk, no-faith life—or we can stretch ourselves beyond our natural abilities and achieve a more fulfilling life.

That was Jesus' message for those following Him. The safe life is a life protected from loss and disappointment, a passionless life that is afraid to love and live. But if we embrace the Kingdom of God in the face of a world that wants to reject it, we will discover a life of passion. As Jesus Himself said, "I have come that [you] may have life, and that [you] may have it more abundantly" (John 10:10). Yes, following Jesus involves risk and therefore trust. But without risk, there is no reward.

If you are tempted to hold back, to not take the risk and follow Jesus...it is time to step out in faith and love. Only then will you find (and save) your life.

JUNE 19
Three in One

No one has seen God at any time. The only begotten Son,
who is in the bosom of the Father, He has declared Him.

JOHN 1:18

Bible teachers have tried to find an illustration that helps explain the Trinity—the three forms of water, the sun, a three-leaf clover, or an egg. But all of the illustrations proposed fall short of explaining the Trinity. All three persons in the Trinity—Father, Son, and Holy Spirit—are coeternal and coequal. Each member is fully God, not a part of God. The Trinity is a mystery beyond our human understanding; however, it is so clearly taught in Scripture that we can accept it by faith.

One of the places where we see the Trinity is at Jesus' baptism in Matthew 3:16–17. Jesus, the Son, is being baptized. The Holy Spirit descends like a dove, and God, the Father, speaks from heaven saying, "This is My beloved Son, in whom I am well pleased." All three members of the Trinity are distinct and active at the same time. The Father and the Holy Spirit are invisible, but in the divine scheme of things, God the Son manifests and reveals God in a personal, tangible way. Through our study of Jesus in Scripture, Jesus shows us who God is and what God is like.

Then [Jesus] said to them, "These are the words which I spoke to you while I was still with you, that all things must be fulfilled which were written in the Law of Moses and the Prophets and the Psalms concerning Me."

LUKE 24:44

In the last few years people started sharing on social media facts and tips about life that they recently learned. They coined these posts "I was _____ years old when I learned_____." The posts range from a more efficient way to clean an electric stove to what a frog's tongue is like. While the content varies greatly, the posts communicate a sense of wonder at the fact the person did not know the piece of information.

When we open our Bibles and study Jesus in the Old Testament, we also develop a sense of wonder and excitement. As we read from Genesis 1 to Malachi 4, we see Jesus in new and profound ways. We find Him in Genesis and Judges as the Angel of the Lord. We read of His future sufferings in Isaiah. And we discover promise after promise about Jesus' first coming, each of which God kept. Jesus in the Old Testament strengthens our faith, encourages our heart, and increases our hope. "For whatever things were written before were written for our learning, that we through the patience and comfort of the Scriptures might have hope" (Romans 15:4).

For by grace you have been saved through faith,
and that not of yourselves; it is the gift of God.
EPHESIANS 2:8

In 2020, 95-year-old *Mary Poppins* star Dick Van Dyke stopped in front of a California nonprofit and reached out to people who were unemployed and seeking assistance. The non-profit organization was helping job seekers who were struggling during the COVID-19 pandemic. The actor walked up to individuals who were unknown to him personally and handed them a financial gift in cash as they stood in line. His presence there that day was a great encouragement to them in their time of difficulty. He gave out of his abundance to those in need.

When we are overwhelmed with the grace of God, we also want to share it with everyone we know—even people standing in line on the street! When we receive a tremendous gift, we want to share it with others as well. And we have received the greatest gift in existence—the gift of grace and salvation from our Heavenly Father. When we experience the Good News in our life, we overflow with joy, and it makes us want to share it—it is a gift worth sharing!

JUNE 22
Limitless God

Not that I have already attained, or am already perfected; but I press on, that I may lay hold of that for which Christ Jesus has also laid hold of me.
PHILIPPIANS 3:12

Seven-year-old Michael Martinez from Texas was the only one who woke up when the carbon monoxide alarm in their house went off. Michael has cerebral palsy, a disorder that doesn't allow him to walk. In the middle of the night, Michael crawled through the house to warn his family so they could get to safety. He saved all their lives—they call him their little miracle and thank God that He saved them. On the family's GoFundMe page, they give "all the honor and glory to the Lord."

No matter what limitations this world may tell you that you have, God can use you. He used Moses, with a speech impediment to lead a nation. Samson was ultimately used by God after he had been blinded. After Jacob wrestled the angel of the Lord, he had a permanent limp, yet God still had plans for him. God is not fazed by our human limitations. He can use anyone to fulfill His purposes. He does not judge our ability by the world's standards but by His own abilities—which are limitless!

JUNE 23
Plans We Cannot See

For you have need of endurance, so that after you have done the will of God, you may receive the promise.
HEBREWS 10:36

Adoniram and Ann Judson were the first American missionaries to Burma (now known as Myanmar). They spent years witnessing to the Burmese people. They endured numerous hardships including Adoniram being imprisoned and tortured—but through it all they never gave up on their calling. By the time they both had passed, the couple had only established a few churches in the country, but they contributed one of the greatest gifts they could: the Word of God in the Burmese language!

Sometimes the efforts we make may seem slow, but we can't see the big picture like God can. What may seem futile to us now may have a great impact in the future. We can only see the short-term solutions, but God has long-term plans—greater than anything we can imagine. The next time you feel your work is in vain—remember that God will not allow your labors to go to waste—He has a plan.

JUNE 24
Too Busy?

For if these things are yours and abound, you will be neither barren
nor unfruitful in the knowledge of our Lord Jesus Christ.

2 PETER 1:8

In his book *Walking with God*, Andrew Murray wrote, "No knowledge of the air or the food around me can nourish me, except it enters into my inward life. And no knowledge of the truths of God can profit me, except as He, by His Spirit, enters into my inmost being and dwells within me. It is with the heart I must wait upon God. It is into the heart God will give His Spirit and every spiritual blessing in Christ."[14]

Amid our business and busyness, we can mentally know we are Christians without enjoying that precious fellowship that makes us one with Christ. Our desire should be to move toward Jesus, not away from Him, but that takes waiting upon Him in prayer, Bible study, quietness, and confidence.

Try to slow down a little bit today, and be still for a few moments, enjoying the knowledge—the true personal character—of the Lord Jesus Christ. How incredible that He longs to meet with us, if we will only pause a moment and take the time!

[14] Andrew Murray, *Walking with God* (Alachua, FL: Bridge-Logos, 2008), 55.

JUNE 25
An Unnatural Choice

You love righteousness and hate wickedness; therefore God, Your God, has anointed You with the oil of gladness more than Your companions.

PSALM 45:7

People who live exclusively in one culture live much of their life subconsciously. That is, they are so used to the ways and traditions of their homeland that they don't have to think before acting. But when they go to another culture to visit or to live, every choice is a conscious one because everything is new. They have left their natural state and are living in an unnatural one.

Jesus' "culture" was one of intimate fellowship with the Holy Spirit. From eternity past, He had lived with the Father and the Spirit in heaven; and when He came to earth, that relationship continued. He was human and had to submit to the Spirit, but He was without the sin nature that we encounter, so He did not wrestle against the Spirit. Not so with us. Our sinful, fleshly nature is not naturally at home with the Spirit. So, moment by moment, instead of walking in darkness, we now choose to walk as "children of light" (Ephesians 5:8).

Choose today to follow the leading of the Spirit in your life and seek to do what is pleasing to the Lord. Humanly it is an unnatural choice, but it is one that your new nature in Christ will gladly agree with.

JUNE 26
Wilderness Training

For the Lord your God has blessed you in all the work of your hand.
He knows your trudging through this great wilderness.
DEUTERONOMY 2:7

Many adventurous people are signing up for wilderness training, seeking to learn the survival skills that will keep them safe in rough terrain and remote regions. The dictionary defines *wilderness* as a wild and uncultivated region, one that is either uninhabited or inhabited only by wild animals.

The word *wilderness* shows up quite a bit in Scripture. The Bible has a lot to say about believers trudging through wilderness areas—the Israelites, who traveled to Canaan; David, who hid from King Saul; Jesus, who was tempted by Satan in the wilderness of Judea.

That word seems to describe the rough patches of life, so we all need wilderness training and survival skills in a spiritual sense.

The most important aspect of wilderness training is having the right Guide. The wilderness doesn't threaten the Lord Jesus. He created the wastelands of earth, and He formed the vast wastelands of the universe. He inhabits it all, and He knows every step of the way.

Don't worry today. With God leading us, we can make it through the wilderness.

JUNE 27
The Key to Happiness

He who heeds the word wisely will find good,
and whoever trusts in the Lord, happy is he.

PROVERBS 16:20

Happy birthday, Adell Julie Green Thompson! When the "rock" of her family turned 105, she gave all the credit to the Lord. Her daughter, Maxine, said, "She trusted God from a little girl. She was always worshiping God and praying. She's just a unique person…. She likes reading her Bible." And her grandson Anthony added, "Her faith is so inspiring. Even at her age, she's still reading her daily devotional. It's just remarkable how the grace of God and the love of God have just been on her life."[15]

Trusting God is a tonic for the body, mind, and soul. The Bible doesn't often use the word *happy*. The biblical writers preferred to write about joy. But Proverbs 16:20 doesn't hesitate to tell us that trusting God brings happiness to our heart. It enables us to cast our cares on Him, focus on His nearness, feed on His promises, anticipate His coming, and share His message.

No matter what is happening around us, we can always trust God.

[15] Dionne Gleaton, "'She's the rock of our family': Santee woman celebrates 105 years with parade," *The Blue Mountain Eagle*, October 14, 2020.

Delight yourself also in the Lord,
and He shall give you the desires of your heart.
PSALM 37:4

No resource was more valued in biblical lands than pure water. Cities grew up around water supplies. In fact, Jerusalem relied upon the waters of the fresh-water Gihon Spring during the Old Testament era. (And it still flows today.) It is no wonder the biblical writers used a spring or well as a symbol of life. Solomon called the heart a "wellspring of life" (Proverbs 16:22). Thus, the heart was to be kept pure and righteous; the health of the life depended on the health of the heart.

So when David wrote that God would give "the desires of your heart" to the one who delights in God, he had a pure heart in mind. Such a heart would be consistent with one who delights in God and His ways. It's the equivalent of Jesus telling His disciples to abide in Him and His words in order to receive whatever they asked for (John 15:7). Getting our prayers answered, or being given the desires of our heart, presupposes a heart that delights in God.

God delights in meeting the needs of His children and satisfying them with every good thing (Deuteronomy 26:11). His goodness to us is an ever-flowing spring of blessing.

JUNE 29
Follow God's Calling

Then He said to them, "Follow Me, and I will make you fishers of men."
They immediately left their nets and followed Him.
MATTHEW 4:19–20

Mary Slessor grew up hearing her mother read the mission paper every month. She could feel in her heart a desire growing to share the love of Jesus with others. When David Livingstone, a missionary to Africa, died, Mary decided she wanted to continue his work in sharing the Gospel. She became a missionary to Africa, and she crossed territories where no Europeans had been before her—fighting danger and hardship—and she was able to spread the Gospel to areas where no other missionaries had been able to go.

Following God can be dangerous. You may face uncertain circumstances and uncharted territory as you follow Him. Some people may try to discourage you, but what God has set in your spirit, no one can take away. God has placed a calling in each of our hearts, and it's our responsibility to follow His direction for our lives. When an opportunity comes our way—it's up to us to seek God's will and pursue it. What has God laid on your heart today? Listen for His still, small voice and follow God's calling.

JUNE 30
Pay It Forward

For the grace of God has appeared, bringing salvation for all people.
TITUS 2:11, ESV

A California student raised nearly thirty thousand dollars for his former substitute teacher after learning that he lived out of his car. After retirement, the teacher, Mr. Jose Villarruel, was struggling to make ends meet and found himself homeless. His former student recognized him and decided to raise donations online. The teacher's response? He wants to pay it forward. "The greatest feeling that I have right now is like an obligation that I need to do a lot for the world and the greatest feeling is I can do it and I'm going to find a way to do it," he said.[16]

Being part of God's family is truly the greatest blessing in the world. As we consider this bountiful gift and thank God for His mercy to us, it is only natural to share it with those around us—to pay it forward. If someone is hurting and needs to hear the message of the Gospel—share Christ with them—pass it on and encourage others to join the family of God!

[16] Janine Puhak, "Man Raises $27K for Former Teacher After Learning He Became Homeless During Pandemic," *New York Post*, March 16, 2021.

JULY

JULY 1
God Will Wipe Away Our Tears

God Himself will be with them and be their God.
And God will wipe away every tear from their eyes.
REVELATION 21:3–4

What do you call a drop of water that contains mucin, lipids, lysozyme, lactoferrin, immunoglobulins, glucose, urea, sodium, and potassium? It's a tear. All land mammals (except goats and rabbits) produce tears, but only humans do so as part of the emotional responses of life. For humans, tears are often sparkling drops of emotion from the depths of our hearts.

There's nothing wrong with tears, for Jesus wept, and He was perfect in every way. Weeping is often therapeutic. Yet at the beginning of the eternal state on the new earth, God will somehow wipe His finger across our eyes, and remove our need for weeping. Most of our earthly tears come from sorrow, grief, loneliness, and heartache. But there will be no such experiences in heaven—"No more death, nor sorrow, nor crying. There shall be no more pain, for the former things have passed away" (Revelation 21:4).

Imagine a place without pain, suffering, or sadness—ever! That's heaven, and that's our home.

Bless You!

Blessed is the man who walks not in the counsel of the ungodly,
nor stands in the path of sinners, nor sits in the seat of the scornful.

PSALM 1:1

Sometimes you'll hear the German word *gesundheit* when someone sneezes. It literally means "health," so saying it after a sneeze means "Good health to you!" The English expression "God bless you" was intended the same way: "May God bless you with good health!"

But what does *blessing* mean? Why do we say, "God bless you," upon parting, or sign our emails with "Blessings"? In both the Old Testament and the New Testament, the words for blessing literally mean "happiness." The Old Testament word *osher* came from a root meaning "to be level or right, to go forth in properness and rightness." The New Testament *makarios* also means to be happy—that is, "to live in God's favor." So when we say, "God bless you," we are invoking the happiness only God can provide. And we find that happiness by living according to His guidelines for life—full of the Spirit and based on the Word.

Who wouldn't want to live a happy life? While the world promotes many paths to happiness, only God's blessing can bring *true* happiness.

For you, brethren, have been called to liberty; only do not use liberty as an opportunity for the flesh, but through love serve one another.
GALATIANS 5:13

When the coronavirus struck China, millions of people fled or were quarantined, as fear spread across China to the world. One group of people, however, had a different response. Christians in the city of Wuhan went into the streets distributing face masks, passing out Gospel brochures, and sharing the message of Jesus. One pastor said, "It is readily apparent that we are facing a test of our faith. The situation is so critical, yet [we are] trusting in the Lord's promises, that his thoughts toward us are of peace, and not evil, and that he allows for a time of testing, not to destroy us, but to establish us."

Christians find joy through serving and helping others. Even in trying times, we can encourage and assist others—especially those who are sick and alone. If you can't leave your home, you can still reach out with a card, an email, a phone call, or through prayer. It is our joy as followers of Jesus Christ to minister to others in His Name. He brings joy to the world!

Liberty at Risk

What persecutions I endured.
2 TIMOTHY 3:11

What do we do when everything we believe in is under attack? It seems that in the past year places of worship were especially set apart for rules and regulations that prevented us from gathering together. The blatant anti-Christian attacks by our secular society have intimidated many Christians in the western world, but God is on our side in this battle for truth!

According to the Bible, every godless culture will view Christians with hostility; and according to Church history, every generation of believers has faced opposition and hatred. The Bible says, "Yes, and all who desire to live godly in Christ Jesus will suffer persecution" (2 Timothy 3:12). But Paul also told Timothy to persevere and lean on the "Holy Scriptures, which are able to make you wise for salvation through faith which is in Christ Jesus" (verse 15).

God is at work in our lives, even when we're being pressured or persecuted for our faith. Don't be intimidated by the world. Be motivated by the Word!

Establish Your word to Your servant, who is devoted to fearing You.
PSALM 119:38

In his book, *Knowing God*, J. I. Packer writes, "There can be no spiritual health without doctrinal knowledge; but it is equally true that there can be no spiritual health with it, if it is sought for the wrong purpose and valued by the wrong standard.... Our aim in studying the Godhead must be to know God better. Our concern must be to enlarge our acquaintance, not simply with the doctrine of God's attributes, but with the living God whose attributes they are."[17]

Many Christians have developed a healthy appetite for God's Word, but the focus must remain on the God who gave His wonderful words to us. As we find precious Scriptures to study and learn, it's for the purpose of getting to know Him better. Think of a wife whose husband is stationed overseas. Despite modern communication, nothing is sweeter than a love letter in the mail. The letter deepens the love between the couple.

The more time we spend in God's Word, the more we come to know, love, and cherish God Himself.

[17] J. I Packer, *Knowing God* (Downers Grove, IL: IVP Books, 1973), 22-23.

JULY 6
Have Mercy

And be kind to one another, tenderhearted,
forgiving one another, even as God in Christ forgave you.
EPHESIANS 4:32

There are several key words in the biblical lexicon that are similar, but different. And their difference makes all the difference! *Justice* means getting what we deserve. *Mercy* means *not* getting what we deserve. And *grace* means getting what we don't deserve. All have their importance, and each has its place in our life.

Justice we leave to God, of course (Hebrews 10:30). Grace we can generously dispense toward others. But mercy? That's a harder one. Remember: Mercy means *not* giving someone what they deserve. We have received mercy from God in that He spared us from the punishment for our sins and punished His Son instead. So what do we do when someone offends us and we feel they deserve our reproach? We should do what God has done for us—show mercy. Instead of dispensing judgment or vengeance, we show love, forgiveness, and understanding. In short, we show mercy. Why? Because God has shown mercy toward us.

The next time you are impulsively or deliberately inclined to judge or retaliate, remember to show mercy. Give to others what God has given you.

JULY 7

Rewards Now and Forever

So Jesus answered and said, "Assuredly, I say to you, there is no one who has left house or brothers or sisters or father or mother or wife or children or lands, for My sake and the gospel's, who shall not receive a hundredfold now in this time... and in the age to come, eternal life."

MARK 10:29–30

Grocery and drug stores issue reward cards that provide immediate discounts on purchases. And there is a reward credit card to suit every desire: travel discounts, airline miles, cash rebates, gas discounts, and more. Some rewards are immediate; others accumulate over time.

Jesus said a lot about rewards—again, some immediate and some long-term. In fact, He warned about the pursuit of immediate, short-term rewards, such as receiving praise from men. Instead, we should seek the rewards that come from God in eternity (Matthew 6:16–21). That is not to say that God doesn't reward faithfulness in this life—He does. He is a rewarder of all who seek and follow Him, both now and in eternity (Hebrews 11:6).

We don't follow Christ to be rewarded, but His grace assures us that His blessings will doubly be ours: in our present life and for all eternity.

JULY 8
The Lost Planet

He counts the number of the stars; He calls them all by name.
PSALM 147:4

Poor Pluto! Many of us remember when it was one of nine planets circling the sun. But the International Astronomical Union decided he wasn't a full-sized planet after all, so now there are only eight. Yet mathematicians insist there are nine planets, so astronomers are searching day and night for "Planet X," which is believed to be ten times the mass of earth and lurking in the outer reaches of our solar system.

God knows the number and names of the stars, and He also knows the planets. He created the universe with a precision that baffles the wisest scientist and with beauty that outstrips the greatest artist.

Don't let the skeptics disturb you. False theories about the origin of the universe abound, and the psychological harm they inflict is appalling. They fill the minds of entire generations with despair. But the message of our Creator God is one of love. He made us. He knows us. He has a roadmap for our lives. And the more we learn of Him, the more we understand who we are and why we're on earth. Trust in the knowledge that you are known and loved by God.

Made for Himself

Lord, what is man, that You take knowledge of him?
Or the son of man, that You are mindful of him?

PSALM 144:3

The population of the world is quickly approaching more than 7.8 billion people—of which you are one individual. If that isn't humbling enough, consider this: Recent estimates show that the total number of people who have ever lived on planet Earth range from 90–110 billion. And again, each one of us is a single individual in that vast number. Numbers that large make us think of sand on the seashore or stars in the heavens.

Yet, in spite of the seeming insignificance of a single human life, Jesus taught that God sees every sparrow that falls and knows the number of hairs on your head (Luke 12:6–7). Such truths made the psalmist, David, look into the heavens and wonder how it could be possible for the mighty God who created the world and everything in it to know and care for him (Psalm 8:3–4). David also wrote that God knows us because He fashioned us, individually, in our mother's womb (Psalm 139:13–14).

You may be only one, but you are unique and precious to God. He created you for Himself!

JULY 10
God Is Shining on You

The grace of the Lord Jesus Christ, and the love of God,
and the communion of the Holy Spirit be with you all. Amen.
2 CORINTHIANS 13:14

The earliest archaeological discovery of God's covenant name—Yahweh—was found on two silver amulets near Jerusalem. Amulets were small pieces of jewelry, typically thought to be protective of evil or harm. What did the amulets have inscribed on them? The Aaronic blessing found in Numbers 6:24–26, in which God's name, Yahweh—"the Lord"—occurs three times.

The blessing is well known to church-goers as it is often used as a benediction: "The Lord bless you and keep you; the Lord make His face shine upon you, and be gracious to you; the Lord lift up His countenance upon you, and give you peace." It is perhaps the most beautiful benediction known to Jews and Christians alike. Paul gives a New Testament equivalent in 2 Corinthians 13:14. It's not hard to see why amulets would have the Aaronic blessing inscribed on them. What harm could come to one who is so cared for by Yahweh?

God is blessing you and making His face shine upon you at this very moment—giving you peace that only He can give. Walk in His blessing today.

JULY 11
Moment by Moment

Do not boast about tomorrow, for you do not know what a day may bring.
PROVERBS 27:1

We should plan tomorrow's work as best we can. We should anticipate tomorrow's blessings and prepare for tomorrow's burdens. But we can never boast about tomorrow, for we don't know what will happen from day to day. The epistle of James says something similar in James 4:13–16. Life is brief and, to us, often seems uncertain. We're not omniscient, so none of us can predict what will happen from moment to moment.

But our times are in God's hands (Psalm 31:15), and the Lord knows every detail of every day allotted to us on earth and in heaven. That's why we should keep in mind that our human planning is contingent on God's perfect will.

It is a reminder to pray in this way: "Lord, if it's Your will, let me enjoy this vacation. If it's Your will, bless this upcoming decision." "Dear God, tomorrow appears to be a busy day; give me strength and wisdom. Be with me through every moment according to Your will."

Our Good Shepherd knows what's around the next turn, and He will never lead us astray. He guides us in one-day increments, and His plans are sealed with His blessings.

JULY 12
Worship the King

He was clothed with a robe dipped in blood.... Now out of His mouth goes a sharp sword.... And He has on His robe and on His thigh a name written: KING OF KINGS AND LORD OF LORDS.

REVELATION 19:13–16

Our culture continues to be fascinated by royalty. Young girls enjoy princess-themed toys. Adults all over the world follow the British royal family, watching interviews, reading news articles, and streaming the series, *The Crown*. However, the grandeur of royal ceremonies and the elaborate royal weddings are nothing compared to the Second Coming of Christ, the King of kings and Lord of lords, in Revelation 19.

When Jesus returns as King of kings and Lord of lords, He will destroy the Beast and his armies before setting up His throne and reigning for a thousand years. Unlike today's human royalty, He will not reign over a nation or group of nations. He will reign perfectly over the entire earth. And peoples' fascination with royalty pales in comparison to the worship Jesus will receive one day. "At the name of Jesus every knee should bow, of those in heaven, and of those on earth, and of those under the earth, and that every tongue should confess that Jesus Christ is Lord, to the glory of God the Father" (Philippians 2:10–11).

Come worship the King of kings and Lord of lords!

JULY 13
A Tale of Two Rulers

Then Jesus, looking at him, loved him, and said to him, "One thing you lack: Go your way, sell whatever you have and give to the poor, and you will have treasure in heaven; and come, take up the cross, and follow Me."

MARK 10:21

One of Charles Dickens' most famous novels is *A Tale of Two Cities*, set in London and Paris before and during the French Revolution. We can paraphrase Dickens' title to suggest one of the Bible's underlying themes: a tale of two rulers.

The two rulers are the Lord Jesus Christ and human beings who are born choosing self-rule as a way of life. Some people submit to the lordship of Christ; others choose to rule their own lives. Scripture gives examples of both. One was a rich young ruler whom Christ called to follow Him, but who ultimately refused the follow Him. Another was Saul of Tarsus who was rich in prestige as a young Pharisee. Paul submitted himself to the lordship of Christ; he considered everything else to be worthless compared to following the Lord (Philippians 3:7).

Who rules your life? Choose today to submit yourself to the lordship of Jesus Christ. Let your life be a tale of someone who follows the one true Ruler.

JULY 14
Follow Me

Imitate me, just as I also imitate Christ.
1 CORINTHIANS 11:1

In his book, *The Fifth Discipline*, Peter Senge wrote, "Most of the outstanding leaders I have worked with are neither tall nor especially handsome; they are often mediocre public speakers; they do not stand out in a crowd; they do not mesmerize an attending audience with their brilliance or eloquence. Rather, what distinguishes them is their clarity and the persuasiveness of their ideas, the depth of their commitment, and their openness to continually learning more."[18]

Not many of us are tall and handsome orators who project a JFK-like persona of Camelot. But we can all influence others, and we can influence others for Christ. Leadership requires responsibility; and whether we're young or old, our lives need to be living examples for others to follow.

What about your habits? Your words? Your attitude? Your disciplines? Your priorities? Your personal standards? We never know who is watching us, and only in eternity will we know the full extent of our spoken and unspoken influence.

How wonderful to say as Paul did: Follow me as I follow Christ!

---

[18] Peter Senge, *The Fifth Discipline*, (New York: Currency Doubleday, 1994), 359.

Lions in the Road

My soul is among lions.
PSALM 57:4

In John Bunyan's classic story, *The Pilgrim's Progress*, Christian was traveling toward the Celestial City when he saw two lions on the roadside ahead of him. They were hungry and angry, and they appeared ready to attack and kill any passerby. Christian stopped in fear and studied them from a distance. Finally, he saw they were both chained, one on each side of the road. Christian had a conversation with himself. He told himself not to be afraid of the lions, for if he stayed in the middle of the road they couldn't hurt him. It was simply a test of his faith, he said. And in this way, he advanced. Though the lions roared on his left and right, they couldn't touch him.

From time to time on our journey through life, we pass down the same road. The lions are still there, and we're apt to fear. But the trials of life are there to test and strengthen our faith. When we stay in the middle of God's highway of holiness and advance forward, we are safe and we are strengthened.

JULY 16
Cannot Help Rejoicing

And why do we stand in jeopardy every hour?
1 CORINTHIANS 15:30

The apostle Paul, stalwart as he was, still felt himself in jeopardy every hour—from persecution, from the devil's attacks, from his own weaknesses. He needed the Lord every single hour of his life. So do we! We need the Lord every hour of our life.

The Bible describes our world as "this present evil age" (Galatians 1:4), and Satan makes sure we're in constant jeopardy from trials and temptations. Life's distractions can make us feel overwhelmed instead of overjoyed. A bad night's sleep can leave us drained. A confrontation with someone can leave us disheartened. And with these many challenges we find it difficult to live each day as we'd like. We are not alone.

Bob Jones, Jr. wrote, "A day-by-day experience of God's mercy develops the Christian's joy. As he trusts his Lord for comfort in the time of sorrow and finds the comfort supplied, as he leans upon Him for strength in a moment of weakness and finds himself upheld, as he turns to Him in the hour of need and finds the need met, he cannot help rejoicing."

The Lord is available every hour. He protects us in jeopardy, forgives us during lapses, strengthens us for His service, and is available to us for all time—moment by moment.

These things I have spoken to you, that My joy
may remain in you, and that your joy may be full.
JOHN 15:11

A new museum has opened in Denmark, sponsored by the Happiness Research Institute. It's the Museum of Happiness, located in Copenhagen's historic district. There are eight rooms dedicated to different theories about happiness. Maps display the world's happiest and unhappiest regions. You can study the history of happiness there, and there's a lab devoted to the relationship between happiness and brain chemistry.

You don't have to travel to Copenhagen, however. Whenever you open the Bible, you're opening the book of joy. The world really doesn't understand it. Happiness is an emotion that comes and goes, but joy is an attitude that comes and grows, and it's piped into our hearts by the Holy Spirit. The world doesn't give it to us, nor can the world take it away.

William A. Swets wrote, "The joy Christ gives is for time and eternity, for soul and body, for adversity and prosperity. Our joy is rooted in the unspeakable blessedness of forgiveness, the assurance of salvation, and the hope of heaven."

Decide to have a joyful heart today!

JULY 18
Beyond Our Imagination

But as it is written: "Eye has not seen, nor ear heard,
nor have entered into the heart of man the things
which God has prepared for those who love Him."
1 CORINTHIANS 2:9

You watched videos; you read copious tourist guidebooks; you talked with neighbors who had been there; and you planned an itinerary that included every part of your destination. But when you returned home and your neighbors asked, "How was the trip?" your answer even surprised you: "We had no idea! It was beyond anything we ever expected!"

If it's possible to gather unlimited amounts of information about a destination on earth, yet still be surprised when we get there, how much more likely are we to be surprised by what we find in heaven? When Paul wrote 1 Corinthians 2:9, he wasn't specifically referring to heaven; he likely had both temporal and eternal blessings in mind. His point was this: The mind of man is incapable of knowing and discovering all that the mind of God contains. His ways are as far above our ways as the heavens are above the earth (Isaiah 55:8–9).

If you ever think you have God figured out, think again. His love and plans for His children, for now and for eternity, are beyond our imagination.

JULY 19
Refreshed by Prayer

Now it came to pass in those days that [Jesus] went out to the mountain to pray, and continued all night in prayer to God.
LUKE 6:12

Life is marked by events, and our life is lived either in anticipation of those events (looking to the future) or in reflection upon them (looking to the past). In either situation, stress is a possibility. We may be concerned about what is coming, or we may be exhausted by what has happened.

Prayer can be a sure way of relieving stress. David poured out his heart to God as his circumstances dictated. When Jesus was faced with choosing twelve disciples to follow Him, He spent the night resting in God's presence and in prayer (Luke 6:12–16). When those same disciples experienced the ascension of Jesus into heaven, the culmination of the forty days following Jesus' resurrection, they gathered in a room in Jerusalem to pray (Acts 1:12–14). The previous forty days, as well as the day of the Ascension, were no doubt taxing. They found refreshment together in prayer to God.

Whenever life drains you of strength, go to God in prayer. Make prayer your first choice, not your last resort. He will restore your soul (Psalm 23:1–3).

JULY 20
A New Kind of Armor

Put on the whole armor of God, that you may
be able to stand against the wiles of the devil.
EPHESIANS 6:11

When we think of "armor," our mind goes immediately to the shiny metal suits worn by European combatants in the late Middle Ages. But armor is older than that. In the Old Testament, Goliath was covered from head to toe in various kinds of bronze armor (1 Samuel 17:5–7). And Saul tried to clothe young David in his own armor (1 Samuel 17:38–39). Throughout history, armor has served to protect the wearer *physically*.

But Paul wrote that we Christians "do not war according to the flesh [physically]. For the weapons of our warfare are not carnal [physical]" (2 Corinthians 10:3–4). For the first time in history, a new kind of armor was introduced to protect the Christian: spiritual armor (Ephesians 6:10–18). Like physical armor, our spiritual armor—the "armor of God"—covers us from head to toe. Our armor consists of truth, righteousness, the Gospel of peace, faith, salvation, and the Word of God. Clothed in this armor, we are "able to stand."

Do not contemplate engaging in spiritual warfare (the daily Christian life), without being fully dressed in the armor of God. Fully armed, we are prepared for any spiritual challenge!

JULY 21
A Problem Halved

Two are better than one, because they have a good reward for their labor.
ECCLESIASTES 4:9

According to a classic proverb, there is a sure way to reduce the size of a problem by half: share it with someone who can help you sort it out. That's what the proverb says: "A problem shared is a problem halved." But what if there is no one with whom to share your problem or to help carry your burden? For the Christian, there is always Someone.

When Jesus prepared to leave this earth and return to heaven, He knew He would no longer be there to counsel and teach His disciples. So He told them the Father was going to send them a Counselor (comforter, helper)—the Holy Spirit. The Greek word for Counselor is *parakletos*, a word made from two Greek words: *para* (beside) and *kaleo* (to call). So the *parakletos*—the *Counselor*, the Holy Spirit—was to be called alongside the followers of Christ as a guide, a teacher, and a comforter. So even when there is no human friend with whom to share your burden, you have the divine Counselor, the Holy Spirit, who was sent by the Father for that very purpose.

You are not alone.

Behold, I stand at the door and knock. If anyone hears My voice and opens the door, I will come in to him and dine with him, and he with Me.

REVELATION 3:20

The English artist, William Holman Hunt (1827–1910), is famous for his painting titled, *The Light of the World*. The painting is based on Revelation 3:20; Christ is standing at the vine-covered front door of a house. In His left hand, He carries a lantern (the light of the world), while His right hand knocks on the door. What is not immediately obvious is that the door on which Christ knocks *has no handle on the outside*. It must be opened by the occupant from the inside.

Hunt's painting illustrates the nature of the Gospel itself—an invitation to fellowship with, and be reconciled to, the Creator God through faith in Christ. But we must open the door by grace through faith (Ephesians 2:8). Jesus' words in Revelation 3:20 were spoken to the church in Laodicea, a church which was lukewarm in its faith and works (Revelation 3:14–22). Christ offered Himself to the church to restore their faith and fellowship—but it was up to them to open the door.

If you sense Jesus knocking on the door of your heart to deepen your relationship with Him, don't fail to open the door and let Him in!

JULY 23
How Blessed You Are

But blessed are your eyes for they see, and your ears for they hear.
MATTHEW 13:16

Every man has had this experience: We are looking for a particular item in the kitchen utensil drawer but we can't find what we are looking for. We rearrange the items, take many of them out, and keep looking. In despair, we call our wife: "I know that measuring spoon is in this drawer. I just used it two days ago." We step back and let our spouse have a look. After a couple of seconds of rummaging, she turns, holding up the measuring spoon: "This one?"

Yes, that one! Sometimes our eyes just don't see what is right in front of us. And that happened to the nation of Israel. Because of unrepentant hearts, they had lost wisdom and understanding when it came to spiritual matters. When Jesus arrived, they didn't understand who He was or what He was saying. Their eyes and ears had been closed since the days of Isaiah (Isaiah 6:9–10). They could "see" but they couldn't "perceive" (Matthew 13:14). But Jesus told His disciples how blessed they were for being able to both see and hear spiritual truth.

All who are filled with the Holy Spirit and have a humble, repentant heart toward God are recipients of spiritual truth. If that is you, you are blessed today with spiritual eyes and ears!

So I say to you, ask, and it will be given to you; seek,
and you will find; knock, and it will be opened to you.
LUKE 11:9

Think about a college basketball player who is struggling to make free throws from the foul line. His coach might say, "Well, if you practice a bit every day you might get better." Or, the coach might say, "I want you to shoot one hundred free throws every day. If you do that, you *will* get better. Trust me." Which approach do you think will produce better results?

We could apply the same two approaches to prayer, according to Jesus. In English, the basketball coach's two approaches are markedly different. But in English, Jesus' words about prayer don't convey the underlying urgency: "Ask … seek … knock." In English, those words might be a suggestion to pray once, or they might be a command to keep on praying. In Greek, Jesus is saying, "I'm instructing you to keep on asking … keep on seeking … keep on knocking." In Greek, these verbs are imperative commands that continue day after day. They aren't a suggestion to pray once and see what happens. Jesus is being authoritative: Keep on praying!

Are you still waiting on an answer to prayer? If so, keep on asking, and you will receive an answer. How do we know that is true? Because Jesus said so!

JULY 25
The Hidden Years

And Jesus increased in wisdom and stature, and in favor with God and men.
LUKE 2:52

You may have wondered why the Bible does not reveal more about Jesus' upbringing or His years as a youth or young adult. We know about His birth in Bethlehem, a glimpse of one event when He was 12 years old (Luke 2:41–52), and then nothing until the beginning of His ministry around the age of 30 or so (A.D. 30).

But the incident at age twelve tells us a lot about how the rest of Jesus' development progressed. It happened when He and His parents traveled to Jerusalem for the Passover Feast. When His parents left to return home, they assumed Jesus was in the crowd with which they were traveling, but He wasn't. He had stayed behind in Jerusalem—Mary and Joseph found Him in the temple courts discussing matters of faith and practice with rabbis and learned men. The elders were "astonished at His understanding and answers" (Luke 2:47). And then Luke gives us this clue: He continued to mature in wisdom and stature, finding favor with God and men. In other words, in His humanity, Jesus was like us—He grew and matured over time.

Don't be discouraged when you feel you aren't progressing. Do what Jesus did: Study, search, ask questions, seek answers—and you will increase in wisdom and stature.

JULY 26
Choose Your Reward

Therefore, when you do a charitable deed, do not sound a trumpet before you as the hypocrites do in the synagogues and in the streets, that they may have glory from men. Assuredly, I say to you, they have their reward.
MATTHEW 6:2

Large-scale charitable donations can be tricky. Do we allow our name to be put on the new hospital wing, or give the money anonymously? Even small donations present a challenge. Is it okay to mention the gift we made to help a family in need? There are no easy answers. But rewards are something to consider—let Jesus explain:

In the Sermon on the Mount (Matthew 5–7), Jesus gave a theological facelift to common religious practices among Jewish religious leaders. Take actions like giving, fasting, and prayer (Matthew 6:1–18). These are all commendable practices. But when we do them to show off our spirituality to others, they lose some of their credibility—and all of our rewards from God. Jesus said if we give to impress others, then we have our reward from the applause of men. Better, He said, to give in secret and let God reward you in His time and way.

Do we want our reward from men or from God? Choose your reward.

*And this is eternal life, that they may know You,
the only true God, and Jesus Christ whom You have sent.*
JOHN 17:3

The Apostles' Creed is one of Christendom's best-known statements of what Christians believe. The closing paragraph of the Creed summarizes Christian belief this way: "I believe in the Holy Spirit: the holy catholic [universal] Church, the communion of saints, the forgiveness of sins, the resurrection of the body, and *the life everlasting*. Amen" (emphasis added).

There it is: "life everlasting"—or what we commonly refer to as "eternal life." Ask the average Christian what eternal life is and they may say something like "heaven." That's not a bad answer, but it's not much clearer than "eternal life" as to its meaning. Thankfully, Jesus tells us what eternal life is: "And this is eternal life, that they may know You [the Father], the only true God, and Jesus Christ whom You have sent." Do you know the Father through faith in His Son? Then you have eternal life—now, not just when you die. The apostle John wrote his first letter "to you who believe" in Christ, "that you may know that you have eternal life" (1 John 5:13).

We know God by believing in Christ; we gain eternal life by knowing God through Christ. If you believe in Christ now, you have eternal life now!

JULY 28
Abide and Grow

And now, little children, abide in Him, that when He appears,
we may have confidence and not be ashamed before Him at His coming.
1 JOHN 2:28

Gardeners know there are two types of tomato plants: determinate and indeterminate. Determinates are tomato bushes that produce fruit for a limited time. Indeterminates are tomato vines that continue to grow and bear fruit for as long as the growing conditions are favorable.

In Jesus' parable of the vine and branches (John 15:1–8), He talked about grapevines. And modern grapevines don't bear fruit forever; they have a season of growth which are then harvested. But He introduced an important spiritual concept: abiding or remaining. As long as we (the branches) abide (remain) in Jesus (the Vine), and His words abide (remain) in us, we will bear much fruit. We will know the Father (the Vinedresser) so well that we can ask for whatever we need and it will be given to us (verse 7). God's will becomes our will as we abide and grow.

What does it mean to abide in Jesus? It means to live in close fellowship with Him—in worship, in obedience, in service, in love, and in ministry. In that way, we are always prepared for His Second Coming.

*But we all, with unveiled face, beholding as in a mirror
the glory of the Lord, are being transformed into the same
image from glory to glory, just as by the Spirit of the Lord.*
2 CORINTHIANS 3:18

One of the greatest mysteries in nature occurs when a caterpillar spins a cocoon around itself and, after a time, emerges as a beautiful butterfly. Changing from a caterpillar to a butterfly is a mystery, but not as great as the transformation of a human sinner into the image of Jesus Christ—the goal of our salvation (Romans 8:29).

The apostle Paul reveals the precondition for that transformation: Beholding Christ in faith (2 Corinthians 3:13–18). When Moses came down from the mountain, having met with God, he had to cover his face with a veil to hide the radiance of God's glory. That veil, Paul says, is like a veil that covers the heart of the unbeliever who fails to see the glory of God in Christ. When our hearts are unveiled by faith, when we see Christ as clearly as in a mirror, we begin to be transformed into His image, "from glory to glory."

Removing the veil means seeing God's glory in Christ and embracing it by faith—and being transformed into His image.

JULY 30
The Sound of the Trumpet

In a moment, in the twinkling of an eye, at the last trumpet.
For the trumpet will sound, and the dead will be
raised incorruptible, and we shall be changed.
1 CORINTHIANS 15:52

Years ago, a strange phenomenon had residents of Hawaii scratching their heads. It's the occasional sound of a trumpet that can't be explained. Some people have speculated the eerie sounds are caused by tidal waves, underground earthquakes, or shifting sand dunes. Some people have called the sounds "unearthly." A few people wonder if the sounds come from extraterrestrial beings.

Who knows? Strange phenomena happen all the time.

But one thing we know for sure: One day the trumpet will sound, signaling the return of Jesus Christ in the skies above our planet. The Bible says, "For the Lord Himself will descend from heaven with a shout, with the voice of an archangel, and with the trumpet of God" (1 Thessalonians 4:16). It's going to be a trumpet loud enough to awaken the dead!

Despite the chaos of the world around us, we can be confident that Christ will return for us. We can almost hear the trumpet sounding now!

JULY 31

The Price of Service

For even the Son of Man did not come to be served,
but to serve, and to give His life a ransom for many.

MARK 10:45

In the ancient world, a ransom was money paid to purchase, then set free, a slave. "Ransom" appears twice in the New Testament when Jesus gave His reason for coming to earth: He came "to give His life a ransom for many" (Matthew 20:28; Mark 10:45). That is, He purchased with His own life those who were slaves to sin and set them free to live a new life.

What's interesting about the ransom Jesus paid is what the payment is connected to: service. Jesus said He came to serve by giving His life a ransom for many. Jesus' own life and actions illustrate that there is a price to service. In Jesus' case, the price was extremely high. We may never be called on to serve others by dying for them physically, but we are called on daily to serve others by dying to our selfish desires. When Paul wrote about Christ as a servant, he wrote, "Let this mind be in you which was also in Christ Jesus"—that is, the mind of a servant (Philippians 2:5).

Be prepared today to pay whatever price Christ-like service requires.

AUGUST

But Simon Peter answered Him, "Lord, to whom shall we go?
You have the words of eternal life."
JOHN 6:68

Most families have them, and all kids love them: a favorite uncle or aunt who is "way more fun" than the parents—especially the uncle or aunt who is younger than the kids' parents and is still single. Those beloved relatives are the ones who liven up the family reunions at Christmas and Thanksgiving or whenever they come to town. Life is always more enjoyable, adventuresome, and exciting when they're around. Being with Jesus is much like that.

Many unbelievers have never encountered the real Jesus—they may have an idea of who He is, but their preconceived ideas do not align with who He truly is. He is like no one else who has ever lived on this earth. The three years that the disciples spent with Jesus left them in a state of amazement: restoring the blind, the sick, and the lame; displaying acts of mercy and forgiveness; and breaking the social and religious barriers of the culture are just a part of what Jesus did during His earthly ministry. But most of all, it was His "words of eternal life" that inspired them to follow Him. What could be more exciting than to spend eternity in heaven?

If your spiritual life has become predictable and dull, it may be because you have not kept close to Jesus—that is something you can change today—draw close to the Savior and begin your adventure with Jesus.

AUGUST 2
The Seventy

Nevertheless do not rejoice in this, that the spirits are subject to you,
but rather rejoice because your names are written in heaven.

LUKE 10:20

We know about the twelve apostles, but Jesus had seventy other disciples who walked with Him and whom He sent on a ministry tour in Luke 10. In verse 17, these seventy returned with joy, saying, "Lord, even the demons are subject to us in Your name." Jesus acknowledged their success, but gave a gentle warning. Their joy should be based on more than their perceived success; it should rest in the simple fact that their names were written in the Lamb's Book of Life.

Ministry is a difficult task, the results of which are not always immediate or obvious. If we base our morale on visible success, we may become proud of our accomplishments or discouraged over momentary setbacks or prolonged struggles. Whatever we're doing for the Lord, the Lord expects us to be faithful—and to rejoice that our names are written in the Lamb's Book of Life in heaven!

AUGUST 3
Everything We Need

As His divine power has given to us all things that pertain to life and godliness, through the knowledge of Him who called us by glory and virtue.
2 PETER 1:3

Often, we gather what we think we need: everything we need to begin life in college, everything we need to welcome a firstborn child into our home, everything we need to get our children back to school in September—but invariably we discover we have forgotten something. Try as we might, it's hard to be fully prepared for life.

Or is it? The apostle Peter wrote that God has "given to us all things that pertain to life and godliness." That isn't a guarantee that our checklist for every life circumstance will be perfectly completed. But it does mean, when it comes to living a godly life, we have everything we need in Christ. By knowing God through Christ, we have access to His character and resources that abide in us. Paul characterized these traits in Galatians 5:22–23 as the fruit of the Spirit. Peter's list includes faith, virtue, knowledge, self-control, perseverance, godliness, brotherly kindness, and love (2 Peter 1:5–7).

Just as Christ lacked nothing in His life, we have everything we need to be successful in our walk of faith through Him, "who called us by glory and virtue."

AUGUST 4
Be an Influencer

Therefore comfort one another with these words.
1 THESSALONIANS 4:18

The new era of social networking has given an old word a new meaning: influencer. Traditionally, an influencer was someone who influenced others. That's the new use of the word as well, but in a new context: social media platforms. Influencers are mostly young people who can sway lifestyle trends by their endorsements, videos, product placements, brands, and appearances. Influencing is a neutral idea—it all depends on the goal of the influence.

The apostle Paul seems to have thought of Christians as influencers. In his description of the Church as the Body of Christ, he viewed all Christians as being connected, as having influence on others. Indeed, 33 times in his epistles (63 times in all the epistles), the phrase "one another" occurs. The New Testament expects believers to (1) be in proximity with one another and (2) to stimulate and influence one another to become spiritually mature. Hebrews 10:24–25 exhorts Christians to meet together to "stir up love and good works."

Are you living in close proximity to other Christians? The only way we can influence one another is to strive for spiritual maturity and Christlikeness.

Thus says the Lord: "Stand in the ways and see, and ask for the old paths, where the good way is, and walk in it; then you will find rest for your souls. But they said, 'We will not walk in it.'"
JEREMIAH 6:16

One wonders if Jesus sees the world today as He saw the people of Israel: "He was moved with compassion for them, because they were weary and scattered, like sheep having no shepherd" (Matthew 9:36). God had seen them that way for centuries. He implored the nation, through the prophet Jeremiah, to turn back to "the old paths, where the good way is, and walk in it; then you will find rest for your souls."

Jesus quoted Jeremiah's phrase, "rest for your souls," in His own invitation to the people to turn to God: "Take My yoke upon you and learn from Me... and you will find rest for your souls" (Matthew 11:29). Sadly, most of the nation failed to turn to the old paths; they failed to find rest for their souls in Jesus. While many since the first century have turned to Jesus, many have not. And Jesus no doubt looks with compassion upon them.

If you need a shepherd for your soul, take Jesus' yoke upon you (be joined to Him) and learn from Him.

AUGUST 6
Commandments or Traditions?

[Jesus] said to [the Pharisees], "All too well you reject
the commandment of God, that you may keep your tradition."
MARK 7:9

Throughout history, churches have formed new denominations
over what were perceived to be biblical and theological issues.
That's one thing, but when churches divide over non-biblical issues
such as man-made traditions, that's another—like the shape of
the new Sunday school wing, the presence of guitars and drums in
worship, or whether to use wine or juice in Communion.

Jesus pointed out the difference between the commands
of God and the traditions of men when His disciples were
criticized by the Pharisees. The disciples were observed eating
with unwashed (ceremonially unclean) hands. So the Pharisees
asked Jesus why His disciples didn't abide by the traditions of
the Pharisees. And Jesus made it clear: The commands of God
are one thing; the traditions of men (like the Pharisees' rules and
regulations) were another. For example, the command of God is to
love one another (John 13:34). Love supersedes all the traditions,
opinions, and differences between well-meaning men and women.

If you have a difference with another person—especially
if the other person is a fellow believer—make sure your view is
God's, not just your own. Don't let non-biblical traditions rule the
day. Let love be the pathway to compromise and reconciliation.

AUGUST 7
Giving and Receiving

Give, and it will be given to you: good measure, pressed down,
shaken together, and running over will be put into your bosom.
For with the same measure that you use, it will be measured back to you.
LUKE 6:38

Many sermons have been preached on financial stewardship using Luke 6:38 as a basis: "Give, and it will be given to you." But Jesus' words apply to a much broader spectrum as summarized by Paul in Galatians 6:7: "Whatever a man sows, that he will also reap."

When Jesus says "give" in Luke 6:38, He is following up on His words in the previous verse where He covered three ways of giving: do not give judgment; do not give condemnation; but do give forgiveness. *Then* He says, "Give, and it will be given to you." If we give judgment, we will receive judgment; if we give condemnation, we will receive condemnation; if we give forgiveness, we will receive forgiveness. In fact, in each case, it appears we will receive *more* of each than we give: "pressed down, shaken together, and running over." Whatever we give—and that could surely include generous financial giving—will be given to us.

Was Paul thinking of this teaching when he wrote Galatians 6:7? Possibly. In any case, both Jesus and Paul say the same thing: We will receive in the same manner (or measure) as we have given.

AUGUST 8
A Foundation for Life

And so it was, when Jesus had ended these sayings, that the people were astonished at His teaching, for He taught them as one having authority, and not as the scribes.

MATTHEW 7:28–29

Today we can listen to the words of almost any modern preacher via the Internet. Can you imagine what it would be like to listen to Jesus teach the Sermon on the Mount (Matthew 5–7)? It must have been something when He taught it the first time, for "the people were astonished at His teaching, for He taught them as one having authority."

The last illustration He gave in the Sermon on the Mount illustrates the power and authority and trustworthiness of all the Sermon: "Therefore whoever hears these sayings of Mine, and does them, I will liken him to a wise man who built his house on the rock" (Matthew 7:24). "These sayings" refers to everything in Matthew 5–7 that preceded verse 24. This body of teaching would prepare one for a life of stability and strength, able to withstand the storms of life. Ignoring His words would be akin to building a house (a life) on shifting sand.

Have you spent time reading and meditating on Matthew 5–7? It's the next best thing to having been there for the original. You may be as astonished as Jesus' original audience.

AUGUST 9
God's Helicopters

Therefore those who were scattered went everywhere preaching the word.

ACTS 8:4

Long before aviators invented helicopters, maple trees were sending whirlybirds into the air. These natural aircraft are maple seeds with wings attached—the technical name for them is samara—and they're designed by God to travel a long distance from the tree itself. Botanists tells us samara have near-perfect engineering, with the weight of the seed balanced by the size of the wings. If you have a maple tree near your garden, you'll likely be pulling up hundreds of sprouting seeds each summer. They can be prolific.

There's a lesson for us as Christians. We should be prolific in spreading the Gospel and reproducing in others our faith in Christ. Just as a maple tree can't be responsible for the success of its seeds, we aren't responsible for all the results of our witness. But we should use every opportunity every day to say a word for the Lord.

When our testimony is scattered abroad, some of the seed will fall on good soil and produce a harvest, as Jesus said, "Some a hundredfold, some sixty, some thirty" (Matthew 13:23). Let's sow bountifully and expect a bountiful blessing.

AUGUST 10
Are We Almost Home?

For He Himself said, "I will never leave you nor forsake you."
HEBREWS 13:5

The foster care system in the United States currently has more than 400,000 children in the system, with ages ranging from infant to 21, with the average age being 8 or older. Many of these children are in foster care for years. The most precious gift for these children would be a permanent home with people who love and care for them close by.

Praise God for the many wonderful foster families who welcome these children into their families and homes, and for the many adoptive parents as well. No doubt you have seen the smiling faces of children on the day of their official adoption—the day they are part of a forever home. They live in expectancy of that day just as believers in Christ long for our forever home.

Anyone traveling with a child in the car has heard the words, "Are we almost home?" at least once. And for us as God's children encountering the challenges of the cares of this world, we may also ask that same question—wondering when the Lord will return. But while we wait for that day, we have His promise that He will never leave us for we are His priceless adopted children.

AUGUST 11
Every Day's Work

So he left Asaph and his brothers there before the ark of the covenant of the Lord to minister before the ark regularly, as every day's work required.
1 CHRONICLES 16:37

When King David transferred the Ark of the Covenant into a new location, the entire nation celebrated. David gave everyone in the kingdom a loaf of bread, a cake of dates, and a cake of raisins (1 Chronicles 16:3, NIV). They sang psalms, accompanied by cymbals, harps, lyres, and trumpets (verses 4–6). The musicians sang a special hymn written by David for the occasion (verses 7–37). And then, after all the celebration and festivities were over, David left the Levites there "to minister before the ark regularly, as every day's work required."

We're not in church all the time, and we don't always hear the celebrations of choirs and music. We appreciate those times of joyous public worship, but our daily job in life is to praise and serve Him, doing what each day's work requires.

We never have two days alike. Every single day is different. Some are easier than others. A few days will be so special we'll always remember them, and perhaps a few will be unbelievably hard.

But one thing is always true: It is our joy and privilege to serve Jesus every day—He is our life!

AUGUST 12
Emergency Power

They all were trying to make us afraid, saying,
"Their hands will be weakened in the work, and it will not be done."
Now therefore, O God, strengthen my hands.
NEHEMIAH 6:9

All over the world, people are adding portable generators to the emergency items stashed away in their basements or closets because power interruptions can occur at any time.

In life, we often need extra strength. As Nehemiah led the effort to rebuild the walls of Jerusalem, his enemies taunted and threatened him. Local authorities tried to frighten the wall builders and make them afraid. But Nehemiah kept working, and as he worked, he uttered a prayer: "Now therefore, O God, strengthen my hands."

The relationship we have with God and our ability to pray to Him at any time or place is like an emergency generator that provides us with power in our inner being. We can stay strong in the Lord even when our physical strength is reduced. Even when our burdens increase. His strength isn't diminished, and it's always available for His children. From the Lord we have the strength needed to face each day.

AUGUST 13
Submit and Resist

Therefore submit to God. Resist the devil and he will flee from you.
Draw near to God and He will draw near to you.
JAMES 4:7-8

The laws of physics say that two different objects cannot occupy the same space at the same time. We could also say that God and Satan cannot occupy the same place at the same time. Or, we cannot submit to God and Satan at the same time. In the words of James 4:7-8, if we are submitted to God, we are resisting the devil. If we submit to God and resist the devil, the devil must flee from us.

The Bible restates this principle of God's superiority in different ways. First John 4:4 says, "[God] who is in you is greater than [Satan] who is in the world." And Romans 8:31 says, "If God is for us, who can be against us?" Satan cannot stand against us. All of this is to say, God is greater than the tempter. When we submit to God, He is able to deliver us from the evil one who seeks our allegiance through temptation.

When you are tempted by Satan, stop and affirm your submission to God. When you resist him, the tempter must flee. Praise God for His deliverance!

AUGUST 14
Not...Nothing...

And I do not seek My own glory.
JOHN 8:50

It's not easy to write about humility, but the devotional writer Andrew Murray did so in a little book titled, simply, *Humility*. He suggested we can learn true humility by studying the Gospel of John, which records the inner life of Jesus. Murray was amazed at how often Jesus used the words *not* and *nothing*.

Jesus said, "I say to you, the Son can do nothing of Himself.... I can of Myself do nothing" (John 5:19, 30). He said, "I do nothing of Myself.... If I honor Myself, My honor is nothing" (John 8:28, 54). In John 5:30, Jesus said, "I do not seek My own will but the will of the Father who sent Me." And in John 6:38, He said, "For I have come down from heaven, not to do My own will, but the will of Him who sent Me."

Murray wrote: "Because Christ had thus humbled Himself before God, and God was ever before Him, He found it possible to humble Himself before men too, and to be the Servant of all."

The only way to live humbly before God is by following the example of Jesus and yielding oneself fully to the will and to the glory of the Heavenly Father.

AUGUST 15
You Are God

Even from everlasting to everlasting, You are God.
PSALM 90:2

God, in His wisdom and might, created the universe and everything in it with a purpose and a timeline for its existence. While the lifecycle of an insect can be as short as 24-hours, a mighty oak tree can live for 150 years. In God's timeline we know: "To everything there is a season, a time for every purpose under heaven" (Ecclesiastes 3:1). Just as a beautiful rose will bloom and then wither away, our days on earth are also known and numbered by God. We are surrounded by the beauty of His creation—from the majestic mountains to the unquantifiable stars in the heavens—for they all reflect their Maker. And above it all enthroned on high is our Creator—the immutable, unchanging, unchangeable, irreplaceable, and sometimes unfathomable God.

The more we learn about Him, the more we are filled with wonder, for God's holiness never changes. His power never wavers. His knowledge never dims. His love never fluctuates. His presence never fades. His righteousness never evolves. His mercy never fails. His truth is unfailing, and His promises are true.

Because He is unchanging and unchangeable, every word He says is consistent, unshakable, and utterly dependable. We can place our hope and confidence in Him for each day here on earth and for all eternity—for He is "from everlasting to everlasting."

Listen carefully to Me, and eat what is good,
and let your soul delight itself in abundance.
ISAIAH 55:2

In Christ, we have abundant life, as He promised in John 10:10. But how should we define the word *abundant*? The thesaurus defines it as: "lavish, overflowing, bountiful, plenteous, teeming, more than is needed."

Think of it! God is abundant in mercy (Numbers 14:18). That is, His mercy is lavish, overflowing, bountiful, plenteous, teeming, and more than enough to forgive any guilt we've been feeling. He gives abundant joy (Philippians 1:26), more than is needed for any trial. We can delight ourselves in the abundance of peace (Psalm 37:11), and He is able to do "exceedingly abundantly above all that we ask or think" (Ephesians 3:20). When we get to heaven and look back on our earthly days, we'll find that He answered our prayers with lavishing, overflowing, bountiful, plenteous, teeming generosity.

He gives so much more than is needed!

Just think of the eternal abundance of our inheritance in heaven! Jesus is not insolvent. The abundant life is ours through Him. We should delight in the abundance of Christ, who is our life.

AUGUST 17
Now! No Condemnation!

There is therefore now no condemnation to those who are in Christ Jesus.
ROMANS 8:1

Notice the word "now" in Romans 8:1. The moment we receive Christ, we're immediately given the righteousness of Christ.

There's an old story of a man unjustly sentenced to death by a Spanish court. This man had dual citizenship from both the United States and England. The ambassadors of those two countries visited the man on death row and wrapped their flags around him—both the Stars and Stripes and the Union Jack. Spanish authorities could not shoot him without the bullet going through the flags and risking war with two great powers. The man was released.

When we receive Christ as our Savior, God wraps us in the banner of the cross. Even though we don't become perfect or sinless the moment we receive Christ, in God's sight we're wrapped in the flag of Jesus Christ and covered with His blood. The devil cannot have us. We belong to our Lord. Our citizenship is in heaven!

There is therefore now no condemnation!

AUGUST 18
Become Childlike

[Jesus] said, "Assuredly, I say to you, unless you are converted and become as little children, you will by no means enter the kingdom of heaven."
MATTHEW 18:3

Adults marvel at the receptivity and unpretentious nature of little kids. If a child asks an adult a question and is given an answer, the answer is believed—no questions asked! As children mature into adults, they become more discerning—and rightfully so. Yet Jesus suggested that the innocent nature of children is something adults would do well to emulate.

In fact, Jesus said that anyone who is not "converted" (turned) and does not become like a little child *will not enter the kingdom of heaven*. Those are strong words, especially when the New Testament teaches we are saved by faith alone (Ephesians 2:8–9). So what did Jesus mean? He meant that we should be humble, as believing, non-argumentative, receptive little children when it comes to believing God. So those who enter the kingdom will not be the smartest or the most distinguished—nor will the proud enter the kingdom, but those who humble themselves as little children.

How are you when it comes to taking God at His word? Are you satisfied with His provisions, His plan, and His purposes in your life? Determine to believe God like a child would—with eagerness and humility.

AUGUST 19
A Daily Decision

Then He said to them all, "If anyone desires to come after Me,
let him deny himself, and take up his cross daily, and follow Me."
LUKE 9:23

Sadly, much of the Bible has become trivialized in cultural conversation. One of the examples of misappropriation of biblical truth is Jesus' reference to "take up [one's] cross daily." In modern society, taking up one's cross refers to any burden or difficult situation one has to deal with—at work, in a relationship, a financial burden, or other non-Christ-related circumstance. These examples could not be further from the real meaning of Jesus' words.

Simply put, Jesus was warning His followers that, not only was He destined to die a cruel death on a Roman cross, but any who chose to follow Him must be prepared to suffer the same fate. That kind of "cross to bear" is a bit different from getting a traffic ticket. In the context of Luke 9, Jesus went on to say that attempting to save one's life by avoiding the threat of death would only result in losing one's life in the end. To be ashamed of Christ now will result in Jesus being ashamed of that one when He returns.

Every Christian needs to reflect on his or her preparedness on a regular basis. Am I ready to follow Christ, regardless of the cost? Make the decision—and begin today.

AUGUST 20
Be Reconciled

Moreover if your brother sins against you, go and tell him his fault between you and him alone. If he hears you, you have gained your brother.
MATTHEW 18:15

Let's say something has come between Bob and Joe, and they are estranged from one another. Bob believes Joe has acted inappropriately toward him—a personal offense of some kind. Joe is unaware that he has offended Bob, but he knows something is wrong since Bob has been avoiding him of late. What should they do?

Bob. Jesus' words in Matthew 18:15 are for Bob, who believes Joe has sinned against him. Jesus said Bob should go to Joe and explain why he feels Joe has acted inappropriately toward him. If Joe receives Bob and acknowledges the offense and seeks forgiveness, all is well. If Joe resists Bob's entreaty, then Jesus has further instructions in Matthew 18:16–20.

Joe. As soon as Joe realizes Bob has something against him, he should go immediately to Bob and be reconciled to him. Discussion, prayer, humility, confession, forgiveness—whatever it takes. In fact, Jesus said this matter should be settled even before going to church (Matthew 5:23–26).

Ideally, Joe and Bob should meet each other on their way: "I was just coming to see you. We need to talk!" Don't let disagreements turn into estrangement and bitterness. Solve them Jesus' way.

AUGUST 21
God's Best

Do not fear, little flock, for it is your Father's
good pleasure to give you the kingdom.
LUKE 12:32

Your children are excited about a planned weekend at a mountain resort. Staying in a log cabin, horseback riding, river rafting, hiking, and nightly bonfires and cookouts. Then—an unavoidable conflict with Dad's work schedule arises. Oh, the disappointment! Until the kids learn that Dad has rearranged his vacation schedule. Instead of a weekend, the family will now have an entire week at the resort.

We often worry about the details of life without remembering that God has provided all we need. In the Sermon on the Mount, Jesus' advice not to worry about food and clothing is well known (Matthew 6:25–34). He concluded by saying, "But seek first the kingdom of God" and all the rest will be provided (verse 33). In Luke's account of the same teaching, he adds one other statement by Jesus, not recorded in Matthew: "Do not fear, little flock, for it is your Father's good pleasure to give you the kingdom" (Luke 12:32). We are to seek the kingdom (Matthew) because it is already ours (Luke). Jesus has already conferred the kingdom on us (Luke 22:29).

Don't settle for a weekend when you can have a whole week. It is "your Father's good pleasure to give you the kingdom."

AUGUST 22
Be a Peacemaker

Blessed are the peacemakers, for they shall be called sons of God.
MATTHEW 5:9

There was not a lot of *shalom* in the first century. (*Shalom* was the Hebrew word for peace and well-being, personally and corporately.) Indeed, there had not been for several centuries. Zealous Jewish factions fought to evict Greeks from Judea prior to Rome's dominance. Then, after the Greeks, Romans and Jews maintained an uneasy, combustible relationship. During Jesus' day, the Pharisees, Sadducees, Samaritans, Essenes, and other groups all vied for attention.

Into this unpeaceable mix came the "Prince of Peace" as prophesied by Isaiah (Isaiah 9:6–7). The peace He brought and advocated was a wholistic peace—first with God, then with man. It was a peace of unity, not of division, a peace that recognized everyone's equal standing before God as bearers of His image. Through faith in Christ's redemptive work, all people—male, female, slave, free, Jew, Gentile—were made sons of God (Galatians 3:26–29). In the Sermon on the Mount, Jesus said that those who promoted that peace were the true sons of God.

Peace is the fruit of the Spirit (Galatians 5:22). Wherever you go today, take God's peace with you. Calm troubled spirits, soothe wounded souls, and heal broken hearts with the love of Jesus. Bearing His *shalom*, His love, is how others know we come in His Name (John 13:35).

AUGUST 23
This Old House

For this purpose the Son of God was manifested,
that He might destroy the works of the devil.
1 JOHN 3:8

It always draws a crowd—and attracts lots of viewers when the video is posted online: a demolition. Sometimes very large buildings, giant smokestacks from power plants, large bridges that are beyond repair...just need to go. Demolition experts are called in; explosive charges are laid; people are moved out of harm's way—and BOOM!—the structure comes down in a great heap. Then the rebuilding can begin—something new and better.

It's possible to cite several reasons for Jesus coming to earth, but one that rarely gets cited is His role as a destroyer of the work of the devil. "He [came to] destroy the works of the devil," John wrote. And Acts 10:38 paints a picture of how Jesus accomplished His undoing of the devil's work: "God anointed Jesus of Nazareth with the Holy Spirit and with power, who went about doing good and healing all who were oppressed by the devil, for God was with Him." When this work is completed, God will set up "a new heaven and a new earth" (Revelation 21:1).

If you belong to Jesus, the renovation work has no doubt commenced in your life: You are a new creation; the old has gone away and the new life has begun (2 Corinthians 5:17).

AUGUST 24
Bear With Me

Keep your heart with all diligence, for out of it spring the issues of life.
PROVERBS 4:23

Residents of a nursing home in Asheville, North Carolina, had surprise visitors last year. Two curious young black bears figured out how to work the front door, and they wandered in to see the inhabitants. After they went back outside, the two cubs wrestled and frolicked to the delight of everyone until they wandered off. Bears, even when young and cute, aren't safe!

There's a lesson there for us. When we leave the doors of our heart unlatched, some wild things may creep in, looking cute and cuddly. Many addictions and sinful patterns begin with small things we allow. When it comes to destructive habits, it's best to keep the door closed from the very beginning.

One woman said the best advice she ever received was from her mother: "Just don't open the door to it," referring to any questionable habit. Proverbs 4 goes on to say: "Ponder the path of your feet, and let all your ways be established. Do not turn to the right or the left; remove your foot from evil" (verses 26–27).

That's good advice to bear in mind.

AUGUST 25
Thanks Be to God!

But God be thanked that though you were slaves of sin, yet you obeyed
from the heart that form of doctrine to which you were delivered.
ROMANS 6:17

During World War I, Sgt. Maj. Robert S. MacCormack saved
the life of his commanding officer, Maj. Harry D. Parkin
while in the thick of a battle in France. When the two men
returned home, Parkin became a real estate agent in Los
Angeles. He began the habit of writing to MacCormack once
a year, thanking him for saving his life. On the twenty-fifth
anniversary of the letter, Parkin wrote, "Dear Bob, I want to
thank you for the twenty-five years of life that ordinarily I
would not have had were it not for you. I'm grateful to you."

For the believer, it's a privilege to thank God every single
day for the gift of eternal life that we share in Jesus Christ.
Although the stress of the day can weaken us, thanksgiving
always revives us. We're to be always "giving thanks to the
Father who has qualified us to be partakers in the inheritance
of the saints in the light" (Colossians 1:12).

Today take a moment and say: "Thanks be to God for His
indescribable gift!" (2 Corinthians 9:15)

AUGUST 26
Strength for Today

As your days, so shall your strength be.
DEUTERONOMY 33:25

Are you weighed down with burdens today, or are your tasks overflowing? Each day's stress can be overwhelming, and even more so when we consider all the unexpected interruptions that distract us. But God has our lives planned on a daily basis (Psalm 139:16). He assigns our daily tasks, bestows our daily bread, and imparts His daily strength.

Take a moment to compare your stress with God's strength. He has much more strength than you have stress. We can't do yesterday's work or tomorrow's work—we can only do today's work today. And we don't have yesterday's strength or tomorrow's strength—we only have today's strength. But that is sufficient.

Our Lord gives daily strength for daily needs. Why not pray now for God's strengthening grace? We're told in Ephesians 3 to ask Him to strengthen us out of His glorious riches and by His Holy Spirit, and to infuse us with strength in our inner personalities.

When we ask, He will answer.

AUGUST 27
Sand Trap

O God, You are my God; early will I seek You; my soul thirsts for You;
my flesh longs for You in a dry and thirsty land where there is no water.
PSALM 63:1

David was trapped in the desert, blistered by the sun, and choked by blowing sands. The armies of Saul were closing in on him, and the nation that had once honored him with their songs was now his enemy. The desert was Satan's sand trap—a dead-end route of barren circumstances and bleak hopes.

But it was also God's school, for only in the desert could David see himself clearly. Only there could he discover and acknowledge his own weaknesses. Only there could he prove the power of his mighty God.

"Because You have been my help, therefore in the shadow of Your wings I will rejoice.…Your right hand upholds me" he wrote in Psalm 63:7–8.

If you're in a desert now, don't think of it as a sand trap, but as a school. It's a place of discipline and development where you can begin to see your weaknesses and the insufficiency of your own strength. There you can prove God as never before. We often mature most and grow fastest when circumstances are roughest. It's often in the desert that we become thirsty for God.

Don't despair. Rejoice in the shadow of His wings and in the shadow of a mighty rock within a weary land. Charles Spurgeon put it this way: "A weary place and a weary heart make the presence of God the more desirable."

AUGUST 28
Happiness

Bless the Lord, O my soul; and all that is within me, bless His holy name!
PSALM 103:1

Everyone has a different idea of happiness. The inspirational speaker and writer Dale Carnegie once wrote: "Success is getting what you want. Happiness is wanting what you get." But the Bible teaches that happiness comes from being happy with who God is.

- Deuteronomy 33:29 says, "Happy are you, O Israel! Who is like you, a people saved by the Lord, the shield of your help."

- Psalm 144:15 says, "Happy are the people whose God is the Lord!"

- Psalm 146:5 says, "Happy is he who has the God of Jacob for his help."

- Proverbs 16:20 says, "Whoever trusts in the Lord, happy is he."

Whose definition of happiness are you going to follow—Dale's or God's? God has made us with great gifts, He has cleansed us with the blood of Christ, and He wants to use us. He doesn't want us being unhappy with ourselves, but all true happiness comes—not from ourselves—but from Him. Those who look to Him are radiant.

AUGUST 29
Authentic Faith

By this all will know that you are My disciples,
if you have love for one another.
JOHN 13:35

In the first century, there were many religious groups with which one might identify—and they were all known for something different. The Pharisees were known for their strict adherence to the Torah, the laws of Moses. Sadducees were known as the political party among the Jews. Zealots advocated for the overthrow of Rome by violent means. Samaritans would worship only on Mount Gerizim and considered only the five books of Moses to be from God.

And then came Jesus and His followers. They had no geographical, political, or zealous agenda; they were mostly lower-class people. At first, they were known only as "the Way" (Acts 9:2); later they were known as "Christians" (Acts 11:26). Was that their only distinction—a name? No, Jesus told them if they were His true followers they would be known by the love they had for one another. This was totally new! A religious movement based on love, like the love Paul describes in 1 Corinthians 13. That "brand" of love still applies today.

What should distinguish Christians from the world? Authentic love—love for God, for one another, for our enemies, and for our neighbors.

AUGUST 30
Awaiting the Resurrection

And he who had died came out bound hand and foot with graveclothes,
and his face was wrapped with a cloth. Jesus said to them,
"Loose him, and let him go."
JOHN 11:44

There are two resurrections in the Gospel of John—that of Lazarus and that of Jesus. When the blessed day comes for our resurrection, we'll not be raised like Lazarus, but like Jesus. Lazarus came hobbling out, still wrapped in graveclothes. Jesus passed through His graveclothes and left them deflated on the slab. Lazarus, though alive, was still trapped inside the tomb until someone rolled away the stone and let him out. Jesus passed right through the stone walls of the tomb, and the angels only opened it to let the disciples look inside.

Lazarus eventually grew sick and died all over again, and was wrapped in graveclothes, and was buried again. His decayed body is somewhere in the dust of that tomb. Jesus arose, never again to face illness or death. In fact, His resurrection body is incapable of dying. The Bible says it is imperishable.

Our body will be like His (Philippians 3:20–21)! We will be raised imperishable, and that's something to consider and praise God for every day!

AUGUST 31
A Song in My Heart

Now when they began to sing and to praise, the Lord set ambushes
against the people of Ammon, Moab, and Mount Seir,
who had come against Judah; and they were defeated.
2 CHRONICLES 20:22

Years ago, the Methodist preacher, Charles Cardwell McCabe, who loved to sing, was standing on a railroad platform waiting for his train. Another man was there, too, and he began swearing viciously and taking the name of Jesus in vain. McCabe winced at the profanities, but instead of rebuking the man, he just starting singing, "Jesus, lover of my soul, let me to Thy bosom fly, / While the nearer waters roll, while the tempest still is high." He kept singing in his beautiful tones, "Hide me, O my Saviour hide, till the storm of life is past; / Safe into the haven guide, O receive my soul at last."

The words of the song cut into the blasphemous man's heart, and he came over to McCabe. "Sir, I beg your pardon. If Jesus is the lover of your soul, as he was of my mother's, I shall respect your feelings and not use His name in blasphemy again."

Sometimes the best way to confront evil is with a spirit that sings to Him who is the lover of our souls.

SEPTEMBER

SEPTEMBER 1
What Troubles Reveal

And Pharaoh said to his servants, "Can we find such a one as this,
a man in whom is the Spirit of God?"
GENESIS 41:38

It has been said that difficulties don't *determine* who we are. Rather, they *reveal* who we are. Said another way, the same heat that softens butter can make mud hard as a brick. It all depends on how the thing being heated responds. The same is true with the human heart. Difficulties can soften one heart and harden another.

Joseph, in Egypt, and Daniel, in Babylon, both revealed their character to their pagan masters. Their difficulties caused the presence of God to be manifested through them. In the New Testament, no one endured more difficulties over a longer period of time than the apostle Paul (2 Corinthians 6:3–10; 11:23–29). He described his difficulties as being "hard-pressed," "perplexed," "persecuted," and "struck down." But never "crushed," "in despair," "forsaken," or "destroyed" (2 Corinthians 4:8–9). He called his troubles "the dying of the Lord Jesus" so that "the life of Jesus also may be manifested in [his] body" (verse 10). His troubles revealed the "treasure" of Christ within (verse 7).

Troubles in life are normal (Job 5:7). Our response to trouble will manifest Christ to the world—or not.

Therefore, having been justified by faith, we have peace with God through our Lord Jesus Christ, through whom also we have access by faith into this grace in which we stand, and rejoice in hope of the glory of God.

ROMANS 5:1–2

Joseph Oldendorf was running in Washington's Olympic National Forest when he slipped on ice and broke his leg. He had no cell coverage. "I wasn't counting on my phone ever working," he said. He crawled for hours to a spot where his phone picked up a signal, and he was able to call 911 just after midnight. Rescuers found him about 4:30 a.m. and airlifted him to the hospital. He survived the ordeal, but barely.[19]

When something awful happens to us, we need access. We need communication. We need instant help.

With our Lord, there's never a break in service or a blackout area. Ephesians 2:18 says, "For through Him we both have access by one Spirit to the Father." And Ephesians 3:12 says, "In whom we have boldness and access with confidence through faith in Him."

Wherever we go, God is immediately accessible to us. Never let yourself feel stranded in a crisis. You have instant communication with heaven. You have uninterrupted access with your Heavenly Father.

[19] "Runner Breaks Leg, Crawls 10 Hours Before Rescue From Wash. Trail," *FOX19*, February 24, 2020.

SEPTEMBER 3
Harvest Time

Do you not say, "There are still four months and then comes the harvest"?
Behold, I say to you, lift up your eyes and look at the fields,
for they are already white for harvest!
JOHN 4:35

The Lord had a special burden for Samaria—the little territory north of Judah inhabited by those who had survived the Assyrian Invasion of 701 B.C. and who had intermarried with pagan settlers. The Jewish leaders disparaged these people, but Jesus visited the region, told a parable about the Good Samaritan, and directed His disciples to take the Gospel there after His resurrection (Acts 1:8). In Acts 8, the evangelist Philip led a revival in this region. Paul and Barnabas also made a trip into the area (Acts 15:3).

Jesus foresaw all this in John 4, when He led His disciples through a village in Samaria. There He sat by the well talking to an immoral woman, sharing the redeeming love of the Father for her. Deeply moved, she went into town and told everyone about Him. As the townspeople returned to meet Him, Jesus told the disciples that even though it wasn't harvest time, they were seeing a spiritual harvest.

Where others saw riffraff, Jesus saw revival.

Let's look at the world like that today—white for harvest!

Work shall be done for six days,
but the seventh is the Sabbath of rest, holy to the Lord.
EXODUS 31:15

Researchers talk about the "paradox of busyness." Many of us feel compelled to be busy all the time, yet it burns us out. We want to be productive, but it leaves us exhausted. How about you? Can you remember the last time you took off a day? Do you awaken tired every morning? Does your "to do" list get longer by the hour?

As Christians, we don't have to keep the Sabbath in the same way as the ancient Jews, but the principle of one-in-seven still provides the best way to maintain our weekly rhythm and ward off exhaustion. One day in seven needs to be different from the others. It should include worship, for that's the most refreshing activity known to humanity. We should try to get some additional sleep or relaxation. It should be a pleasant day, for we need an interruption from the demands on us.

Set aside one day a week for the welfare of your soul. It's the first step in breaking free from the barrenness of busyness. Try it—for the rest of your life.

SEPTEMBER 5
City of Gold

And he who talked with me had a gold reed to measure the city.
REVELATION 21:15

Autumn trees are never more beautiful than when they burst into gold. It seems incredible that the leaves of summer should change into colors that remind us of wealth.

Few things are more valuable than gold. It's the only metal on earth that is yellow or golden in color, and it is extremely pliable. Almost half of all the gold mined today is used in jewelry. Maybe you have some of it in your dresser drawer. If not, you might want to check with the U.S. Federal Reserve. They have 530,000 gold bars laying around somewhere.

God created gold to delight us, and the Architect of New Jerusalem is using it as a primary building material as He prepares a place for us. Revelation 21:18 says, "The city was pure gold, like clear glass."

If you have a gold ring (or if you simply see a golden tree this fall), let it always remind you of the City of Gold—the City of God—the eternal inheritance for His children.

SEPTEMBER 6
Why Do We Sing?

Be filled with the Spirit, speaking to one another in psalms and hymns and spiritual songs, singing and making melody in your heart to the Lord.
EPHESIANS 5:18–19

Why do people sing? The nineteenth century American poet Henry Wadsworth Longfellow may have said it best: "Music is the universal language of mankind." Even when our spoken words cannot be understood, music can bridge a gap where our words often fail. Joy, sorrow, fear, exaltation, praise, energy—every facet of life can be reflected in music. And when words are added, especially words that edify and inspire and communicate to the heart, all the better.

Why do we sing songs in church? The Early Church did so because of the Jewish culture of singing the psalms in worship. But why did Israel sing? Because they were human and needed to pour out their hearts to God in praise, confession, petition, and love. We also sing in corporate worship because Paul instructed us to praise God with "psalms and hymns and spiritual songs" (Ephesians 5:19). Corporate worship, especially with music, focuses our attention on the Savior we serve.

Do you invest your whole heart in corporate worship in church? Worship is our "sacrifice of praise" to the Lord (Hebrews 13:15).

SEPTEMBER 7
Fuel for Faith

Now faith is the substance of things hoped for,
the evidence of things not seen.
HEBREWS 11:1

James Watt, the eighteenth-century Scottish inventor and engineer, coined the term "horsepower" to compare the power of newly invented steam engines to the power of a draft horse. The horse and carriage gave way to the horseless carriage, or automobile, powered by gasoline. Now we are in another transition—vehicles are being powered by electricity rather than carbon-based fuels.

Everything is powered by something, even the Christian life. First and foremost, the Christian is empowered by the Holy Spirit (Romans 15:13). But from our human perspective, what empowers our life? We could say that faith is the fuel that keeps us moving forward. The New English Translation of Hebrews 11:1 says, "Now faith is being sure of what we hope for, being convinced of what we do not see." Can you see God? Heaven? Rewards? Eternal life? Why would you keep pressing on for what you cannot see? Because of the faith and hope which anchor our soul (Hebrews 6:19).

Freedom Fighter

Stand fast therefore in the liberty by which Christ has made us free,
and do not be entangled again with a yoke of bondage.
GALATIANS 5:1

A "freedom fighter" is someone who fights to overthrow a government or authority perceived to be oppressive. There have been freedom fighters all over the world. Those who participated in the American Revolution in the eighteenth century could be called freedom fighters. They sought to throw off what they considered an oppressive yoke of burdensome taxation and subjugation without representation.

The apostle Paul can be considered a freedom fighter as well. When he began spreading the Gospel of grace through Jesus Christ apart from the law, some Jewish believers attempted to impose the yoke of the law on Paul's Gospel. His response? "To whom we did not yield submission even for an hour, that the truth of the gospel might continue" (Galatians 2:5). Paul took the Galatian Christians to task for replacing freedom in Christ with an obligation to the requirements of the law. Once Paul tasted true spiritual freedom, he never looked back.

If you have found freedom in Christ, "you shall be free indeed" (John 8:36). Join Paul as a freedom fighter for the Gospel!

SEPTEMBER 9
How to Pray

Now it came to pass, as [Jesus] was praying in a certain place,
when He ceased, that one of His disciples said to Him,
"Lord, teach us to pray, as John also taught his disciples."
LUKE 11:1

Some days, our prayers flow unbidden. Other days, an outline can help. The outline for prayer that Jesus gave His disciples can work as well for us as it did for them. Using the version of "the disciples' prayer" in Matthew 6:9–13, consider the following headings as an outline for prayer.

Praise (verse 9): Begin by praising God for who He is and what He has done in your life. *Petition* (verse 10): If there are no burning needs you have to pray for, pray that God's Kingdom will fill the earth; pray His perfect will would be done in all things. *Provision* (verse 11): If you have needs, bring them before Him. If all your needs are met, give Him thanks for His provision. *Pardon* (verse 12): Ask for forgiveness for your own sins, and ask for grace to forgive any who have sinned against you. *Protection* (verse 13): Pray for protection against the schemes of the devil; pray to take the way of escape from temptation that God provides.

As you pray through this outline, many things will come to mind to expand your prayers and deepen your time with God. Write them down and then as your prayers are answered, make a note of how and when God met your need.

Extravagant Forgiveness

Jesus said to [Peter], "I do not say to you,
up to seven times, but up to seventy times seven."
MATTHEW 18:22

The pre-Flood actions of early humanity leave much to be desired, especially among the descendants of Cain, the murderer of his brother Abel (Genesis 4). God graciously spared Cain from death for his sin of murder, even putting a mark of protection on him. If anyone killed Cain, God would judge that person seven times over. When Cain's arrogant descendant, Lamech, killed a man for wounding him, he swore that if anyone tried to harm him he would seek vengeance "seventy-sevenfold" (Genesis 4:24). Lamech's threat of extravagant judgment was a way of saying, "I, not God, determine how much judgment is appropriate."

Not surprisingly, Jesus seems to use Lamech's arrogance and extravagant judgment to set a new standard for forgiveness when wronged. When Peter asked how often he should forgive others, Jesus replied, "[Not] seven times, but up to seventy times seven [times]." Instead of being extravagant in judgment and unforgiveness, be extravagant in grace and forgiveness.

Be part of Jesus' mission of extravagant forgiveness. Don't count. Simply forgive the way God forgives you in Christ (Ephesians 4:32).

He who testifies to these things says, "Surely I am coming quickly."
REVELATION 22:20

A group of researchers conducted a study with participants who were given sheets of paper containing mazes. Every sheet had a little mouse near the middle, and the participants had to get the mouse through the maze. At the top of the page for one set of participants was an owl, looming over the puzzle and hunting the mouse, ready to snatch him up if he took the wrong route. The other set of participants had no owl. Instead there was a morsel of cheese awaiting the mouse at the end of the puzzle.

Which group did the best with their puzzles? The people with the cheese consistently did better. The researchers explained we do much better in life when we're moving forward toward a goal, not looking backward at a threat. We don't need to look back in fear, but to look forward in hope and expectation.

World events seem dire; the daily headlines are frightening. And our 24-hour news cycle is enough to keep anyone on edge. But Jesus is coming quickly. He is coming soon. And He is coming for us. Let's keep our eyes fixed on that promise—"Surely I am coming quickly."

SEPTEMBER 12
Fretting

Do not fret.
PSALM 37:1

Fretting is such a descriptive word! Parents fret over little signs they notice in their teenagers. Athletes fret when they fall into a slump. Politicians fret when their poll numbers drop. The dictionary defines fretting as "feelings of nagging worry that can torment you"—vexing, irritating, distracting fears that gnaw into your feelings of happiness. It comes from an Old English word meaning "to eat up, to consume, to gnaw away at."

Dr. John Henry Jowett, the British expositor, said, "Fretfulness is an irritation disquietude; it is a form of uneasiness which vents itself in... complaints." He said that when you are fretting about something, it's usually the first thing you thought about in the morning and the last thing on your mind in the evening.

Perhaps you know what that's like.

In Psalm 37, the Lord said: "Do not fret.... Do not fret.... Do not fret—it only causes harm" (verses 1, 7, 8). Keep those phrases in your mind today and repeat them to yourself over and over—do not fret; do not fret; do not fret! Replace your fretting with trusting in God's provision and supervision of your life.

SEPTEMBER 13

The Only Right Fear

Let all the earth fear the Lord; let all the
inhabitants of the world stand in awe of Him.
PSALM 33:8

One of Jesus' most cryptic teachings is found in His words to the scribes and Pharisees: "Woe to you lawyers! For you have taken away the key of knowledge" (Luke 11:52). Jesus didn't say specifically what the "key of knowledge" was. But wouldn't it be good to know?

The clue to the key may be found in Isaiah 33:6—a verse Jesus may have had in mind: "Wisdom and knowledge will be the stability of your times, and the strength of salvation; the fear of the Lord is His treasure." Interestingly, one modern translation says, "The fear of the Lord is the key to this treasure [of wisdom and knowledge]" (NIV). Could the fear of the Lord be the key to gaining wisdom and knowledge about God and living rightly with Him? Scripture seems to think so, as described in Psalm 111:10; Proverbs 1:7; 2:5, 9:10, 14:26–27, 19:23. In fact, we are to be "zealous for the fear of the Lord all the day" (Proverbs 23:17).

Honor, reverence, awe, submission, obedience—all these characterize the fear of the Lord. The whole earth should fear the Lord...and "stand in awe of Him."

Living for the Lord

Surely goodness and mercy shall follow me all the days of my life;
and I will dwell in the house of the Lord forever.
PSALM 23:6

When Hester Ford passed away on April 17, 2021, she left a legacy of twelve children, 68 grandchildren, 125 great-grandchildren, and at least 120 great-great-grandchildren. That's a family of 325 people! She was born on a farm in Lancaster County, South Carolina, either in 1904 or 1905—the records are unclear, and she lived to the age of 115 (or 116). At the time of her death, she was the oldest living American.

Her secret was, in her words, "Living for the Lord." She believed in memorizing Scripture, and even after she developed dementia she could still recite her Bible verses perfectly. Her favorite passage was Psalm 23. Near the end of her life, she told her children she was ready to "go home to be with Jesus."

Few of us will live to be 115 or 116, but those who live for the Lord and hide His Word in their heart have the joy of anticipating the day when they will be at home with Jesus. The secret to a well-regulated life is maintaining a day-by-day walk with our Savior, Sustainer, and Shepherd. His goodness and mercy will bless our lives here on earth, and we will dwell with Him forever.

SEPTEMBER 15
Never a Day

So it was always: the cloud covered it by day,
and the appearance of fire by night.
NUMBERS 9:16

When the children of Israel escaped their Egyptian captors, the Lord went with them, encamping among them, and manifesting His presence. Every day, a bright cloud of glory appeared above the tabernacle, and every evening a column of fire shot into the sky. At some point after the Israelites entered the Promised Land, the visible phenomena ceased, but the Lord was still near, still dear, and still dwelling close among them.

In the same way, He is near, dear, and close to us. An old hymn says: "There is never a day so dreary, but God can make it bright; / And unto the soul that trusts Him, He giveth songs in the night."

There is never a day when God's presence isn't as near to you as your very breath. He lives with you, within you, around you, before you, behind you, above you, below you; and He surrounds you with favor as with a shield. If you have trouble grasping this, imagine His cloud of glory and His pillar of fire above your head. He is there just as truly as He dwelt among the Israelites.

SEPTEMBER 16
The Morning Watch

And in the morning the word of the Lord came to me.
EZEKIEL 12:8

The Student Volunteer Movement was an organization founded in 1886 to mobilize university students for the mission field, and it had a deep impact on thousands of young people. One of its emphases was the "Morning Watch"—the practice of personal prayer and Bible study each morning. In one SVM publication, Grace Wilder wrote, "A mark of the divine origin of the Student Volunteer Movement is the fact that early in its history, the Morning Watch became one of its prominent features."

She wrote of a missionary who, after eighteen years of service, said, "When I first came to India, I was on the supernatural plane; now I am on the natural plane. When I first came I saw results; now I rarely see them."

Wilder continued, "It was her conviction that neglect of the Morning Watch accounted for this leakage of power. If Satan can deprive us of our Morning Watch in this land, he has little to fear from us in any land."

Whether we call it the Morning Watch, our quiet time, daily devotions, or just our daily time of prayer and Bible study, don't neglect spending this precious daily time with God.

Like a shelter from the wind and a refuge from the storm, like streams of water in the desert and the shadow of a great rock in a thirsty land.
ISAIAH 32:2, NIV

Isaiah 32 speaks of the King who will reign in righteousness and be a shelter, a refuge, streams of fresh water, and a welcoming shadow.

Evangelist Robert E. Lee was caught in a tornado, which sounded like a prolonged "fierce, shrill, titanic shriek." He said, "All the evening, the clouds dashed hither and thither without aim or drift. In the gusts from every quarter, the wind came and went. All night I heard it, moaning and groaning, as if it were some human being crying from the harm he had done. That day I got a better conception of what the Book says: 'They are like the chaff which the wind drives away.' I also got great comfort in recalling the truth: 'A man shall be as a hiding-place from the wind.'"

The Bible compares our difficulties to storms, but our Savior is a shelter from the wind, a refuge from the storm. Think of Him today as streams in the desert and as the shadow of a mighty rock within a weary land. He is your safe place—your refuge from the storms of life.

But each day the Lord pours his unfailing love upon me,
and through each night I sing his songs, praying to God who gives me life.
PSALM 42:8, NLT

The tallest uninterrupted waterfall in the world is Angel Falls in Venezuela, where the Churún River plunges off the summit of the Auyán-Tepui mountain and descends for 3,212 feet. Most people only see Angel Falls in videos because the location is difficult to reach.

Perhaps God created waterfalls to give us spectacular images of His outpouring grace. No waterfall can compare with the cataract of love that the Lord pours on us every morning. His grace streams all the way from heaven, lands in our life, and fills us to overflowing. Romans 5:5 says "The love of God has been poured out in our hearts." And Titus 3:5–6 talks about the "renewing of the Holy Spirit, whom He poured out on us abundantly through Jesus Christ our Savior."

The next time you visit a waterfall—or see an image of one—think of Psalm 42:8, Romans 5:5, and Titus 3:5–6. Visualize yourself standing under the waterfall of God's unfailing love. It is poured out on you each new day.

Don't you think there will be massively beautiful waterfalls on the new earth?

SEPTEMBER 19
Morning 'Till Evening

*So when they had appointed him a day, many came to him at his lodging,
to whom he explained and solemnly testified of the kingdom of God,
persuading them concerning Jesus from both the Law of Moses
and the Prophets, from morning till evening.*

ACTS 28:23

From morning 'till evening. That's how long we're to serve the Lord. And then from evening 'till morning. God assigns our work daily, and one of the best prayers we can offer daily is: "Lord, what do You want me to do today?"

The apostle Paul found himself under house arrest in Rome for two years while awaiting trial. He was chained to guards, but he had the freedom to stay in his own rented house. During this period, he didn't have the rigors of travel or the threat of violence. He didn't have to worry about bandits on the trails or shipwrecks on the sea. He could write letters to his churches and entertain the guests wanting to see him. Paul accepted this as a time assigned by God for sharing Christ and teaching how Jesus fulfilled "the Law of Moses and the Prophets." And this he did from morning till evening.

Every new day is a fresh opportunity to serve the Lord. We'll never retire from that calling, and we will never resign from His will. As long as we're on earth, He'll have something for us to do... from morning 'till evening.

SEPTEMBER 20
Eager to Forgive

*When [Jesus] saw their faith, He said to [the paralytic],
"Man, your sins are forgiven you."*
LUKE 5:20

Certain experiences in modern society have garnered the reputation as being unpleasant—or at least not to be looked forward to. Examples might include: Renewing your driver's license at the DMV, having a root canal at the endodontist, or meeting with an IRS agent for an audit of your tax return. The anticipation regarding any of these experiences is usually negative. What a surprise it is, then, when the experience turns out to be not as bad as expected—even pleasant!

Imagine you are a sinner seeking to meet with Jesus to receive forgiveness for your sin, and perhaps for the healing of a physical affliction. Will it be rigorous? Embarrassing? Will He ask probing, personal questions? Not if this example of Jesus healing a paralyzed man is any indication. In fact, in this instance, Jesus didn't interact with the man at all. The paralytic was healed and forgiven based solely upon the faith of this man's friends, the same friends who brought him to Jesus. Jesus is not only able to forgive—He is eager to forgive! That should have been no surprise since Psalm 103:3 praises God for forgiving all iniquities and healing all diseases. Jesus' actions revealed that the same God was in their midst.

Do you need forgiveness? Healing of some sort? Jesus welcomes you with open arms to come to Him. He is eager to meet your need.

Rejoicing in hope; patient in tribulation; continuing instant in prayer.
ROMANS 12:12, KJV

During the past couple of years, the U.S. Postal Service has grappled with serious delays, partially because of COVID. One Connecticut landscaper nearly went bankrupt because his post office box was empty for 45 days. When he complained, postal authorities found some of the missing mail—nearly a hundred pieces, many of them containing checks from customers. At the time of this writing, he was still waiting for more of the lost mail to be found.

Sometimes we feel God's answers to our prayers are lost or delayed, but, no, each comes as a special delivery at just the right moment in His blessed will. The King James Version tells us to be "instant in prayer." We can pray in an instant, and God instantly hears. No request is ignored, no plea is unheard, and no prayer is unanswered if we pray with humble hearts in Jesus' Name.

In a day of instant communication, nothing is more instant than our connection with the Heavenly Father.

Grace Day by Day

And He said to me, "My grace is sufficient for you."
2 CORINTHIANS 12:9

Imagine a silver lamp—a gas lamp like people of earlier days had on their kitchen tables. This one has a beautiful clear globe and an ornate silver bowl or reservoir for the oil. A wick stretches from the bowl up to the globe, and the flame casts a golden glow over the room. The glow, in fact, is quite unusual. It allows anyone in the room, even in the distant corners, to read every word of their Bibles without strain. And it casts a cheerful mood that dispels sadness.

We are God's lamps, and the oil is His sufficient grace. The oddest thing, however, is there is no way to replenish the oil, nor does it need replenishing. Somehow it's fed by an invisible source, and its level never diminishes. When we're filled with the Spirit, the fire in our heart never falters, its globe is never blackened with soot, and our light can never be blown out.

Our Lord's invisible grace flows constantly from Calvary into our hearts to keep us bright, cheerful, and useful. By His invisible operation, He keeps the supply of His grace full and overflowing, both day and night.

*Now hope does not disappoint, because the love of God has
been poured out in our hearts by the Holy Spirit who was given to us.*
ROMANS 5:5

How would you define *disappointment*? According to
Wikipedia, *disappointment* is a "feeling of dissatisfaction that
follows the failure of expectations or hopes to manifest." Dr.
Bill Thrasher suggested another definition he once heard:
"Disappointment is God's way of dimming the glamour of the
world and deepening our ability to enjoy Him."[20]

Of all our emotions, disappointment can hit us the hardest.
It's a form of destroyed hope, delayed expectation, failed
plans, and abandoned dreams. Think of a young woman whose
boyfriend leaves her, a couple whose hope for pregnancy is
crushed, an actor whose show is canceled, an entrepreneur
whose business fails, or a high school student who doesn't make
the team.

Sturdy faith processes the disappointments of life and
recognizes that if God doesn't allow us to achieve a goal, it's
because He has a different and a better plan. Disappointment
can be God's way of showing us a better way. Yes, that takes raw
faith, but we have an unfailing God!

[20] Bill Thrasher, *Living the Life God Has Planned* (Chicago: Moody Press, 2001), 36.

SEPTEMBER 24
Living on Purpose

But Daniel purposed in his heart that he would not defile himself with the portion of the king's delicacies, nor with the wine which he drank; therefore he requested of the chief of the eunuchs that he might not defile himself.

DANIEL 1:8

Our English word *purpose* derives from an old Anglo-French verb meaning "to propose." When a man proposes marriage to a woman he says, "It is my purpose to spend my life with you and with none other." The advantage of such a proposal, as it transitions to a life purpose, is that it eliminates a multitude of decisions that might present themselves. Anything that conflicts with one's purpose in life is not even considered—or shouldn't be.

When young Daniel was taken as a captive to Babylon, he *purposed* in his heart not to defile himself in that pagan land. So he *proposed* to the one in charge an alternative to the diet he was offered. He didn't have to wonder, "What should I do?" That decision had been made before God many years before. His purpose was to live a life of purity and obedience to God.

How would you describe your purpose in life? Make your future easier by declaring a clear purpose today.

SEPTEMBER 25
His Majestic Handiwork

He hangs the earth on nothing.

JOB 26:7

In his book, *Taking Back Astronomy*, Dr. Jason Lisle wrote, "This verse expresses (in a poetic way) the fact that the earth is unsupported by any other object—something quite unnatural for the ancient writers to imagine. Indeed, the earth does float in space. We now have pictures of the earth taken from space that show it floating in the cosmic void. The earth literally hangs on nothing, just as the Bible teaches."[21]

Creation reveals God's majesty to us. We can see His handiwork in the tiniest creatures He has made, but it's the vastness of the universe that truly boggles our mind. The Bible says, "For since the creation of the world His invisible attributes are clearly seen, being understood by the things that are made" (Romans 1:20).

The Lord has surrounded us with His majesty—the blades of grass beneath our feet, the twinkling stars above our head. We're surrounded by His beauty and grace, which should always remind us of His power and glory.

How majestic is His Name!

[21] Dr. Jason Lisle, *Taking Back Astronomy* (Green Forest, AR: Master Books, 2011), 28.

He declared to you His covenant which He commanded you to perform,
the Ten Commandments; and He wrote them on two tablets of stone.
DEUTERONOMY 4:13

In the Ten Commandments, the infinite character and holy requirements of God are reduced and recorded for our welfare. They're the foundation of ethics. Obeying them is the secret of happiness. So eternally true yet so simple! An old English verse found in the *McGuffey Reader* says it this way:

> *Above all else love God alone;*
> *Bow down to neither wood nor stone.*
> *God's name refuse to take in vain;*
> *The Sabbath rest with care maintain.*
> *Respect your parents all your days;*
> *Hold sacred human life always.*
> *Be loyal to your chosen mate;*
> *Steal nothing, neither small nor great.*
> *Report, with truth, your neighbor's deed;*
> *And rid your mind of selfish greed.*

These rules are not designed to hinder our happiness, but to teach us how to live our life to the fullest.

Defeating Fear

For God has not given us a spirit of fear,
but of power and of love and of a sound mind.
2 TIMOTHY 1:7

Medical science has made it possible for humans to live longer. But ask the average senior citizen if that excites them and the answer may be, "Yes and no." Yes, we want to live longer but not while battling a disease. Disease remains a potential source of fear for all humans, regardless of age.

But does it need to be? We know all of creation has been impacted by sin. When creation malfunctions or begins to break down, we shouldn't be surprised. We know death is coming for all. But we need not be afraid of death or any disease that may hasten its arrival. Rather, we should echo the apostle John's prayer: "I pray that you may prosper in all things and be in health" (3 John 2). Health is a desire we should pray for and work toward, while leaving the answer to God.

One deadly condition we can eliminate today is fear! Fear is not from God (2 Timothy 1:7). Live well, pray well, and be well—one day at a time.

Swallowing Fog

Out of weakness were made strong.
HEBREWS 11:34

In a sermon on this text, Charles Haddon Spurgeon said:

"When I rise, as upon eagle's wings, in joyous rapture, I feel right glad to be capable of the blissful excitement. Yet if you soar to the skies, you are very apt to drop below the sea-level. He that can fly, can faint…. If you are a creature that can be excited, and that can be depressed; and, worse still, if you happen to have been born on a foggy day, and to have swallowed so much of that fog that you have found it shading your spirit many a time ever since; then you can only be strong by faith."

"The only cure for depression is faith," said Spurgeon. "Settle this in your heart: 'Whether I am up or down, the Lord Jesus Christ is the same. Whether I sing, or whether I sigh, the promise is true, and the Promiser is faithful'…. If you will stand firm in Christ Jesus, even in your weakness you will be made strong."

We are emotional creatures, and some of our emotions are difficult to manage. But God's promises aren't emotional. They are solid, stable, firm, strength-imparting, and true. The Lord will strengthen you in your weakness today.

SEPTEMBER 29
O Lord, Save!

Then the multitudes who went before and those who followed cried out,
saying: "Hosanna to the Son of David! 'Blessed is He who comes
in the name of the Lord!' Hosanna in the highest!"

MATTHEW 21:9

Two Hebrew words, rendered into English, are often used as synonyms—but they have different meanings. *Hallelujah* means "Praise the Lord" (Psalm 104:35), while *hosanna* literally means "O Lord, save!" However, by the first century *hosanna* had come to be used like *hallelujah* as a shout of praise, as in, "Praise the One who can save us!"

When Jesus made His entry into Jerusalem a week before His crucifixion, the crowds that accompanied Him were shouting the words of Psalm 118:25–26: "Save now, I pray, O Lord [hosanna!]…. Blessed is he who comes in the name of the Lord!" It was clearly an acknowledgement of Jesus as the Messiah of Israel. Sadly, in a matter of days, most of the city turned on their Messiah and rejected Him. They shouted "Hosanna!" ("O Lord, save!") not realizing that salvation was at hand if they would simply receive it. Knowing what was coming, Jesus wept over the city (Luke 19:41).

If you have ever prayed, "Save me, Lord!" know that He is ready to answer your prayer. Confess His lordship and believe in your heart and you will be saved (Romans 10:9).

SEPTEMBER 30
Do You Believe This?

Jesus said to [Martha], "I am the resurrection and the life. He who believes in Me, though he may die, he shall live. And whoever lives and believes in Me shall never die. Do you believe this?"

JOHN 11:25–26

Winston Churchill made specific requests about his anticipated funeral. It was held in the massive St. Paul's Cathedral in London, where music would have echoed gloriously. He specified that two bugle pieces be played: "Taps," the military signal that the day is over, and "Reveille," the military signal that the day is just beginning. Churchill believed that, yes, his earthly "day" was over, but his eternal "day" was just beginning. That night, as Churchill's widow, Clementine, prepared for bed, she told her daughter, "It wasn't a funeral, Mary—it was a triumph."

That was the message Jesus conveyed to Martha and Mary, sisters of His friend, Lazarus, as they mourned the death of their brother. It was the bittersweet message of death from a Christian perspective. Yes, death brings sorrow, but it also brings hope and victory for the one who dies in faith in Christ. Christ's resurrection removed the sting from death forever. Death has been swallowed up in victory (1 Corinthians 15:54–55).

Do you believe this? As you consider the end of life on earth, think of it as the continuation of life in Christ—forever.

OCTOBER

OCTOBER 1
He Restoreth My Soul

I will give you the treasures of darkness and hidden riches of secret places, that you may know that I, the Lord, who call you by your name, am the God of Israel.
ISAIAH 45:3

In his book *As a Tree Grows*, W. Phillip Keller, studies several occasions in Scripture where God compares His people to trees. Trees need darkness, said Keller. Darkness provides respite from the oppressive heat of the day. "Darkness brings dew and refreshment to the foliage of the tree. In mountainous country like Lebanon, where the forests lie close to the sea, nighttime brings its banks of cloud and mist and fog that enshroud the trees in refreshing coolness, saturating the cedars with mineral-laden moisture from the ocean deeps."

Sometimes we go through seasons of darkness, when our circumstances are not sunny, and our spirits aren't as bright as usual. But God works in our hearts during such times, and He can use these periods to increase our sturdiness and fruitfulness.

He also makes the sun rise right on time, replacing fear with joy and sadness with gladness. With Him near, we never need to fear the dark—His presence can turn the darkness into pictures of grace.

OCTOBER 2
Great Is Your Faithfulness

Through the Lord's mercies we are not consumed, because His compassions
fail not. They are new every morning; great is Your faithfulness.
LAMENTATIONS 3:22–23

"What if Your blessings come through raindrops? What
if Your healing comes through tears? What if a thousand
sleepless nights are what it takes to know You're near? What
if trials of this life are Your mercies in disguise?" Singer and
songwriter Laura Story wrote these words after her husband
was diagnosed with a brain tumor. As the couple wrestled
with his diagnosis and prayed for healing, Laura expressed her
prayers to the Lord through her song, "Blessings," which has
encouraged many others as they walk through trials.

No matter your trial—illness, unemployment, family
struggles—God is still blessing you. The blessing may come
through a comforting verse in His Word or through an
encouraging card from a friend. It might appear in the
unexpected gift from a family member or the worship song
sung at church. His blessings are all around us. These small
blessings bring great joy to our hearts, but perhaps the greatest
blessing we receive during times of trial is the blessing of
drawing closer to God. As we trust Him and cling to His
promises, our relationship with the Father deepens. What an
indescribable blessing!

*Nor is there salvation in any other, for there is no other name
under heaven given among men by which we must be saved.*
ACTS 4:12

The Roman Emperor Caesar Augustus established a "zero-mile" monument in Rome to measure distances throughout the empire. It eventually led to, "All roads lead to Rome." A variant on that idea is found in modern computer and phone software that maps various routes from "city A" to "city B"—different roads leading to the same destination.

Sadly, this idea of "multiple roads, one destination" has made its way into theology: "All roads lead to God." Proponents of this idea suggest that all religions have the same ultimate destination. Said another way, "There are many ways to get to God." However, the Bible doesn't support this idea. The apostle Peter was clear when speaking to the Jewish elders after Pentecost. He stated clearly that the Name (Person) of Jesus is the only means of salvation. Paul echoed this position when he wrote that there is only one Mediator between God and man, "the Man Christ Jesus" (1 Timothy 2:5).

Don't be confused by non-biblical positions on salvation. There is only one road to God and His heaven. That road begins and ends with Jesus.

OCTOBER 4
Memorize and Obey

How can a young man cleanse his way?
By taking heed according to Your word.
PSALM 119:9

There are many ways that health-conscious folks try to ensure the purity of their physical bodies and improve their health. Eating organically-grown foods, drinking pure water, breathing clean air, engaging in cleansing fasts, cutting out junk food—are all ways to help detox our body. Our world grows less pure, from a physical standpoint, every day due to pollution and other toxicities.

What about our spiritual life? Our world certainly seems to grow more spiritually toxic all the time, and it is impossible to avoid encountering snares and temptations. So how do we keep our spiritual "body" pure? The psalmist had a solution: Store up God's Word in our heart so that we might not sin against Him and apply the wisdom and direction His Word offers into our life (Psalm 119:9, 11). Think about it: If we obey (apply) God's Word, we won't choose to sin. And if we memorize (store up) God's Word, it will be within a thought's reach when we are faced with temptation.

The more we live "in" God's Word, the purer our life will be in the midst of a toxic world.

OCTOBER 5
Energizing Love

Simon, son of Jonah, do you love Me?
JOHN 21:16

Tony Evans wrote, "Our fundamental problem as Christians is not really obedience. Our problem is keeping our love for Christ fervent, for love makes obedience a delight. A decline in obedience is the outgrowth of a decline in love."[22]

Just before He returned to heaven, Jesus asked Peter three times if he loved Him. This is undoubtedly because Peter had earlier denied Jesus three times. But the question wasn't to reassure Jesus. Jesus already knew the exact temperature of Peter's love. He wanted to provide an opportunity for Peter to reaffirm and express his love. Jesus also wanted Peter to realize that genuine love would propel him into his future ministry of feeding Jesus' sheep and tending Jesus' flock.

We affirm our love for Jesus by telling Him we love Him, and by doing what He says. Furthermore, our love for Jesus will spill over into our relationships. We love others because we love Him. Love is the energy of life. It motivates us in our service and in our servanthood.

---

[22] Tony Evans, *Life Essentials for Knowing God Better, Experiencing God Deeper, Loving God More* (Chicago: Moody Publishers, 2003), 249.

OCTOBER 6
Sharing God's Love

For all the law is fulfilled in one word, even in this:
"You shall love your neighbor as yourself."
GALATIANS 5:14

Founded in 1987, Straight Ahead Ministries has reached thousands of juvenile offenders around the world with the Gospel. Not only do they lead Bible studies for the youth while they are incarcerated, but they also help the youth prepare for and adjust to life once they are released. They desire to give "every juvenile offender the opportunity to hear and respond to the Gospel and grow into all that God intends them to be."[23] One young man whom they helped put it this way, "They've seen my record but they've never judged me. They want to see you do good and they don't want nothing in return."[24]

The men and women who invest in the lives of these youth are living out Christ's command to "love your neighbor as yourself" (Mark 12:31). Reaching out and loving those that others ignore or forget shows God's love not only to the ones we are reaching but also to those who are watching. A life spent loving others as Jesus commands is a life well lived for Him. Whether it's sharing the Gospel with juvenile offenders, meeting the needs of the homeless, or being a listening ear at a crisis pregnancy center, showing Christ's love to others always brings Him glory!

---

[23] "Our History," *Straight Ahead Ministries*, https://www.straightahead.org/international.
[24] Daniel Olasky, "Sharing a Vision," *World*, July 1, 2010.

OCTOBER 7
Day by Day

Therefore we do not lose heart. Even though our outward man is perishing, yet the inward man is being renewed day by day.
2 CORINTHIANS 4:16

Lina Sandell-Berg was born in Sweden in 1832. Her father, Jonas, was a Lutheran minister, and Lina was very close to her dad. From an early age, Lina developed a paralysis that disabled her. Her parents prayed for her healing. One Sunday, when she was twelve, Lina stayed home from church and spent much time in serious Bible reading and prayer. Somehow her paralysis lifted, and her parents returned to find her dressed and walking around the house.

Years later, Lina accompanied her father on a boat trip across a Swedish lake. He fell overboard and drowned as she watched helplessly. She learned to accept what she could not change, trusting God with her daily burdens. Out of her experiences, Lina wrote many hymns, one of which said: "Day by day, and with each passing moment, / Strength I find to meet my trials here; / Trusting in my Father's wise bestowment, / I've no cause for worry or for fear."

Living by faith is the experience of drawing on God's strength day by day, trusting in His ability "[to give] unto each day what He deems best."

OCTOBER 8
He Will Do It

Now may the God of peace Himself sanctify you completely; and may your whole spirit, soul, and body be preserved blameless at the coming of our Lord Jesus Christ. He who calls you is faithful, who also will do it.

1 THESSALONIANS 5:23–24

This is a great passage for those of us who become discouraged with our spiritual progress. We're beset with temptations, interruptions, adjustments, weaknesses, and relapses. It's often two steps forward and one step backward.

If that's the way you feel today, study these verses and notice: (1) God is the One who will sanctify you and cause you to mature into the image of Christ. Yes, it takes work on your part, which is detailed in the book of First Thessalonians. But God is the source and strength of our progress. (2) One day you'll be completely whole, perfect, and pleasing to God in every way. (3) This will happen at the Second Coming of our Lord Jesus Christ. (4) Until then, we're works in progress—and it involves our whole spirit, soul, and body.

He has called you, and He will be faithful to work in you what is pleasing to Him.

OCTOBER 9

The Shepherd Boy

You come to me with a sword, with a spear, and with a javelin. But I come to you in the name of the Lord of hosts, the God of the armies of Israel.

1 SAMUEL 17:45

The story of David and Goliath is a classic. The shepherd boy arrived at the battlefront to find the armies of Israel quaking because of the Philistine army and its outsized champion. In front of everyone, David confidently selected five smooth stones, and the rest is history.

What we sometimes forget is this: One chapter earlier, the prophet Samuel arrived at Jesse's house, met his sons, and anointed David with the anointing oil that represented the Holy Spirit. Samuel anointed the boy as king, "and the Spirit of the Lord came upon David from that day forward" (1 Samuel 16:13).

It was the Holy Spirit in David's heart that gave him the wisdom to fight rather than to flee. How greatly we need the same anointing! As Christians, we have the Spirit living within us. Let's ask for a fresh empowering by our indwelling Spirit for every giant we face in our daily lives.

And [the expert in the law] said [to Jesus],
"He who showed mercy on him."
Then Jesus said to him, "Go and do likewise."
LUKE 10:37

The verse above is the conclusion to one of the most famous of Jesus' stories, popularly known as the story of the Good Samaritan. Jesus told an expert in the law (and tells us), to do what the main character in His story did to a stranger. Generally, to show compassion and love to anyone who is in need. But specifically—and more importantly—to show mercy when it is required.

In Jesus' story, a (presumably Jewish) man was set upon by robbers and left for dead on the road. Two Jewish religious leaders passed by the man without stopping to help him. But then a Samaritan came by—Samaritans and Jews had hated each other for centuries. Yet the Samaritan stopped and helped the beaten man, taking him to an inn and paying for his care. The Samaritan showed the helpless man *mercy*—love when it is least expected. The Samaritan man treated his enemy as a neighbor, something the two Jewish religious leaders failed to do. And Jesus said, "Go and be like the Samaritan; go and show mercy."

If you have the opportunity to show mercy today, be like the Good Samaritan. Demonstrate love where it is least expected.

I have shown you in every way, by laboring like this, that you must support the weak. And remember the words of the Lord Jesus, that He said, "It is more blessed to give than to receive."

ACTS 20:35

It happens on lots of occasions—the opportunity to give. Maybe a needy person holds up a sign at a busy intersection asking for money to buy food. Or a youth sports team might be soliciting donations outside a large store on a Saturday morning. Then there are the familiar "red kettles" manned by bell ringers during the Christmas season. All are worthy causes, it seems. But sometimes we wonder if we should give.

When bidding farewell to the elders at Ephesus, the apostle Paul reminded them of something Jesus said—something not found in any of the four Gospels—"It is more blessed to give than to receive." He was reminding the elders how he had asked for no financial support from them, but how he had worked to support himself and to support those in need. One wonders if Paul had Jesus' words in Matthew 5:38–42 in mind—where Jesus exhorted us to give generously when asked.

To give is to be like God—who so loved that He gave (John 3:16). Let the Holy Spirit direct your giving—and "remember the words of the Lord Jesus."

OCTOBER 12
All Deserve Mercy

So when [the Jewish religious leaders] continued asking Him,
He raised Himself up and said to them, "He who is without
sin among you, let him throw a stone at her first."

JOHN 8:7

John 7:53–8:11 is not found in all ancient Greek manuscripts of the Gospel of John. But it is included in all modern translations because it was a true event in Jesus' life, and is found in more than nine hundred manuscripts. And it is consistent with the character and teaching of Jesus. It is the story of the woman caught in adultery and forgiven by Jesus.

Jewish religious leaders presented a woman to Jesus who had been caught in adultery; they asked Jesus what should be done with her. It was a trap. If He said, "Stone her according to the Jewish law," He would have to answer to the Romans who did not permit Jews to carry out the death penalty. If He said, "Let her go," He would seemingly be violating Mosaic law. As usual, He did something unexpected: He said any of the Jewish leaders who had never sinned could cast the first stone—and no stones were thrown. Jesus' mercy saved the woman and convicted her accusers.

Paul wrote that we are to forgive others as God through Christ has forgiven us (Ephesians 4:32). All have sinned; all deserve mercy.

And take the helmet of salvation.
EPHESIANS 6:17

Football players wear helmets. Ice hockey players wear helmets. Baseball and softball players wear helmets when they bat. Jockeys wear helmets when they ride. Cyclists wear helmets when they race their mountain or road bikes. Those and other athletes put a premium on protecting their brains from injury.

And soldiers protect their heads as well. No surprise, then, that Paul included the "helmet of salvation" in his list of the Christian's spiritual armor. Paul draws much of his armor imagery from Isaiah where God is pictured as wearing spiritual "armor" (Isaiah 59:17) as well as the coming Messiah (Isaiah 11:5). Why the helmet of salvation? In short, because of the emphasis in Scripture on the mind. We have "the mind of Christ" (1 Corinthians 2:16). We are to renew our mind (Romans 12:2). The main battleground of spiritual warfare is the mind, the thought life (2 Corinthians 10:4–5). If Satan can cause us to have thoughts of doubt concerning our salvation, the battle tilts in his favor. We protect our mind with God's promises concerning salvation.

When you have doubts or insecurities, go to the Word! Renew your mind; protect your thought life. Meditate on what is true (Philippians 4:8).

*How beautiful are the feet of those who preach the gospel of peace,
who bring glad tidings of good things!*
ROMANS 10:15

When the city of Flint, Michigan, declared a state of emergency due to its water crisis, one church stepped up to help those in search for clean water. The North Central Church of Christ worked to provide clean drinking water to those in their community that were in need. Church members volunteered all day to distribute water. "I always want to hear, 'Well done, my good and faithful servant,'" one volunteer said. Another added, "We just want to make sure we're reflecting Christ, because sometimes we are the only Bible that people see."[25]

Many people are filled with loss and heartache in our broken world. During crises, we have the opportunity to share the love of Christ with others by helping to fill a need in their lives. For many souls, we are the only reflection of Christ they will ever see. What a commission! We bear the magnificent responsibility of being Jesus' hands and feet to our fallen world. Let us never forget our calling to represent our Savior to "thirsty souls"!

---

[25] Bobby Ross Jr., "Thirsty Souls: Churches Help Victims of Flint Water Crisis," *ChristianChronicle.org.,* February 17, 2016.

He Knows

But the very hairs of your head are all numbered.
MATTHEW 10:30

Modern technology has provided unparalleled views of the vastness of our planet and the universe. Via aerial photography we can sweep across endless plains and skim the peaks of immense mountain ranges—often without a single person or animal in sight. The thought might strike us, "If I was lost down there, no one would ever know." No one on earth might know, but Someone in heaven would.

The psalmist David didn't have access to the visual vistas that we have, but he knew enough about the immensity of the universe to know that God is everywhere and knows everything. David confesses in Psalm 139 that it is impossible to hide from God; He sees us wherever we are—beginning with our first heartbeat in our mother's womb. Jesus amplified this truth when He encouraged His disciples not to be afraid. Not even a sparrow falls without God's knowledge, and He knows the number of hairs on our head (Matthew 10:29–31)!

Yes, the world and the universe are big—but God is bigger! Never forget that He knows you and your needs.

OCTOBER 16
On a Mission

Go therefore and make disciples of all the nations, baptizing them
in the name of the Father and of the Son and of the Holy Spirit,
teaching them to observe all things that I have commanded you.
MATTHEW 28:19–20

Most corporations have a mission statement of some kind.
But suppose a corporation has a thousand employees. It's a long
way from the mission statement down to the tasks of the line
workers in the organization. Someone has to decide which
tasks need to be completed in order to advance the mission.

The Church is not a corporation, but it does have a mission
statement (to use modern terminology). The clearest expression
of that statement is in Matthew 28:19–20, commonly referred
to as "the Great Commission." There is one command—make
disciples—and three means to that end: go, baptize, and
teach. It's incumbent upon all Christians to play a part in that
Commission, but how do we know what our part is? There are
lots of ways to tell: spiritual gifts, talents, interests, calling, and
the affirmation of leaders and others. And prayer: "Lord, what
can I do to help disciple the nations?"

Have you discovered your part in the Great Commission?
You have a role to play; ask God to make it clear. Never lose
sight of the fact that you are part of a Grand Mission!

OCTOBER 17
An Intelligent Man

He was amazed at the teaching about the Lord.
ACTS 13:12, NIV

Acts 13 is the story of the first missions endeavor to be officially sponsored by a local church. The Christians in Antioch sent Barnabas, Saul of Tarsus, and John Mark on an evangelistic tour of Cyprus and Asia Minor. The first convert of this first missions endeavor was a very smart man—Sergius Paulus. He was the governor of Cyprus and "an intelligent man" (verse 7). This man shows up in archaeology, and we believe he was the same Sergius Paulus who wrote an ancient text on natural history.

The governor was "amazed at the teaching about the Lord."

The story of Christ and the message of the Gospel should always be amazing to us. The entire Bible should never fail to fascinate us. It is truth revealed by God Himself, which we could never have learned on our own. In our Lord's day, people marveled at His words and His works. Don't let familiarity or apathy or busyness steal the wonder from your heart today. Don't let Satan steal the sunshine. Faith in God's Word displays utmost intelligence.

Take a moment today and stand amazed in the presence of Jesus.

OCTOBER 18
God's Strength Made Perfect

He gives power to the weak, and to those
who have no might He increases strength.
ISAIAH 40:29

Christiana Tsai (1890–1984) was converted to Christ in missionary school in China. Her family was furious, yet over time Christiana managed to win 55 of her loved ones to Christ. In 1930, she was stricken with malaria, which left her debilitated. She became sensitive to light and noise, and she remained confined to a dark room from 1931 until her death in 1984. But her ministry grew despite her weakness, with many people visiting her bedside and finding Christ.

"From her bed as a pulpit, she led countless people to accept Christ. Drawn by the Holy Spirit, people traveled from many parts of the world to visit her. She seldom refused to see anyone no matter how unwell she felt."[26]

All of us long for good health, and at times we worry about sickness, illness, injury, and disease. While our concern is normal and natural, we need to remember how mightily God can use us regardless of how we feel from day to day. We can be spiritually strong in Christ, even when we are physically weak.

[26] Margaret Lamberts Bendroth and Virginia Lieson Brereton, ed., *Women and Twentieth-Century Protestantism* (Urbana, IL: University of Illinois Press, 2002), 158.

OCTOBER 19
As Each Day May Require

And may these words of mine, with which I have made supplication before the Lord, be near the Lord our God day and night, that He may maintain the cause of His servant and the cause of His people Israel, as each day may require.

1 KINGS 8:59

It was a special day when the priests of Israel bore the fabled Ark of the Covenant into its new home in the glorious temple envisioned by David and built by his son, King Solomon. After the priests deposited the precious chest in the holy of holies and came out of the temple, a massive cloud of glory filled the entire place. Solomon lifted his hands toward heaven and prayed a long prayer. Then he turned and blessed all the assembled worshipers with a benediction. The Living Bible says: "And may these words of my prayer be constantly before [the Lord] day and night, so that he helps me and all of Israel in accordance with our daily needs" (1 Kings 8:59).

We have daily needs, and through prayer God meets them. He provides daily strength, daily encouragement, daily provision, daily protection, and a daily word for our souls in His Bible. That's why every day with Him is a good day!

OCTOBER 20
Facing Financial Failure

*Therefore, do not worry, saying, "What shall we eat?" or
"What shall we drink?" or "What shall we wear?"... For your heavenly
Father knows that you need all these things.*
MATTHEW 6:31–32

Recent years have brought financial hardships for many people, including many Christians. Stock market crashes, the Great Recession of 2008, financial advisors who embezzled their clients' money, economic downturns that caused jobs to evaporate, the closure of businesses due to COVID-19, and the list goes on. Being a Christian doesn't inoculate one from the fear of financial calamity.

So how should we face the possibility of financial loss? The psalmist, David, starts at a good place: "Trust in the Lord, and do good; dwell in the land, and feed on His faithfulness" (Psalm 37:3). Facing all fears—including the fear of financial loss—begins at the same point: Trust and obey. "Do good," in this case, might mean to be a good steward, save, spend wisely, give generously, plan for the future—and don't worry! That was Jesus' message in the Sermon on the Mount when He said not to worry about your financial needs (Matthew 6:25–34). What is the recommendation when facing financial distress? Be good stewards, trust God, live in hope, and don't worry.

OCTOBER 21
Then He Arose

And suddenly a great tempest arose on the sea,
so that the boat was covered with the waves.... Then He arose
and rebuked the winds and the sea, and there was a great calm.
MATTHEW 8:24, 26

Missionary Amy Carmichael often sent insights to her workers from her own daily devotions. One day she told them how she had been helped by two phrases in Matthew 8: *And suddenly a great tempest arose.... Then He arose*. She pointed out that when the storms arise, that's when Jesus arises to deal with them.

"There are almost always waves," Amy wrote. "Now and then we have times of quietness—little lulls, I used to call them—but far more often the wind is blowing from one quarter or another, and so there are waves.... But that is not the whole story."

No, that's not the whole story! The storms and the waves are a part of life; they arise. But our Lord also arises to deal with them, to help us, to protect and navigate us, to accompany us, to work on our behalf, and to turn the storms into streams of mercy.

OCTOBER 22
Receive and Give Comfort

For Demas has forsaken me.... Only Luke is with me.
Get Mark and bring him with you.
2 TIMOTHY 4:10–11

"Why?" is one of the most asked—or thought, if not asked—questions in the Christian experience. When we go through difficult circumstances in our lives, we don't rebel against them as much as we want to know why God has allowed them. What is the purpose behind our pain or our problems?

There is one possible reason for every discomfort we experience: So that we might comfort others in the same way God comforts us. Paul describes God as the "God of all comfort" who comforts us in our troubles "that we may be able to comfort those who are in any trouble, with the comfort with which we ourselves are comforted by God" (2 Corinthians 1:3–4). He goes further: "Now if we are afflicted, it is for [our] consolation [or comfort]" (verse 6). God lets us have troubles and receive comfort so we can comfort other people who need comfort.

The next time you are hurting, go to God for comfort. Then ask Him, "Who can I comfort with this same comfort?"

OCTOBER 23
The Fear of Being Alone

I alone am left a prophet of the Lord.... I alone am left.... I alone am left.
1 KINGS 18:22; 19:10, 14

Church history is filled with examples of those who stood alone for God at risk to their own lives. When Martin Luther dared to proclaim a biblical Gospel in 1517, he was called to account before the Diet of Worms in 1521. When told to take back his teachings, he refused: "I cannot and will not recant anything."

Standing alone can be a fearful experience. Martin Luther no doubt was thinking what the prophet, Elijah, said when he stood alone: "And they seek to take my life" (1 Kings 19:10, 14). The apostle Paul probably thought the same thing before Emperor Nero took his life. But all who stand alone for Christ do so because they have confidence in God's promise never to forsake His own.

We may never be called upon to stand alone for God in the face of death. But even in the face of criticism, or being ostracized or ridiculed for our faith, we can stand firm because God stands with us. Remember: God has said, "I will never leave you nor forsake you" (Hebrews 13:5).

This is My commandment, that you love one another as I have loved you.
JOHN 15:12

Mary Soames, daughter of Winston and Clementine Churchill, edited a collection of hundreds of her parents' letters, notes, and telegrams to one another (*Winston and Clementine: The Personal Letters of the Churchills*). Their personal correspondence revealed not only the Churchills' international standing and influence, but it revealed something else: They were best friends. They communicated everything to each other: love, longing, joys, sorrows. And most of all, when Winston's political and military duties separated them, how they longed to be reunited.[27]

Jesus did something unheard of in religious circles between rabbis and students: He became His disciples' friend! He revealed to them what the Father had revealed to Him. He spent time with them in intimate conversation. He traveled with them, ate with them, and taught them. And most of all, when it was time for Him to go away, He assured them He would return for them (John 14:1–4).

Jesus invites everyone to become His friend (Matthew 11:29; Revelation 3:20). If you haven't done so already, become a friend of Jesus today by trusting Him as your Savior and Lord.

---

[27] Mary Soames, *Winston and Clementine: The Personal Letters of the Churchills* (New York: Houghton Mifflin Co., 1998).

OCTOBER 25
Don't Fear Trouble

Yet man is born to trouble, as the sparks fly upward.

JOB 5:7

One of the most iconic images to come out of the 2001 attack on the World Trade Center's Twin Towers was this: One group of people was running away from the towers, and another group of people was running *toward* the towers. Those running away were citizens trying to save their lives; those running toward the towers were firefighters trying to save the lives of others.

Naturally, many of us fear trouble to one degree or another. But some people don't, especially those called to a mission. Trouble deters most people, but it is an obstacle to be overcome for others. Jesus was a good example of the latter. Described as the Servant of the Lord in Isaiah 42, the Messiah would "set [His] face like a flint" and not be deterred by the troubles He would face (Isaiah 50:7). When Jesus fulfilled the Servant's role, "He steadfastly set His face to go to Jerusalem" (Luke 9:51). Why? Because He knew God would help Him; that He would not be disgraced or ashamed (Isaiah 50:7).

Do you fear trouble? Don't! Better to be with God in trouble than to be without trouble and without God.

OCTOBER 26
Never Doubt His Word

On the same day, when evening had come, [Jesus] said to them, "Let us cross over to the other side."

MARK 4:35

Children grow up learning to trust their parents' word. In the vast majority of cases, what parents tell their children is true. Promises are kept, plans are fulfilled, advice is sound. But inevitably, a day of disappointment arrives when a parent fails to live up to his or her word.

When a child becomes a follower of Jesus, he learns something new: God's Word never fails. Jesus' disciples learned that when He summoned them to cross the Sea of Galilee and a dangerous storm arose, threatening to sink them. The disciples were full of fear until Jesus quieted the storm and they continued their trip. Here's what they learned: When Jesus said they would cross the Sea of Galilee; *they would cross the Sea of Galilee!* No storm or circumstance would prevent them from reaching the other side. There was a storm, yes. But it was only a challenge, not a change.

God's Word tells us we will reach "the other side" for eternity with faith in Jesus. Never let a circumstance in life be a reason to doubt God's promises.

OCTOBER 27
God's Curriculum

Come, you children, listen to me; I will teach you the fear of the Lord.

PSALM 34:11

Think about how much time we invest in learning in our modern society. We begin with one year of kindergarten, then twelve years of graded school, then four years of college, then up to five years of graduate school. Then, for some professions, like the medical field, there are three to seven more years of specialty training. Some people spend twenty years or more learning because education is valuable and usually contributes to greater success in life.

But how often do we think about learning to fear the Lord? That is, do we consider growing deeper and deeper in our relationship with Him as a "curriculum" of sorts? A curriculum that lasts a lifetime? This was a common theme in the nation of Israel. Citizens of Israel were expected to be taught how to fear the Lord—how to honor Him, trust Him, love Him, worship Him, and more. And the main vehicle for that learning was the Word of God—the words of His law (Deuteronomy 31:12–13).

When you read and study your Bible, think of it as learning about God's marvelous plan for us as His children—it is a curriculum that lasts a lifetime.

OCTOBER 28
Every Spiritual Blessing

Blessed be the God and Father of our Lord Jesus Christ, who has
blessed us with every spiritual blessing in the heavenly places in Christ.
EPHESIANS 1:3

What if your real estate agent's only description of a house she has found for you is this: "You're going to love it! It's got everything you need!" Would you sign on the dotted line based only on that description? Because the agent knows your family's needs and desires, her description of the house is probably accurate. But there's something about knowing the details that gives you assurance that this house really will meet your needs going forward.

The apostle Paul wrote a statement in Ephesians 1 similar to the real estate agent's general description. He wrote that we have been "blessed... with every spiritual blessing... in Christ" (verse 3). That covers it, right? What more do we need to know? Thankfully, Paul went on to enumerate eight of those spiritual blessings for our comfort: We are chosen (verse 4), adopted (verse 5), accepted (verse 6), redeemed (verse 7), enlightened (verses 8–9), given an inheritance (verses 11), sealed (verse 13), and secured (verse 14).

Are you blessed today? Yes, in at least eight different ways—blessed with every spiritual blessing in Christ.

OCTOBER 29
Wait Patiently

You also be patient. Establish your hearts,
for the coming of the Lord is at hand.
JAMES 5:8

When societies were agrarian, children grew up learning about how things grow. They learned that some crops grow underground—like potatoes, beets, carrots, garlic, radishes—and must be pulled out of the ground when harvested. More than one impatient child over the years has made the mistake of pulling a tiny plant out of the ground prematurely because, "I wanted to see how well it was growing!" A lesson in patience soon followed.

The New Testament's world was agrarian; it is filled with illustrations related to agriculture. The apostle James used such an illustration when writing about Christ's Second Coming. His exhortation was for his readers to be patient—just as the farmer has to wait for his "precious fruit… until it receives the early and latter rain" (James 5:7). Only then is the harvest ready. But such waiting is not idle waiting. It is anticipatory, preparatory, and proactive. And so is our waiting for the return of Christ.

Our preparation involves standing firm, establishing and keeping our hearts in faith, our hands busy with the Lord's work. As we patiently, but actively, wait for the harvest, we wait for Jesus' return.

OCTOBER 30
Alive in Christ

But God, who is rich in mercy, because of His great love with which
He loved us… made us alive together with Christ.

EPHESIANS 2:4–5

Most everyone is familiar with the expression, "You can't see the forest for the trees." It means we have become so focused on the details of a project that we have lost sight of the big picture. At such times, it is helpful to step back from "the trees" and remind ourselves of what "the forest" is like.

Here is the Christian Big Picture: We were dead in sin; we were without hope; we were without God in the world. Even though we were dead, we have been made alive in Christ (Ephesians 2:5). A cemetery is a picture of humanity apart from God—no life and no hope. That's the big picture. It was God's love "with which He loved us" that "made us alive together with Christ."

There are many people physically alive today who are without God and without hope in this world. Consider ways to give them hope—a gift, an encouraging word, an act of service, or the Gospel. As you demonstrate Christ's love to the unsaved, some may come alive in Christ.

Jesus said to him, "If you can believe,
all things are possible to him who believes."

MARK 9:23

Modern references to "Ponzi schemes" refer to the fraudulent investment plan started by Charles Ponzi in the 1920s. He promised unrealistic rates of return—and succeeded for over a year—by paying initial investors with money from new investors instead of from actual profits from investments. In all such swindles, the victims have absolute faith that the conman will be true to his promises.

Such swindles reveal the most important truth about faith: More important than the amount of faith is the trustworthiness of the object of the faith. A lot of faith in a liar produces terrible results, but even small faith in a truthful person yields guaranteed results. When a man approached Jesus about healing his demon-possessed son, he asked Jesus if He could heal him. In other words, he had little confidence in Jesus. But Jesus reminded the man that faith in the real thing will always be rewarded. Putting one's faith in Jesus guarantees His attention and His response.

If you have a need today, put your confidence in Jesus, not in the amount of your faith. He will reward even the tiniest amount of trust (Matthew 17:20).

NOVEMBER

NOVEMBER 1

A Line of Praise

Rejoice in the Lord, O you righteous!
For praise from the upright is beautiful.

PSALM 33:1

Charles Spurgeon once told of an old clergyman who said that a line of praise was even better than a page of prayer—that "praise was the highest, noblest, best, most satisfying, and most healthful occupation in which a Christian man could be found."

If that's true, how can we praise the Lord as we go through the day?

When we look out our morning window, we should pause to take in the sky, looking for rays of sunshine, whisps of clouds, drops of rain, flakes of snow—each and every one crafted from the artistry of the Almighty. When we have our breakfast and eat our meals, we should pause to thank God for His generous nature, for He provides us with everything to enjoy. As we drive to work or take up the housecleaning, we should sing a song of praise, even if it's simply in our mind. As dusk and darkness fall over the landscape, we should remember God's faithfulness.

Praising our Savior strengthens our faith, steadies our nerves, and minimizes our troubles.

Make a joyful shout to the Lord, all you lands!
Serve the Lord with gladness; come before His presence with singing.
PSALM 100:1-2

Perhaps the best-known psalm of praise in the Old Testament is Psalm 100. It is short, well organized, and links worship with gladness and joy in singing. In fact, our modern use of choirs has its roots in the Old Testament forms of worship. Choirs of thanksgiving were appointed when the rebuilt walls of Jerusalem were dedicated after the return from exile (Nehemiah 12:31, 38, 40).

Psalm 100 establishes the pattern for worship: We worship God for what He has done and for who He is. There are two exhortations to praise in the psalm. The first is in verse 2, the reason being that He has made us and "we are His people" (verse 3). The second exhortation to praise is in verse 4, and the reason is because of who God is: He is good, merciful, and truthful (verse 5).

If you are ever at a loss for motivation or reasons to praise God with joy, remember Psalm 100. Praise Him with joy for what He has done and for who He is. He is faithful and loving as evidenced by Him making you His child.

Christ Jesus came into the world to save sinners.
1 TIMOTHY 1:15

On fourteen different occasions, the Bible says that Jesus came "into the world." He wasn't simply born. He left heaven and came *into the world*. The Lord Himself said, "I came forth from the Father and have come into the world" (John 16:28). He told Pontius Pilate, "For this cause I was born, and for this cause I have come into the world, that I should bear witness to the truth" (John 18:37).

Only Jesus would say something like that, for He knew His eternal origin and His divine mission.

The apostle Paul picked up on this phrase when he gave his testimony to Timothy, saying, "This is a faithful saying and worthy of all acceptance, that Christ Jesus came into the world to save sinners, of whom I am chief" (1 Timothy 1:15).

Jesus came into the world that He might come into your heart. And He comes into your heart that you might come into His kingdom. The apostle John wrote, "In this the love of God was manifested toward us, that God has sent His only begotten Son into the world, that we might live through Him" (1 John 4:9).

That's God's gift to each of us.

NOVEMBER 4
An Attitude of Gratitude

O Lord my God, I will give thanks to You forever.
PSALM 30:12

Do you ever write out your prayers? How about praying words that were written by others? We often do that when we sing great hymns that are actually prayers, such as "Great is Thy Faithfulness." While personal and spontaneous prayer is critical for our daily lives, sometimes it helps to whisper a prayer that is written out and shared with many others—as we do when we pray, "Our Father, which art in heaven" (Matthew 6:9, KJV).

During November, let's offer some united prayers of thanksgiving.

Almighty God, I want to give thanks to You forever! I want to continually be singing, "How Great Thou Art" for great is Your faithfulness. Great is Your majesty! Great is Your power!

Lord, when all goes well with me, it's because You give me strength. When things fall apart, Your grace is sufficient. You know how to turn my sadness to gladness and my rags to righteousness—and why? So that I can sing my praise to You forever without interruption.

Oh Lord my God, I will give thanks to You forever.

NOVEMBER 5
I Once Was Blind

[The man healed from blindness] answered and said,
"Whether [Jesus] is a sinner or not I do not know.
One thing I know: that though I was blind, now I see."
JOHN 9:25

Sometimes people who have cataract surgery are shocked by how the world now looks to them—brighter colors, crisper details, and sharper contrasts. Because cataracts develop so slowly, the deterioration in eyesight happens slowly. But when their cataracts are removed and new lenses are installed, it's like being given the gift of sight! Science can work wonders when it comes to restoring sight to human eyes. But there is one kind of sight science cannot restore: spiritual sight.

Spiritual blindness is referred to in general when Paul says we were "dead in trespasses" (Ephesians 2:4–5). Specifically, God blocked Israel's spiritual sight as His covenant people due to their sins (Isaiah 6:9–10). But He also promised that the Messiah would come and open their spiritually blind eyes (Isaiah 35:5), something Jesus affirmed when He came (Luke 4:18–19). Spiritual eyes can only be opened by God Himself (Psalm 119:18).

If you have received the grace of God in Christ (Ephesians 2:7), your spiritual eyes have been opened. Praise God today that though you were blind, now you see!

NOVEMBER 6
The Needed Lift

Humble yourselves in the sight of the Lord, and He will lift you up.
JAMES 4:10

Missionary pilot Forrest Zander told of landing on a remote airstrip that was so muddy the plane sunk into the mire to its axles. There was no safe way to take off again, nor was it practical to disassemble the plane and transport it back to base. Forrest decided to try to take off, but how could he work up the speed needed to become airborne? It was a short runway of nothing but mud.

"Lord, help!" was his prayer.

As he lifted his head from prayer, he saw a black rain cloud barreling toward him. As the storm approached, the wind began to blow, and that provided lift to the wings, reducing the load on the landing gear. The wheels began to plow through the mud, and aided by the strong headwinds the plane suddenly popped free from the mire and was unstuck and airborne.

How incredible that sometimes God uses storms to help us!

Your prayers for help are heard by the Lord, and if you feel stuck in life, trust Him for a much needed lift.

NOVEMBER 7
Expressing Gratitude

And one of [the lepers], when he saw that he was healed, returned,
and with a loud voice glorified God, and fell down
on his face at [Jesus'] feet, giving Him thanks.
LUKE 17:15–16

During World War II, Eric Schwam, a Jewish refugee from
Austria, ended up in the French village Le Chambon-sur-Lignon.
The townspeople hid him, his family, and over two thousand
other Jewish refugees. After his death in 2020, the French village
learned that Schwam had left them approximately two million
euros as a thank you for their care for him during the war.[28]
What a generous expression of gratitude!

When Jesus healed the ten lepers in Luke 17, only one
returned to thank Him. When this leper came back to thank the
Lord for his physical healing, he experienced a healing that went
much deeper. He experienced salvation. After he thanked Jesus,
Jesus said to him, "Arise, go your way. Your faith has made you
well" (Luke 17:19). He was a leper who met Jesus and came out
clean inwardly and outwardly. His reward for returning was to
see the real nature of the power of God in cleansing him from
sin. He was healed and made well spiritually and physically. We,
too, should be grateful for Jesus' healing in our life, for the gift of
salvation. As Paul professed, we should also proclaim, "Thanks be
to God for His indescribable gift!" (2 Corinthians 9:15)

[28] Lynde Langdon, "WWII Refugee Leaves Fortune to French Town That Hid Him," *World*, January 29,
2021.

NOVEMBER 8
Heavenly Worship

Then I looked, and I heard the voice of many angels around the throne…
saying with a loud voice: "Worthy is the Lamb who was slain to receive power
and riches and wisdom, and strength and honor and glory and blessing!"
REVELATION 5:11–12

Early in their musical studies, musicians learn the different terms and symbols related to music. One term, and its accompanying symbol, is *crescendo*. A *crescendo* is "a gradual increase in volume of a musical passage." As the musician plays the notes with the crescendo symbol underneath them, they gradually play louder and louder.

In Revelation 5 we read a description of worship that will take place in heaven. This worship of the Lamb begins with the four living creatures and the 24 elders. Then angels, which are too numerous to count, join in the worship, and finally every creature begins to worship the Lamb. The volume increases as each group joins in and as they praise the Lamb for who He is and what He has done by singing, "Blessing and honor and glory and power be to Him who sits on the throne, and to the Lamb, forever and ever!" (Revelation 5:13)

Our human mind is limited—it cannot fathom the beauty and splendor of worship in heaven, but as Christians we have the certain and glorious hope that one day we will worship the Lamb and say: "Worthy is the Lamb who was slain to receive power and riches and wisdom, and strength and honor and glory and blessing!" (Revelation 5:12)

NOVEMBER 9
Why?

But as for you, you meant evil against me; but God meant it for good, in order to bring it about as it is this day, to save many people alive.
GENESIS 50:20

When something bad happens in the life of a new Christian, they will often say, "Lord, why is this happening to *me*?" When something bad happens in the life of a mature Christian, they will often say, "Lord, *why* is this happening to me?" Same question, but different motivations. The new Christian may think it unreasonable that a bad thing happened. But the mature Christian knows problems are part of life in a fallen world. His "Why?" question is to discern from God what he can learn from the difficult situation—how he might grow in faith.

When the teenage Joseph was sold by his brothers into slavery, he no doubt asked the "Why?" question. At first, he may have thought, "What did I do to deserve this?" But later, his "Why?" likely turned into, "Oh, now I see why!" He realized God had sent him to Egypt to prepare a place for Jacob's family to escape the famine in Canaan.

When you experience difficulties in life, it's not wrong to ask "Why?" Just make sure you're asking for the right reason.

NOVEMBER 10
Praise for Forgiveness

Be glad in the Lord and rejoice, you righteous;
and shout for joy, all you upright in heart!
PSALM 32:11

Have you experienced this sheer relief? You are stopped by
a police officer for a traffic violation; you are given a verbal
warning instead of a ticket; you are sent on your way like it
never happened. Relief? No, joy and thanksgiving! We thank
the officer, then we praise God as we drive away. And after our
praise we purpose to be more careful.

If we are grateful for that pardon, how grateful should we
be when Almighty God forgives our sins and sends us on our
way? After a brutally honest retelling of his pre-confession
suffering from sin, David praised the Lord for being forgiven
(Psalm 32:11). Why should forgiveness result in praise? Because
God removes our sin far from us (Psalm 103:12). He buries
our sin out of our sight (Micah 7:19). He puts our sins behind
His back (Isaiah 38:17). He blots out our sin (Isaiah 44:22).
He treats our sins as if they never happened (Jeremiah 31:34).
That's why forgiveness should bring forth praise.

The next time you receive God's forgiveness, give Him
the praise He deserves for forgiving you and restoring you to
fellowship with Him through His unfailing love.

I thank You and praise You, O God of my fathers; You have given me wisdom and might, and have now made known to me what we asked of You, for You have made known to us the king's demand.

DANIEL 2:23

Daniel lived in a pagan land ruled by a ruthless king. But when that king had a troubling dream, Daniel asked God for wisdom, and the Lord gave him its interpretation. Daniel exalted in thanksgiving. In our own days of troubling world events, let's thank God He's still in control.

Dear Lord, the times are in Your hands and so are we. You warned that perilous times would come in the Last Days, but You also told us the Last Days would prepare for the return of Christ. We're apt to be troubled by politics, upset by elections, and wary of rulers. But You, O Lord, direct the affairs of history; and if the prophet Daniel could praise You in Babylon, we can praise You in our modern world. Thank You for being on Your throne. The rulers of this world with their power and pride are no match for Your sovereign rule.

NOVEMBER 12
Perpetual Praise

And looking at Jesus as He walked, he said, "Behold the Lamb of God!"
JOHN 1:36

Ebenezer Erskine was a Scottish minister in the 1700s who faced some serious challenges in his ministry. But he knew how to draw encouragement from the Lord each morning. In his journal for September 20, 1721, he wrote: "This morning, a little after I awakened, I began to turn my thoughts toward the Lord Jesus; and the Lord encouraged me…by a sweet gale of his Spirit; for my meditation of him was sweet. I could say that his love is better than wine; yea, that his loving kindness is better than life…. My heart did burn within me, while I thought of him who is Immanuel, and whose name is Wonderful; and what more can I say?"

We live in a chaotic world, and without the daily encouragement of Christ what would we do? That's why it's vital to start the day with Him. Even before rising from bed, we can say, "Good morning, Lord!" And on a chair or table nearby, we can keep an open Bible.

We're encouraged as we walk with Him each day, and our walk with Him is a pathway of perpetual praise.

But he did not know that the Lord had departed from him.
JUDGES 16:20

Judges 16 tells the tragic story of Samson. In letting his lover cut his Nazirite-vowed hair, he disobeyed God, squandered his opportunities, and undermined his own power—yet he didn't realize it. He reminds us of the church of Laodicea in Revelation 3:17, which thought it was rich and needed nothing—"and do not know that you are wretched, miserable, poor, blind, and naked."

It's frightening to think how easily we can sustain a false impression of ourselves. Being poor in spirit and humble before the Lord means we understand our true condition. Without God, we are miserable even when we think we're happy. We're poor even when we think we're rich. We're doomed to hell even as we're looking forward to our next vacation or special event.

When we know who we are *without* God, we can discover all we can be *with* God. He is the Source of our power, joy, usefulness, and eternal wealth. Be sensitive to His Spirit, responsive to your conscience, and remain close to Him who knows the number of hairs on your head.

NOVEMBER 14
God Sees Our Tears

Those who sow in tears shall reap in joy.
PSALM 126:5

There are many kinds of tears. Some come from chopping onions. Others come from a fit of laughter. A sad movie can turn on the water works. Even smoke from a campfire can make our eyes water. Babies begin their lives with tears. Tears are important for lubricating our eyes and flushing away debris.

But when we think of tears, we usually think of burdens. God sees our tears as seeds. Each tear shed in grief, disappointment, pain, or emotional distress is like a seed that falls from our eyes and lands in the garden of God's grace. He knows the meaning behind every drop, and none of them are unnoticed by Him.

In the same way that Romans 8:28 tells us that all things will work together for our good, Psalm 126:5 tells us that somehow our tears will produce a harvest of joy. How can that be? We don't fully understand the scope of God's grace, the power of His providence, and the depths of His mercy. But every promise in the Bible is true, so you can adopt Psalm 126:5 as your own.

NOVEMBER 15
Always Just

*As for the Almighty, we cannot find Him; He is excellent in power,
in judgment and abundant justice; He does not oppress.*

JOB 37:23

We've all heard young children say it: "But that's not fair!"
And we may have said it ourselves. Life is filled with "unfair"
moments. Tragedies, disasters, genocides, and more lead us to
ask why God allows such things to happen. The Old Testament
character, Job, certainly had grounds for such a complaint.

What Job ultimately discovered is that fairness is not the
issue. Rather, justice and righteousness are. Was it fair for Job's
family and livelihood to be destroyed for seemingly no reason?
Not on the surface. But beneath the surface (which Job didn't
see until the end of his deep dive into God's character), God
was being just in His judgments and His use of power. It was
more important for Job to know God than to have his life of
smooth sailing be undisturbed. At the beginning of Job's saga,
he was angry with God for being unfair. By the end, He was
worshiping God as the all-powerful Creator and Judge of all
things (Job 42:1–6).

God's ways are not our ways (Isaiah 55:8–9), but even when
we don't understand His ways, we can trust in His character.

NOVEMBER 16
Our Heavenly Home

God Himself will be with them and be their God.
REVELATION 21:3

If you ever have the privilege of buying a new house in a development that is under construction, it can be exciting. You sit down with the builder's representative and go through everything: the floor plan, the color schemes, the flooring materials, the appliances, and more. You come away with a picture of what your new home is going to look like. It's exciting!

Given how much fun a new house or apartment can be on earth, think of how exciting it will be to move into our eternal dwelling in the New Jerusalem (Revelation 21:2). We don't know exactly what our eternal home will be like, but given the apostle John's description in Revelation 21, it will be like nothing we have ever seen. Jesus told His twelve disciples that He was going to prepare a place for them, and that means a place for us too. Jesus left His heavenly home and came to earth so He could take us to His home forever.

Jesus endured a hard life on earth so we could enjoy an eternal life with Him in our heavenly home.

Secret Service

But when you do a charitable deed, do not let
your left hand know what your right hand is doing.

MATTHEW 6:3

Dallas Willard once advised Christians to serve the Lord with a certain amount of secrecy—not in deceit but for the purpose of intentionally wanting God to bring our hunger for fame and recognition under control. It's unhealthy when we want all our good deeds to be known.

As we serve others, we are serving God. But if we're eager for everyone to know how well we've served, how humbly we've helped, or how hard we've worked, our motivations are questionable. True humility serves quietly and finds satisfaction in serving as Jesus did.

There is joy to be found in providing a service to someone without any expectation of thanks or notice from the recipient. Perhaps even today, an occasion will arise for serving someone as a member of God's Secret Service.

Praise the Lord! Oh, give thanks to the Lord,
for He is good! For His mercy endures forever.
PSALM 106:1

Martin Rinkart was a Lutheran minister who ministered in Saxony, Germany, during the Thirty Year's War and plague of the 1600s. All around him was death and despair. To sustain his spirits and those of his people, he wrote a powerful hymn of thanksgiving. It may be the only known hymn to include the word "perplexed," for in the second stanza, Rinkart prayed, "O may this bounteous God... keep us in his grace and guide us when perplexed."

Here is the first stanza. Why not sing or say it as a prayer of gratitude to the Lord today?

Now thank we all our God
With heart and hands and voices,
Who wondrous things has done,
In whom his world rejoices;
Who from our mother's arms
Has blessed us on our way
With countless gifts of love,
And still is ours today.

And we know that all things work together for good to those who love God,
to those who are the called according to His purpose.
ROMANS 8:28

Even those who don't believe the biblical story praise the book of Job for tackling one of life's most difficult questions: Why do bad things happen to good people? In fact, critics of the Bible suggest that Job was written in relationship to the Babylonian captivity of Israel with Job representing the nation: a choice servant of God suffering unjustly.

But there is no reason to doubt the biblical record: Job was a historic person who lived in the Middle East. He was righteous and upright and feared God—the greatest man of his era. Yet he suffered miserably when all he had was taken away (Job 1–2). But he refused to curse God, believing both God and himself to be free of blame for his condition (Job 2:10). When his suffering ended, his faith was rewarded (Job 42:10–17). Job's troubles gave him a clearer vision of God than when he lived in ease.

When you go through troubles, believe God will use them for good (Romans 8:28). Wait patiently and expect to see the outcome of your faith.

Blessed are the dead who die in the Lord from now on.
REVELATION 14:13

Many people don't realize that one of earth's greatest revivals will occur during the Tribulation of the Last Days. During this frightening period, multitudes will seek the Lord, aided by 144,000 Jewish evangelists. Yet many of these new Christians will be martyred.

In Revelation 14:13 a loud voice from heaven—apparently the voice of the Lord—shouts: "Blessed are the dead who die in the Lord from now on." And the Holy Spirit replies: "Yes… that they may rest from their labors, and their works follow them."

This wonderful verse applies to the Tribulation martyrs. But in a broader sense, it is true of every believer. We don't simply die, we die *in the Lord*. That brings rest—not the ceasing of activity but the end of strain and stress. And the works we leave behind will create a ripple effect of blessings that will extend to the end of time.

If we live or if we die, all the praise goes to Jesus.

To live is Christ, and to die is gain!

I will set him in the safety for which he yearns.

PSALM 12:5

David Wilson, the police chief of Foley, Alabama, retired after 37 years on the job, and his letter to the community was remarkable. He thanked many individuals who had encouraged him and served alongside him. He thanked his family who had sacrificed that he might serve, and he thanked the community. Then Wilson ended his letter with a special thanksgiving to Jesus Christ.

"He IS my life," said Wilson. "I'm so very thankful for the hedge of protection He has kept around me in the 37 years as a cop with the many close calls I've had…. I'm so thankful that He answered my prayer—my daily prayer to keep the officers I've worked with my whole career safe from death in the line of duty. Thank you for keeping all my employees safe from death with COVID also. Most of all thank you for redeeming this sinner."[29]

Thank God for a police officer who prayed for the safety of his fellow officers every day, and for a God who answered that prayer every day for upward to four decades.

Be thankful for your answered prayers. You have His assurance from His Word that He not only hears but also answers prayers.

[29] Carey Cox, "Foley police chief retiring at the end of August," *News WKRG*, August 3, 2020, https://www.wkrg.com/top-stories/foley-police-chief-retiring-at-the-end-of-august/.

The former account I made, O Theophilus,
of all that Jesus began both to do and teach.

ACTS 1:1

The biblical writer, Luke, wrote his Gospel ("the former account"), telling us of all Jesus *began* to do and teach. Then Luke wrote the book of Acts to tell us what Jesus *continued* to do and teach through His people by His Spirit. The Lord Jesus indwells His people by His Spirit, working and speaking through them.

Each of us is different—utterly unique. There's no other person on earth like you, nor has there ever been, nor will there ever be! Of the billions of people on the world's stage from Creation to the return of Christ, only one person is like you— and it's you. Jesus wants to use your strengths and weaknesses, your idiosyncrasies and quirks, your gifts and talents, your abilities and disabilities.

We are uniquely created by God to serve Him, so we should never bemoan the way God made us. Give Him control over every part of your life and ask Him to work through you to His glory today!

NOVEMBER 23
The Speed of Providence

Lord... all that we have accomplished you have done for us.
ISAIAH 26:12, NIV

George A. Buttrick, a Presbyterian writer, told of an Arctic expedition in which men trudged forward at a very slow pace, making no apparent headway. They were exhausted. But when they took their bearings, they found they were much closer to their goal than they realized. They finally learned that the ice block beneath their feet had been moving, carrying them on.

In our personal life or in our work for the Lord, sometimes we grow weary and discouraged. We think we're making no progress. But when we are walking and working on the basis of God's will, we're making more progress than we know. The Lord Himself is moving us along more quickly than we realize and faster toward the goal than we know.

Isaiah knew the work wasn't getting done by his own human efforts. The Lord was doing the work through Him. The New Living Translation of Isaiah 26:12 says, "Lord, you will grant us peace; all we have accomplished is really from you." Don't be discouraged. You're doing more than you think, for you're traveling at the speed of God's providential work.

NOVEMBER 24

With Thanksgiving

Oh come, let us sing to the Lord! Let us shout joyfully to the Rock of our salvation. Let us come before His presence with thanksgiving; let us shout joyfully to Him with psalms.

PSALM 95:1–2

In America, today is Thanksgiving Day. Its roots go back to 1621 when the Pilgrims celebrated their first harvest in the New World. But it was not until 1863 that it became an official U.S. observance at the instigation of President Abraham Lincoln.

In the most general terms, the way to give thanks was expanded from the Old Testament to the New. In the Old Testament, God was normally thanked "for" things—His works, attributes, and blessings (Psalm 106:1). While that focus is maintained in the New Testament, it is expanded to giving thanks "in" all things (1 Thessalonians 5:18). That is, in all circumstances. We can do that because we know God causes "all things" to work together for our good (Romans 8:28).

Why not do both today? Give thanks to God for His blessings and give thanks for whatever circumstances you are experiencing. Fill this day with thanksgiving to God.

For whoever exalts himself will be humbled,
and he who humbles himself will be exalted.

LUKE 14:11

It happens at every Black Friday sale: People start lining up in front of their favorite retail outlets hours before the doors open. Why? In order to be first in line, of course! Or, if there are only two cookies left, why does a child often take the biggest one?

Why do we need to be first or to get a seat on the front row or to make a name for ourselves? Jesus told a parable about this carnal tendency when He was invited to eat at the home of a prominent Pharisee (Luke 14). When He noticed how the guests were jockeying for position to get a seat at the head table, He issued a warning via a story. If you are invited to a wedding feast, instead of trying to get the best seat at the feast, take the lowest seat. Better to be honored by being moved higher by the host than to be dishonored by being asked to give your seat to another. Jesus summarized: "Whoever exalts himself will be humbled, and he who humbles himself will be exalted."

Be aware of the temptation to exalt yourself, to put yourself ahead of others. Let God move you higher in His time and in His way.

Therefore by Him let us continually offer the sacrifice of praise to God, that is, the fruit of our lips, giving thanks to His name.
HEBREWS 13:15

There's an old song that tells us to count our blessings, but it's not possible! There are too many.

Today, let's offer a prayer of thanksgiving for some of them.

Heavenly Father, at this moment I'm not coming with requests, only with the sacrifice of praise and thanksgiving. Thank You for the sky—its blueness, its clouds, its sunrises and sunsets, its space for the birds to fly. Thank You for the ground—its green grass, brown sand, towering mountains, fruitful plains. Thank You for the seas—the vastness of the watery depths, the fish, the coral, the tides, the marvel of water itself. Thank You for beauty—the petals of flowers, the grins of children, the existence of colors, the blackness of the night sky, and the twinkling sparkle of the stars.

And Lord, thank You for providing everything for me to richly enjoy. The Bible says the cheerful heart has a continual feast, so thank You for all the flavors of life.

Whatever today brings—and tomorrow—Lord, thank You for You!

For you are my rock and my fortress; therefore,
for Your name's sake, lead me and guide me.

PSALM 31:3

A groom in Indonesia was using GPS to get to the site of his wedding, but the device led him to the wrong venue. He arrived at the site where another wedding was taking place. The groom greeted a number of people and took his place, waiting for the bride to appear. Imagine his surprise when he learned he was at the wrong wedding! He made a quick exit, which was caught on camera and went viral on social media. Thankfully, the man made it in the nick of time to his own wedding.

GPS systems are getting better, but most of us know what it's like to end up in the wrong place. Human guidance often fails us. But when we follow God's Providential Shepherding, we're never led astray. The Lord leads His children in the right paths. As we pray and seek His will, He enables us to make wise decisions, to know what we should do, and to take each step at the right time.

Don't doubt God's ability to lead you. He will lead and guide you for His Name's sake, from now until we meet Him in heaven one day.

Now when Paul and his party set sail from Paphos, they came to Perga in Pamphylia; and John, departing from them, returned to Jerusalem.
ACTS 13:13

John Mark was a young man—the cousin of Barnabas—who agreed to travel with Paul and Barnabas on their missionary tour to Cyprus and Asia Minor. Halfway through the journey, he gave up and returned to Jerusalem. Paul was so upset he refused to take Mark with him on his next trip, which tore apart history's first missionary team (Acts 15:36–41).

How easy to become aggravated, disappointed, and disillusioned about someone's failure!

But that's not the end of the story. John Mark later became the associate and translator of the apostle Peter and the writer of the second Gospel—the Gospel of Mark. Some years after the incident in Acts 13, Paul commended Mark in Colossians 4:10. And in his final letter Paul described Mark as a man who had become very useful and valuable to him (2 Timothy 4:11).

If someone has disappointed you, don't give up on them. We all need time to mature, and it's always wise to let mercy and patience prevail during times of growth, and then let God complete the development.

NOVEMBER 29
Head, Hands, Heart

*Now then, we are ambassadors for Christ, as though God were pleading
through us: we implore you on Christ's behalf, be reconciled to God.*
2 CORINTHIANS 5:20

Whenever a presidential election is certified and the new
administration is in place, many important positions become
available throughout the government. One privilege that the new
President immediately has is to assign ambassadors for the United
States to the diverse countries around the world. Depending upon
the size and importance of the country, the status of this position
can be immense. But whatever country the ambassador is assigned
to, it brings with it the status of representing our nation. As an
ambassador, they have a plenipotentiary (full power) authority to
represent the President of the United States.

Imagine how hard it would be for foreign nations to
communicate with our government if we did not have
ambassadors in their land. If he had no ambassadors, our President
would spend all his time traveling to ensure there was dialogue
and understanding between the nations. The apostle Paul says we
are Christ's ambassadors, speaking and acting for Him to those
who do not know Him. He does not appear in person to those
who need Him—instead, He sends us. We are His head (His
mind), His hands (His works), and His heart (His love) to those
who need Him. Wherever we go, we need to show and share
Christ to the world.

Examine yourselves as to whether you are in the faith. Test yourselves.
2 CORINTHIANS 13:5

For a number of years, the British physician, Dr. Martyn Lloyd-Jones, thought he was a Christian. He went to church and even served as overseer of the Sunday school. But he began sitting under the preaching of a minister, Dr. John Hutton, and for the first time in his life he became aware of the genuine, life-changing power of the Gospel. He began to see that the deepest problems of human life were not medical in nature, but spiritual. By the time he was 25, he had become a true Christian.

"For many years I thought I was a Christian when in fact I was not," he said. "It was only later that I came to see that I had never been a Christian and became one." Lloyd-Jones went on to become a prolific Bible teacher and pastor.

All who truly know Christ as Savior can have full assurance of salvation; but if your life has never been changed by the Gospel, don't deceive yourself. The apostle Paul was concerned that some in the Corinthian church had never truly trusted Christ for salvation. Make sure you are in the faith and rejoice in the true, life-saving, everlasting redemption of Christ.

DECEMBER

DECEMBER 1
As White as Snow

Purge me with hyssop, and I shall be clean;
wash me, and I shall be whiter than snow.

PSALM 51:7

Most people love a "white Christmas"—a blanket of fresh snow that has gently fallen like a silent white shroud. But why is snow white when it's actually just made of crystals of ice? The reason is, when light waves of different frequencies (colors) hit the ice crystals, they are reflected off the snow so all the colors blend to create "white"—the color that results when all color frequencies are combined.

While the writers of the Bible may not have understood the science of white snow, they understood this: Snow was the whitest, or purest, thing they knew. Pure white snow doesn't have any marks or stains or blemishes, and thus they equated the image with sinlessness and holiness. Daniel saw the Ancient of Days wearing a garment "white as snow" (Daniel 7:9). John saw Jesus with hair "as white as snow" (Revelation 1:14). When we see our sin, we know we need to be made as "white as snow" (Isaiah 1:18).

The more we see the holiness of God, the more we become aware of our need to be made pure as well (Psalm 51:7).

DECEMBER 2
Evergreen

Most assuredly, I say to you, he who believes in Me has everlasting life.
JOHN 6:47

Imagine your family's response if you brought home a seven-foot-tall oak sapling—a thin trunk, a few scraggly limbs, brown, with no leaves as your Christmas tree this year. Their response would not be joyful! When the custom of decorating a tree for Christmas began in Europe in the sixteenth century, it was the dead of winter. The only green trees in the forests were conifers (evergreens): hemlock, spruce, fir, and the like.

The time of year for cutting a tree may have had something to do with the choice of evergreens, but there was likely a better reason. Christmas is the celebration of the life of God coming to earth in the Christ-Child and His promise of eternal life. Therefore, an evergreen tree, full of life year-round, was the obvious choice to use in a Christmas celebration. We have been decorating at Christmas ever since with evergreen trees, boughs, garlands, and wreaths. Christmas evergreens speak of the ever-living life of Christ in all who believe.

Don't let the significance of the evergreen go unnoticed this Christmas. Rejoice that life in Christ never goes away—not now, not for eternity.

DECEMBER 3
Light of the World

Then Jesus spoke to them again, saying, "I am the light of the world. He who follows Me shall not walk in darkness, but have the light of life."

JOHN 8:12

One of the most famous Christmas trees in the world is the Rockefeller Center Christmas tree in New York City. The tree is anywhere from 69 to 100 feet tall and covered with 50,000 LED lights. These lights are a far cry from the lights that adorned the first Christmas trees in Germany: candles attached to tree limbs with melted wax. When electricity became available in the late nineteenth century, electric lights slowly replaced the candles and small lanterns used for centuries.

Regardless of the kind of lighting, Christmas trees have always displayed lights. Why? Originally lights to illuminate dark houses in the dead of winter were a welcome source of cheer. But for Christians, the reason was obvious: to celebrate the birth of Christ who came as the Light of the World (John 1:3–9). As Simeon declared when seeing the infant Jesus, "A light to bring revelation to the Gentiles, and the glory of Your people Israel" (Luke 2:32).

Be the light of Christ in your world as you celebrate Christmas this year. His light dispels all darkness wherever it shines forth.

DECEMBER 4
Immanuel

Therefore the Lord Himself will give you a sign: Behold, the virgin shall conceive and bear a Son, and shall call His name Immanuel.

ISAIAH 7:14

A father reassures his teenage daughter about her first solo airplane trip: "I'll be with you all the way to the gate, and the flight attendants will be with you after that. Then Grandma will be with you when you arrive." "With you" happens a lot in this life—but there is always a starting point and a stopping point. "With you" never lasts forever in the human realm.

But in the heavenly realm, it does! The name given to the Messiah in the Old Testament was *Immanuel*, which in Hebrew meant "God with us," a name confirmed at the birth of Jesus (Matthew 1:23). When the writer to the Hebrews wanted to convey God's omnipresence, he quoted God's words to Joshua on the eve of Israel's entrance into the Promised Land: "I will not leave you nor forsake you" (Joshua 1:5). Jesus even told His disciples He would be with them "to the end of the age" (Matthew 28:20).

You were not alone yesterday; you are not alone today; you will not be alone tomorrow. Jesus is Immanuel—He is with you.

But you, Bethlehem Ephrathah, though you are little among the thousands of Judah, yet out of you shall come forth to Me the One to be Ruler in Israel, whose goings forth are from of old, from everlasting.

MICAH 5:2

Bethlehem meant "house [beth] of bread [lechem]." It was one of two Bethlehems, the second being in the region of Galilee (Joshua 19:15). To avoid confusion, Jesus' birthplace is referred to as "Bethlehem of Judea" (Matthew 2:1, 5). The Jewish leaders in Jerusalem also confirmed that the Messiah would be born in Bethlehem of Judea, not Bethlehem in Galilee, quoting the prophet Micah (Micah 5:2; Matthew 2:1–6). Jesus was born in the predicted place!

But why was He born in the "city of bread"? Perhaps Bethlehem was given that name because it was a center for growing grain as illustrated in the book of Ruth where Bethlehem is mentioned six times. The climax of Ruth's story centers around the grain harvest of Boaz. More prophetically, the One born in the "house of bread" eventually identified Himself as the Bread of Life (John 6:35, 48).

Be comforted this Christmas by the prophecy and fulfillment that surrounds the birth of Christ. God's promises for you are as certain as His promises were for the birth of Jesus.

And everyone who competes for the prize is temperate in all things. Now they do it to obtain a perishable crown, but we for an imperishable crown.

1 CORINTHIANS 9:25

When Harry Swayne played in the NFL, his teammate, Mark Schlereth, kept inviting him to Bible studies. Swayne politely declined, but he couldn't help noticing the difference in the players who *did* go. They were so kind to Swayne that he came under deep conviction and longed to give his life to Jesus. In January 1999, after the Broncos won Super Bowl XXXIII, he piled into the caravan of limos heading to the celebration.

"I was so convicted that I told my limo driver to take a left, and I made him take me back to the hotel. And I gave my life to Christ."[30]

The greatest gift we can offer our Savior is to yield our life to Him. Compared to knowing Christ, even a Super Bowl victory dims and fades. What the world offers—even the most expensive Christmas present—is perishable. When we give Jesus our heart and life, we become imperishable, and we become the recipients of imperishable riches.

[30] John Ackerman, "Mark Schlereth discusses how he received and gave spiritual guidance on NFL teams," *Sports Spectrum*, June 23, 2020.

I am the Alpha and the Omega,
the Beginning and the End, the First and the Last.
REVELATION 22:13

Most Christians are familiar with the "fish" symbol that appears on bumper stickers, jewelry, Christmas ornaments, and elsewhere. The fish originated as a Christogram—a Christian monogram or Chrismon. It emerged as a form of Christian decoration in churches, tombs, and "graffiti." The Greek word for "fish" is *ichthus*, and those letters were used to represent the Greek words for Jesus Christ, Son of God, and Savior. Many other Chrismons have arisen since then: the Chi-Rho symbol, the IHS symbol, the ICXC symbol, the Alpha Omega symbol, and many others.

Decorations have always been a part of the Christian tradition and celebration. We use lights and a "Bethlehem" star on our trees and outside on our houses, colorful wrapping paper for our presents, and green and red decorations throughout our homes. Some people decorate their vehicles and workplaces. Chrismon trees have even become popular: evergreens decorated with white lights and Chrismon symbols cut out of white styrofoam or cardboard.

Christmas is a celebration! And celebrations demand decorations. Whatever kind of decorations you choose, let them reflect the reason for the Christmas season.

DECEMBER 8
Gift Giving

Thanks be to God for His indescribable gift!
2 CORINTHIANS 9:15

One thing that parents often struggle with is giving their children gifts that not only give joy but will also last beyond a short season in their lives. Even something worthwhile, like a book, is designed for a specific reading level and age, so it will soon lose its value in the life of a child. Along with the desire to give something that will last, part of the joy is seeing the delight of their children when they receive the gift—and that is true of the gift God has given us as well. And His gift is "indescribable"!

The Bible says that our Heavenly Father gives us the gift of eternal life (Romans 6:23); the gift of salvation by grace through faith (Ephesians 2:8); and the gift of the indwelling Holy Spirit (Acts 2:38). James said, "Every good gift and every perfect gift is from above, and comes down from the Father of lights" (James 1:17). Romans 4:17 says, He "gives life to the dead," and Romans 8:11 promises life to our mortal bodies through His Spirit who dwells within us.

We serve a kind and gracious God who gives us good gifts, and the most indescribable gift is Jesus Christ Himself!

DECEMBER 9
God's Providence

There was in the days of Herod, the king of Judea,
a certain priest named Zacharias, of the division of Abijah.
LUKE 1:5

The story of the Gospel didn't start with Mary, Joseph, or Bethlehem. It began with an aged couple in the Judean hills—a priest named Zacharias and his wife Elizabeth. That's where Luke begins the story of Jesus in the first chapter of his Gospel. We don't know the exact year of Zacharias' birth. Perhaps it was 70 B.C. or earlier. But he served quietly and faithfully for decades, not realizing his life was no mere accident on God's calendar. He and Elizabeth had each been born at the precise time to place them in the historical lineup for the coming of the Messiah. They lived in the days of Herod, and despite their age and humble circumstances the fullness of time had arrived—and they were a part of it.

God's ultimate providence over our lives places us where He wants us and when He wants us there. Each of us is born at the exact moment in time that God has ordained. Our times are in His hands. We are here on earth for a reason.

Look around, then, and see how God wants to use you!

And having come in, the angel [Gabriel] said to [Mary], "Rejoice, highly favored one, the Lord is with you; blessed are you among women!"
LUKE 1:28

Life in some families is a continual adventure. On the way to school on a normal morning, Mom may turn at the last minute and head for a local farm and petting zoo for a one-day field trip. Or Dad comes home early from work on a Friday and piles everyone into the car and heads for a weekend in a mountain cabin. Adventures are all the more exciting when they are completely unexpected.

God is a God of adventure as well. A lowly farmer named Gideon was thrust into the role of military commander (Judges 6–7). Saul of Tarsus was called by Jesus to become the apostle to the Gentiles (Acts 9:1–19). And there was a young teenager named Mary whose life was completely turned around by God. When the angel Gabriel announced that she would become the earthly mother of the Son of God... talk about an adventure! She started down a path she couldn't have imagined.

It doesn't matter where Jesus leads us, following Him will always be an adventure. Whenever He says, "Follow Me," do what Mary did: Just say, "Let it be" (Luke 1:38)—say "Yes."

Therefore do not be like [the hypocrites]. For your Father
knows the things you have need of before you ask Him.
MATTHEW 6:8

We sometimes ponder the purpose and procedures of prayer; Jesus' disciples had a learning curve on the subject as well. At times, Jesus' instructions might have seemed contradictory. On one occasion, He told them that God knew what they were going to ask for before they prayed—which probably raised a silent question in their mind, "Then why pray?" Then He immediately taught them how to pray (Matthew 6:8–13)! So His point was not, "Don't pray." His point was "Don't pray long, sanctimonious prayers like religious pagans who use long prayers as a way to influence 'god.'" Instead, He taught them a prayer of just over sixty (English) words.

Jesus' point was that God hears our heart, not just our words. He knows and hears all of our prayers, even when we don't know exactly how to pray (Romans 8:26–27). When the young Mary received the angel Gabriel's message, she likely didn't know exactly how to pray in response. But she pondered his words in her heart (Luke 2:19)—unspoken prayers that God heard and answered.

Be assured that God hears and answers your prayers—even before you pray.

From the beginning were eyewitnesses…
an orderly account… the certainty of those things.
LUKE 1:2–4

The Gospel of Luke begins with a powerful preface in which Luke states his purpose—he aimed to "set in order a narrative" of the historical events related to the Gospel. He interviewed the "eyewitnesses" and gained a factual history, writing an "orderly account" so that we would know "the certainty of those things" we believe (Luke 1:1–4). Scholars rate Luke among history's greatest historians.

Jesus Christ isn't like King Arthur. Most modern historians doubt Arthur ever existed in the late fifth to early sixth centuries in England. The story is made up of folktales with little historical certainty. Arthur appears as a great warrior defending England from human and supernatural enemies, along with his Knights of the Round Table. But is any of it true? Probably not. Probably fiction.

On the other hand, almost no reputable historian denies the existence and impact of Jesus of Nazareth, and the details of His life were recorded four times in the Gospel, down to the events of His remarkable birth in Bethlehem. We have a Book we can trust and a story we can believe!

Jesus isn't a knight in shining armor. He's the risen King of the Ages.

DECEMBER 13
It Could Be Today

Watch therefore, for you know neither the day
nor the hour in which the Son of Man is coming.
MATTHEW 25:13

A few years ago, a Mississippi woman entered the hospital to give birth to triplets. After the three children were delivered, she was shocked to hear the doctor say, "More feet!" A fourth identical child, who had been missed by the ultrasounds, made a surprising appearance.

In the days of Herod the Great, few people expected the birth of the Messiah. The rabbis had misread the ultrasound charts of Old Testament prophecy. But Jesus arrived exactly at the right moment, in the fullness of time.

In our day, few people are expecting the imminent return of Christ. But every sunrise is a reminder of His impending return. J. D. Greear recalls growing up in a church where the pastor would end each service by saying, "Maranatha," meaning, "The Lord is coming." The congregation would respond, "And it could be today." Greear said, "We could use some of that attitude. This may be our last chance—to share the Gospel, to forgive, to repent."[31]

[31] J. D. Greear, "Jesus' Imminent Return," *Ligonier Ministries*, 2021.

Blank Contract

"For I know the plans I have for you," declares the Lord,
"plans to prosper you and not to harm you, plans to give you hope
and a future. Then you will call on me and come and pray to me,
and I will listen to you. You will seek me and find me when you seek
me with all your heart. I will be found by you," declares the Lord.
JEREMIAH 29:11–14, NIV

Have you ever signed your name on a blank check, allowing someone else to fill in the other lines however they'd like? Have you ever signed a blank contract, letting someone else decide all the terms and conditions? Most of us would agree that it is folly to allow someone else to fill in the blanks after we have signed a document.

But the same reasoning cannot be applied to our walk with God. We will never know the will of God if we approach it saying, "I want to find out God's will so I can decide whether or not it fits my plans." God's will is not about your plans, and it's not about your finding His intentions so you can decide whether or not to obey Him. We don't get to vote on the will of God.

Instead, think of it as taking a blank sheet of paper and signing your name at the bottom even before you know what God is going to fill in at the top. We have to say, "Almighty God, I want to know what Your will is, and whatever it is, I will do it." Does that sound scary? It isn't, because we have an all-loving, all-wise God.

DECEMBER 15
Do Not Worry

*Therefore I say to you, do not worry about your life, what you will eat or
what you will drink; nor about your body, what you will put on.
Is not life more than food and the body more than clothing?*

MATTHEW 6:25

The theme of Jesus' words in Matthew 6:25–34 is sometimes
misunderstood. The theme is not, "God will provide everything
you need according to your timetable"; the theme is, "Do not
worry" (verses 25, 31, 34). Why would He exhort us not to
worry if there would never be an occasion (temptation) to
worry—a time when our needs seemed not to be met?

God made similar promises of provision to His covenant
people, Israel (Deuteronomy 15:4–6). But at the same time, He
said, "For the poor will never cease from the land" (verse 11).
How could there be poor in the midst of promises of plenty?
Because we live in a fallen world; things happen; crops fail. In
such cases, the Israelites were to meet the needs of their poor
brethren (verses 7–10), just as the Church would later do (Acts
4:32–37). God's provision comes in many ways.

Jesus said, in essence, "Don't worry. Trust in God. Seek
Him, and He will care for you" (Matthew 6:33–34).

Moses took his tent and pitched it outside the camp.
EXODUS 33:7

When a creative mother in Chicago noticed her son was anxious during the pandemic, she came up with a biblical solution. Together they made a prayer tent—a homemade pup tent—and set it up in a corner of the boy's bedroom. Whenever he felt afraid, he could go there, read his Bible or kids' devotional book, pray, and feel enclosed in safety.

The idea originated with Moses. In Exodus 33, when Moses was frazzled by the idolatry of the children of Israel, he "took his tent and pitched it outside the camp." This wasn't the famous tabernacle, which would be built later. This was an ordinary tent. Some translations use the word "tabernacle," but that's simply another word for tent. This was an ordinary tent, yet whenever Moses entered it, the presence of the Lord descended and met with him.

You may want to literally build a prayer tent for yourself or your children. But truly, any quiet spot where we enter God's presence in prayer is a special place of safety. The Lord longs to be with us, to hear us, and to answer our prayers.

Stand therefore, having girded your waist with truth,
having put on the breastplate of righteousness, and having
shod your feet with the preparation of the gospel of peace.
EPHESIANS 6:14-15

In this day of instant news, it's hard to imagine how information traveled in the ancient world. For example, when armies went out to battle, runners would be dispatched from the battle scene to return and inform the king as to the outcome of the battle (2 Samuel 18:26). The prophet Isaiah wrote about the beauty of feet that came with good news (Isaiah 52:7).

Isaiah was speaking prophetically of the good news that Israel would be returning to her homeland from exile in Babylon. How beautiful were the feet of those who would bring that message! And Israel's return from exile prefigured the spiritual release from sin provided by Christ. Paul quoted Isaiah 52:7 when he noted the Good News of the Gospel of salvation (Romans 10:15). And he also referred to the Isaiah passage when listing the believer's armor: shoes that carry the Good News of the "gospel of peace." How does the Gospel protect us? Because it is Good News! We are free from the captivity of sin.

Make sure to carry the Gospel of peace with you daily. Be ready to share it with those who need and want to hear the Good News (Luke 2:14).

DECEMBER 18
Good Tidings, Great Joy

*Then the angel said to [the shepherds], "Do not be afraid, for behold,
I bring you good tidings of great joy which will be to all people."*
LUKE 2:10

All of us have had the experience of waiting on an outcome—a medical diagnosis, a job application, a missing child—and we wait with a sense of dread. Then the phone rings, or a person approaches, and says, "Good news! All is well!" When that good report comes, we have experienced what the Bible calls evangelism—the receipt of good news that brings joy and relief.

In Luke 2:10, the angel's words, "I bring you good tidings of great joy" contains the Greek word for *evangelism*—the announcing of good news. The shepherds were no doubt anxious when the angel of the Lord appeared. But they were soon put at ease by the angel's words. Dread and fear were replaced by "great joy" at the announcement of the birth of the Savior in Bethlehem. And that is true of us as well. Fear may beset us in life, but the Good News of Christ can alleviate every worry.

This Christmas let the reminder of Christ's birth and life be a source of great joy for you.

DECEMBER 19
Though Troubles Assail Us

The righteous cry out, and the Lord hears,
and delivers them out of all their troubles.
PSALM 34:17

Have you finished your Christmas shopping? Don't forget to give Christ something this year. Give Him your troubles. No one else would want them, but Jesus is glad to bear them because it's an indication of your faith and trust in Him.

When David was running from his enemies, he said, "This poor man cried out, and the Lord heard him, and saved him out of all his troubles.... Blessed is the man who trusts in Him!" (Psalm 34:6, 8) Your Lord will provide answers, peace, hope, and grace for every situation.

John Newton, the author of "Amazing Grace," wrote another hymn that says:

> *Though troubles assail us*
> *And dangers affright,*
> *Though all friends should fail us*
> *And foes all unite,*
> *Yet one thing secures us,*
> *Whatever betide,*
> *The promise assures us,*
> *"The Lord will provide."*[32]

[32] John Newton, "The Lord Will Provide," 1779.

DECEMBER 20
Speak Out! Don't Quit!

Now the Lord spoke to Paul in the night by a vision, "Do not be afraid,
but speak, and do not keep silent; for I am with you, and no one
will attack you to hurt you; for I have many people in this city."
ACTS 18:9–10

We think of Paul as a superhero who wasn't fazed by suffering, danger, or rejection. But if we could join him in Corinth, we might have found him near the end of his resources. In Acts 16 and 17, he was flogged in Philippi and run out of Thessalonica like a scoundrel. In Athens, few responded to his message. Going on to Corinth in chapter 18, he got a job making tents. When he tried to evangelize, he found rejection.

That's when the Lord said: "Don't be afraid! Speak out! Don't quit! For I am with you and no one can harm you. Many people here in this city belong to me" (Acts 18:9–10, TLB). Many souls in Corinth were ready to hear and respond to Paul's Gospel. He stayed there a year and a half.

Through whatever challenges we face, the Comforter will always be at our side, saying: "Don't be afraid. Don't quit. I'm beside you and will bless your efforts."

God is our refuge and strength, a very present help in trouble.

PSALM 46:1

When riots and violent protests struck Portland, Oregon, one pastor fought to share Jesus with his community. Reverend Aaron Bennett of Garden Church in downtown Portland said, "Don't give up on Portland. This is a place filled with people that Christ has died for." He said that his desire was to establish a calming presence in the midst of the unrest because that reflects the presence of God.[33]

Our God is close at hand, not far away, and the very name *Immanuel* means "God with us." When turmoil erupts in our lives—and we never know when things will go wrong—we should stay as calm as possible because this reflects the calming presence of our Savior. He is a "very present help in trouble" (Psalm 46:1). The apostle Paul said, "The Lord is at hand. Be anxious for nothing" (Philippians 4:5–6).

If you feel troubled today, remember that the Lord is at hand. He is with you. He is near. Visualize Him standing beside you, and let His calmness fill your heart.

[33] Tess Schoonhoven, "Despite Unrest, Portland Pastors See the Gospel Moving in the City," *Baptist Press*, July 31, 2020.

Glory to God in the highest, and on earth peace, goodwill toward men!
LUKE 2:14

At the heart of human aspiration has been the longing for peace. While some rulers have destroyed peace willingly, those affected have longed for a return to peace for their families and communities. It was the longing in Israel as well: "Pray for the peace of Jerusalem" was the psalmist's admonition (Psalm 122:6). Gradually, the Messiah was seen as the only One who could restore peace to Israel and Jerusalem.

Such was the prophecy of Isaiah concerning the Messiah. He would be called "Prince of Peace," and of His peace "there will be no end" (Isaiah 9:6–7). So when the angels appeared to the Bethlehem shepherds, glorifying God for the birth of the Savior, their announcement echoed the prophets' desire: "On earth peace, goodwill toward men!" The Savior whose birth they announced was the Prince of Peace foretold by the prophet. Jesus came to bring peace to all who would receive Him—along with comfort, joy, and salvation. And He will bring peace to the whole world at His return.

Do you need peace this Christmas season? It is to be found in Jesus: "My peace I give to you" (John 14:27).

DECEMBER 23
God With Us

And they shall call His name "Immanuel"..."God with us."
MATTHEW 1:23

The days around Christmas can be lonely for many people, but there are ways to instantly recognize the presence of God near us. After all, that's the core of Christmas. God wanted fellowship with us, and He gave Jesus the heavenly name of *Immanuel*—"God with us."

Here are seven ideas for letting the presence of Christ cheer you:

(1) Praise Him aloud, even if you don't feel like it. Start talking to Him out loud, thanking Him for specific blessings you've experienced this year. (2) Listen to hymns and worship music. If the Christmas carols make you melancholy, play an upbeat version of "Blessed Assurance." (3) Read through the book of Philippians, circling the words "joy" and "rejoice" every time they occur. (4) Confess your sins. Often our sense of God's presence is hindered by something in our thoughts or behavior that we should confess. (5) Overhaul your prayer list, bringing it up to date. (6) Find a small task to do in Jesus' Name. (7) Light a candle. The temple contained a lamp, and Jesus said He was the Light of the World.

Don't let yourself become discouraged. Get up, get busy, and remember God is with you!

And the Word became flesh and dwelt among us, and we beheld His glory, the glory as of the only begotten of the Father, full of grace and truth.

JOHN 1:14

A funnel allows us to take a measurable amount of material and focus it into a small place. The apostle John did that when he wrote, "The Word became flesh." The word for "Word" was *logos*, a term used by the Greeks in many broad senses: the first principle, the divine mind, the ground of reason. But John narrowed all those broad ideas down into a single point when he described the first Christmas: "And the Word became flesh and dwelt among us."

Why did John choose *logos* to describe Jesus? Because in Christ all wisdom and knowledge are manifested. He is before all things, and by Him and through Him all things were created (Colossians 1:15–20). "For in Him dwells all the fullness of the Godhead bodily" (Colossians 2:9). Yes, the Christ-Child whose birth we celebrate today was, at first, a helpless infant in a manger. But at the same time, He was the manifestation of all wisdom and power and knowledge.

Praise God today for sending Jesus, the *Logos*, to be the fullness of God fulfilled in the life of our Savior.

DECEMBER 25
O Holy Night

Then the shepherds returned, glorifying and praising God for
all the things that they had heard and seen, as it was told them.
LUKE 2:20

For many people, the true spirit of Christmas is experienced in the last few hours of Christmas Eve. Many churches have a Christmas Eve service as they commemorate and remember the birth of our Savior. Indeed, many non-Christians attend these services to catch an annual glimpse of the true meaning of Christmas.

Beautiful music, soft candlelight, the fellowship of like-minded souls, and a chance to hear the Christmas story read reverently—all this and more makes a Christmas Eve service a holy night for the Christian church. But it's not just the surroundings, meaningful as they are. Holiness is a matter of the heart above all else. And just as the shepherds left the holy stable where they found Jesus in Bethlehem and went back to their fields and their work glorifying and praising God, we should do the same. The holiness of Christmas Eve and Christmas Day should be a prelude to living a holy life that reflects what Christmas means to the follower of Jesus Christ.

Sanctify Christ in your heart today and make a commitment to live each moment and each day for Him in the coming year.

Eternity in Our Hearts

He has made everything beautiful in its time.
Also He has put eternity in their hearts.
ECCLESIASTES 3:11

Most people on this planet, regardless of their religious persuasion, do not think that life on earth ends here. We do not believe that this is all there is. In America, for example, more than seventy percent of the population believe that heaven is a real place.

The Bible teaches that God has placed eternity in our hearts; we're made to live forever, and we instinctively know that there's more life than our threescore-and-ten here on earth. How wonderful to study the subject of heaven in the Bible and learn more about the eternal home for God's children. Revelation 21 and 22 is a virtual travel guide for the new heavens, the new earth, and the New Jerusalem.

Our passport, however, is all important—the key to obtaining one is knowing Jesus Christ as Lord and Savior. He said in John 11:25–26: "I am the resurrection and the life. He who believes in Me, though he may die, he shall live. And whoever lives and believes in Me shall never die."

Our heavenly home is assured for the believer—an eternal destination designed and prepared by God.

Above all, taking the shield of faith with which you will
be able to quench all the fiery darts of the wicked one.
EPHESIANS 6:16

If you watch movies that depict battle scenes between ancient armies, you will see defensive tactics reenacted whereby hundreds of shields are overlapped together to prevent the incursion of arrows. It's an impressive site and illustrates the value of a shield. (See 1 Kings 22:34–36 where the lack of a shield resulted in death.)

No wonder Paul used the Roman shield to illustrate the power of faith to defend us against the "fiery darts of the wicked one" (Ephesians 6:16). Why "fiery" darts? Because often arrow points would be dipped in pitch and set alight before being shot to set fire to whatever they struck. Roman soldiers would soak their leather shields in water to extinguish these fiery missiles when they landed. And why "faith"? How does faith extinguish Satan's hellish attacks? Because Satan's attacks are against the character of God—His words and works. When we have faith in God and His promises, as Jesus did when tempted by Satan in the wilderness (Matthew 4:1–11), we can extinguish Satan's attacks.

How is your faith today? The stronger your faith is, the faster Satan's fiery attacks will be extinguished.

And you shall know the truth, and the truth shall make you free.
JOHN 8:32

People who read the Bible love it because it presents human
life as it really is: the good, the bad, the ugly—and the *funny*.
Take the time when the prophet Elijah challenged the prophets
of Baal to a power encounter on Mount Carmel. The contest
was to see who was greater—the God of Israel or the god Baal.
When Baal couldn't deliver, Elijah spared no sarcastic efforts to
humiliate the false god and his prophets (1 Kings 18:16–45).

Or take the time Jesus spoke to a group of Jews about
spiritual freedom (John 8:31–36). They retorted, "We are
Abraham's descendants, and have never been in bondage to
anyone. How can You say, 'You will be made free'?" (verse
33) Never been in bondage? How about the four hundred
years their ancestors spent enslaved in Egypt? How about the
northern tribes of Israel being enslaved to Assyria? How about
the two southern tribes spending seventy years enslaved in
Babylon? And as they spoke, they were in bondage to Rome! It
would be funny if it weren't so sad.

The spiritual freedom of which Jesus spoke comes only by
grace and truth. It is possible to be free from the bondage of sin
(Galatians 5:1).

DECEMBER 29
Satan's Sway

We know that we are of God, and the whole
world lies under the sway of the wicked one.
1 JOHN 5:19

Why are our public universities, the global media, the global economy, and the governments of the world gripped by wrong thinking and godless conduct? Why is the persecution of Christians reaching unprecedented levels? Why are people screaming at each other on television, and why has pornography overtaken our technology?

It's because the whole world is under the sway of the wicked one.

He is the father of lies (John 8:44), the power of darkness (Colossians 1:13), the ruler of this world (John 14:30), the prince of the power of the air, and the spirit that works in the children of disobedience (Ephesians 2:2). His craft and power are great. But, as Martin Luther said, "Though this world with devils filled should threaten to undo us, we will not fear for God has willed His truth to triumph through us."

We are the children of God, and He has provided us with everything we need when facing spiritual battles. Let's be armored up, prayed up, and filled up—so we can stand up. Our Commander in Chief has already won the war, and He wants us to get in on the victory every day that we live.

DECEMBER 30
Way of Escape

No temptation has overtaken you except such as is common to man;
but God is faithful, who will not allow you to be tempted beyond
what you are able, but with the temptation will also make
the way of escape, that you may be able to bear it.
1 CORINTHIANS 10:13

Many of us have been through the preflight instructions given by
a flight attendant before take-off. How to buckle your seatbelt;
how to use your seat cushion as a flotation device. And the most
important: *How to escape the aircraft through the emergency exits.*
Happily, the escape paths are almost never needed. Sadly, most
people don't pay attention to those instructions—negligence that
could prove fatal.

The Bible gives Christians instructions on how to escape
situations of spiritual danger. It does so by reminding us that the
Israelites failed to take advantage of their escape paths and suffered
dire results (1 Corinthians 10:1–13). Israel was tempted to sin and
suffered in extreme ways. Paul writes that, in every tempting
situation, God provides a way of escape if we will see it and take it.
"Take it" calls for a choice on our part, a decision of obedience.

Don't wait for temptation before you look for the way of
escape. Learn the paths of obedience beforehand and be prepared.

Now may the Lord of peace himself give you his peace at all
times and in every situation. The Lord be with you all.
2 THESSALONIANS 3:16, NLT

To many people around the world, this was a difficult year, even a tragic one, and we have no idea what the new year will bring. But we know this without a doubt: In every situation we face, our Savior is with us.

As the new year dawns, paraphrase 2 Thessalonians 3:16 as an earnest prayer: *Lord, may You, the Lord of peace, give me Your peace at all times and in every situation.*

Remember what Paul said in Philippians 4:6–7: *Do not be anxious about anything, but in every situation, by prayer and petition, with thanksgiving, present your requests to God. And the peace of God, which transcends all understanding, will guard your hearts and your minds in Christ Jesus* (NIV).

He added in verse 12: *I have learned the secret of being content in any and every situation* (NIV).

Every situation means every day, every hour, every circumstance, every location, every need, every fear, every joy, every opportunity, every step. He is more present than you know, and more powerful than you can possibly conceive. Our times are in His hands.